Ecosystem–Aware Global Supply Chain Management

Ecosystem–Aware Global Supply Chain Management

N. Viswanadham
Indian Institute of Science, Bangalore

S. Kameshwaran
IBM Research – India, Bangalore

 **World Scientific**

NEW JERSEY · LONDON · SINGAPORE · BEIJING · SHANGHAI · HONG KONG · TAIPEI · CHENNAI

Published by

World Scientific Publishing Co. Pte. Ltd.

5 Toh Tuck Link, Singapore 596224

USA office: 27 Warren Street, Suite 401-402, Hackensack, NJ 07601

UK office: 57 Shelton Street, Covent Garden, London WC2H 9HE

British Library Cataloguing-in-Publication Data
A catalogue record for this book is available from the British Library.

The V for Voluntary symbol on the bookcover is taken from:
http://en.wikipedia.org/wiki/File:VforVoluntary_normal.svg

ECOSYSTEM-AWARE GLOBAL SUPPLY CHAIN MANAGEMENT

ISBN 978-981-4508-16-2

In-house Editor: Yvonne Tan

Typeset by Stallion Press
Email: enquiries@stallionpress.com

Printed in Singapore by World Scientific Printers.

Preface

This book is about supply chain network (SCN) and its ecosystem, which comprises of elements that affect, control and create competitive advantage for the network. During the last two decades, the subject of supply chains has grown enormously both in terms of theory and applications. Several textbooks were written, research papers and case studies have been published, and new applications and innovations have resulted in blockbuster product and service industries. Outsourcing to low-cost countries has resulted in globalization, which resulted in creating emerging markets and a burgeoning middle-class. Several companies such as component suppliers, contract manufacturers, third party and fourth party logistics providers have emerged, and new state-of-the-art sea ports, airports, container freight stations, and special economic zones have been built. Companies such as SAP, Oracle, and IBM have built software packages for optimizing supply chain strategies and operations. Streamlining the business processes for automation using packaged software and the Internet is very common. The players in the supply chain are highly connected *logistically*, *informationally* and *financially*. In fact, it is often heard that it is not the manufacturing that matters; rather, it is the supply chain that provides the competitive advantage.

However, recent events have demonstrated that the efficiency contributors of SCNs can turn into risk creators. This is evident from the aftermath of the 2008 financial crisis and decline in trade threatening de-globalization, and also the March 11, 2011 earthquake, tsunami, nuclear crisis and the resultant plant shutdowns in Japan that slowed down the supplies of semiconductors to car parts to the globe. There were also lots of government interventions in the production matters in the form of protectionist regulations and preferences to local firms in government procurements. Thus, we see that the supply chains are indeed affected by exogenous factors such as the political and economic climate in the locations of the partners, delivery infrastructure in those locations, availability of the resources, and a host of other factors. It is not B2B and B2C that we need to study anymore; rather, we should concentrate on the ecosystem, which includes the entire supply chain, institutions covered by the supply chain partners, resources, and delivery mechanisms. Indeed, it is the ecosystem that creates competitive advantage for the companies, products, and partners. This creates a tremendous need for supply chain redesign. This book is probably the first step in that direction. After reading the book, we hope that one would find several directions for further research and possible approaches for solving real-world problems.

In this book, we develop the supply chain ecosystem framework for the management of global supply chain networks. In our view, the supply chain ecosystem is a composition of networks of companies, countries and their governments, other industrial, social and political organizations, infrastructure, logistics and information technology services that connect the companies and the countries to the external economic and social environment and resources including natural, financial and human resources with talent, connections, knowledge of the industrial environment, interacting together with the landscape (space or domain) and climate. We develop a comprehensive analysis and design of the global supply chain networks, focusing on the location, planning, performance, risk, governance and innovation involving all the ecosystem players. We also discuss the application to green supply chain design.

How to Use This Book

This book can be used for teaching courses on Global Operations or Supply Chain Networks in MBA classes by supplementing with the Harvard cases mentioned in the book. Such a course provides the students with tools and frameworks to manage globally dispersed manufacturing and service network operations and also effectively deal with multiple strategic and operational issues such as outsourcing, green regulations, tensions with the network partners, increased transportation costs and regionalization. The book can also be used in engineering schools supplementing with topics such as Social Networks and Supply Chains, Orchestrator model for governance of SMEs, Location Selection based on Investment Climate, Tax-Integrated Global Supply Chains, Game Theory and Supply Chain Coordination.

N. Viswanadham
S. Kameshwaran

Acknowledgments

This book has come out of a course on *Global Operations Management* that the first author taught at Indian School of Business (ISB) during 2006–2011. Executive education programs were also given from this book. We would like to thank Kutti Krishnan (ISB) for his help and comments in running the course. Several researchers from the Center of Global Logistics and Manufacturing Strategies (GLAMS) — Usha Mohan, Abhijit Kumar, Ramakrishna Devarakonda, Shilpa Dixit, Prachi, Vinit Kumar, Sai Sailaja, Vikas Garg, Srivastava, Somya Sexena, and Sowmya Vedula — have worked on related logistics and supply chain problems. Some of these contributions appeared in the book released by the Prime Minister of India in 2006. The GLAMS Center of Excellence was financed in part by Hero Honda and TAFE. IBM has instituted a *Collaboractory on Service Science* (COSS) at ISB and several researchers from IBM — Gyana Parija, Vinayaka Pandit, Sameep Mehta, Munish Goyal, Krishna Kummamuru, and Nitya Rajamani — participated on joint research efforts. We have benefited immensely from these high-networth individuals and organizations and would like to thank them for collaborating with us. We greatly appreciate the support extended to us at ISB from Ajit Rangnekar (Dean, ISB), The Munjal Family (Hero Corp), and Mallika Srinivasan (TAFE Motors and Tractors Ltd.). In particular, we would like to thank the students of ISB who took the course and carried out the term projects applying the popularly called PERC framework. The first author (NV) would also like to thank the Indian National Academy of Engineering for the financial support as a distinguished professor from August 2011 to date.

We would like to thank our alma mater Indian Institute of Science for what we are today. The first author (NV) thanks IISc for providing him with students, grandstudents (the second author is one of them) and great-grandstudents for collaborating on research projects, writing books and thought leadership papers. We would like to thank Professor Narahari for his help at the Department of Computer Science and Automation, Professor M. R. Rao for his help at ISB and Roshan Gaonkar for his comments and help in the initial stages of this book.

Along with the academic family of the first author NV, his family also has grown. He has five grandchildren: Sairaj from daughter Sundari and Kaladhar;

Arya, Ananya and Sachin from his son Murthy and Sunita; and Dhruti from his son Kiran and Rupal. They introduce me to new gadgets and teach me new video games and keep me and my wife Subhadra busy with Facetime. I would like to thank my grandkids and children and their spouses for giving me an excellent ecosystem for creative work.

Kamesh would like to thank his wife Navolina (who sacrificed her considerable amount of quality time for this book), grandparents Subramani and Saroja (first teachers), parents Sampath and Mangai (first friends), brother Mak and sister Raji (all-time pals) for their everlasting love and appreciation. Special thanks to colleagues at IBM Research (India) — Ramesh Gopinath (Director), Raghuram Krishnapuram (Associate Director), Ravi Kothari (Associate Director), Gyana Parija, Karthik Visweswariah, and Vinayaka Pandit — for their support and encouragement.

N. Viswanadham
S. Kameshwaran

Contents

PART 1
Ecosystem Framework

Chapter 1

Introduction

In this chapter, we provide an overview of the supply chain networks, the recent developments due to globalization, and introduce the notion of supply chain ecosystem. For the last four decades the supply chains of various verticals are very well studied to optimize the supply-demand matching, lead time, and cost. Taking lessons from manufacturing, particularly from Japan, the supply chains have been designed to be of high performance. Globalization has restructured and stretched the supply chains across the national borders. They are highly connected logistically for flow of goods, through Internet for flow of information, and financially for flow of funds. Dense connectedness has made the supply chains fragile and highly risk prone. The financial crisis of 2007 in USA propagated into global trade crisis affecting the flow of goods across the globe.

Our thesis here is that the supply chain designs of yesteryears are inadequate and one has to think of redesign of supply chain networks taking into account the entire ecosystem. Ecosystem encompasses not just companies that make up the supply chain but also consists of their financial and informational partners, governments and regulators of the host countries, infrastructures that enable flow of goods, information, and finance.

1.1 Supply Chain Networks

A supply chain network is a group of independent companies forming a strategic alliance with the common goal of designing, manufacturing, and delivering right-quality products to customer groups faster than other alliance groups and vertically integrated firms. A service chain network has a similar functionality for delivering service. Products generally have both supply and service chain networks. In a global supply or service network, the companies are geographically distributed. The dimension and complexity of the network vary depending on the vertical, the specific product, and its market. Both the supply and service chains are prevalent in automobile, pharmaceutical, aerospace, electronics, computer, food, apparel, etc. These networks are not generally under single ownership but are group formations of independent companies in alliance for a specific and special purpose. They compete with similar cooperating networks.

1.1.1   *Types of supply chains*

We identify two types of supply chains based on the demographic and governance profiles.

Rural supply chains

The farm-to-fork food supply chain in emerging markets such as India starts with the farmers and ends with consumers buying from retail shops. The supply chain is fragmented and there is no single governing body. The supply chain is not designed but exists as a result of social culture, business practices, and regulations. There are too many intermediaries increasing the cost and unorganized business practices leading to wastage and inefficiencies. Rural supply chains are usually supply driven or push supply chains and hence are subject to high price volatility.

Industrial supply chains

Unlike rural supply chain, an industrial supply chain is created by forming strategic alliance among a group of independent companies with the common goal of designing, manufacturing, and delivering right-quality products to customer groups. We can identify two types of industrial supply chains: domestic and global. In a domestic or local supply chain, all the companies are co-located domestically catering to the local market. A global supply chain is internationally dispersed but with an integrated management strategy that blurs the national borders and treats all the constituent companies as part of the single supply chain network. Industrial supply chains have streamlined business-to-business and business-to-consumer processes supported with logistics, communication, and information technology infrastructure. Global supply chains in addition require international trade management to handle cross-border customs regulations and tax regimes.

Electronics, personal computing, apparel, and toys are verticals that usually have global supply chains. Texas Instruments' high-speed telecommunications chip is conceived by engineers in Sweden, designed in Nice with software tools developed in Houston, produced in Japan and Dallas, and finally tested in Taiwan. Another classic example of disintegration of production is the popular Barbie doll. The plastic and hair are sourced from Taiwan and Japan, and the moulds and paints used for decorating the dolls are supplied from the US. The assembly is done in low-cost locations in Indonesia, Malaysia, and China.

It is important to realize that supply chains involve several stakeholders such as suppliers, contract manufacturers, logistics providers and financial institutions. The cost of the final product is made up of the costs of goods and services the product uses in its journey from suppliers to the customer. For example in the case of Barbie doll, the export value of a doll when it leaves Hong Kong for the US is $2. Out of $2, 35 cents is the value of Chinese labor, 65 cents for the cost of materials, and the rest goes for transport, overheads, and profits. The selling price of a doll is $10 in the US, of which Mattel, the lead manufacturer earns at least $1, and the rest covers transport, marketing, wholesale and retailing expenses in the US.

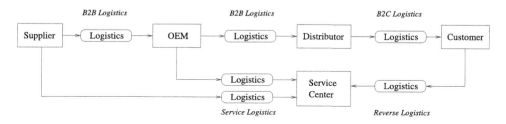

Fig. 1.1   Integrated manufacturing and service network (Cradle-to-Cradle Protocol)

1.1.2   The three flows in a supply chain

A well-designed supply chain network integrates three different flows: material flow, information flow, and financial flow. The logistics network provides a streamlined material flow between all partners, cutting down the lead time and cost of moving the raw materials, sub-assemblies, and finished goods to their destinations. Secure and reliable communications network, information technology, and IT-enabled services link all the companies of the enterprise, providing the information integration. The financial network connects financial institutions, insurance, credit rating agencies and all the other stakeholders enabling financial flow across the supply chain.

1.1.3   The three sub-networks in a supply chain

Operationally, the integrated supply chain network has three sub-networks: demand network, supply network, and service network. The demand sub-network is the fulfillment arm of the supply chain consisting of the manufacturing, distribution, retailing and the associate logistical and finance functions. Timely delivery to the customer is a crucial function. The supply sub-network consists of the suppliers, manufacturers, inbound logistics, and the providers of the documentation needed for exports, imports, and funds transfer. This activity can be termed as primarily business-to-business. The service sub-network connects the end consumer with after-sales service centers, who are connected with the suppliers and manufacturers for spare parts procurement.

1.1.4   *The three business processes in a supply chain*

The three primary business processes that constitute the functionalities in the supply chain are procurement, manufacturing, and distribution.

Procurement

The procurement function involves the acquisition of raw materials and components from the suppliers to produce the product. Procurement is broadly related to various activities such as vendor selection, material selection, outsourcing, negotiation, inventory management, inbound logistics, and to some extent, involvement in design. The supply sub-network is the primary procurer.

Manufacturing or assembly

Manufacturing is the set of production processes which use inputs from the suppliers to produce the products. The manufacturing function could be in a single location or geographically distributed.

Distribution and retail

Distribution consists of packaging and outbound logistics. Outbound logistics includes activities such as transportation planning, packaging, location analysis, and warehousing, as well as inventory management. Examples of typical logistics decisions include options such as direct shipping or hub-and-spoke, central warehouse or distributed network, intermodal or single mode, and third party services or private fleet. But, each of these issues includes tradeoffs among delivery time, responsiveness, quality and cost, as well as environmental performance.

1.1.5   *Supply chain governance*

Governance models such as channel master, third party service providers and fourth party logistics providers exist today for supply-demand matching and in-store replenishment. However, supply chains are treated as simple linear processes of goods or services swiftly passing though an efficient *logistics or IT pipeline* and stakeholders concentrate only on that part of the pipe directly controlled by them or at best their customers and suppliers. The result is that there are three or four masters for the supply chain and each depends on the service-level agreements to keep supply chain smooth. However, uncertainty rules in the practical world. Consequentially, sales routinely deviate from forecasts; components are damaged in transit; production yields fail to meet plan; and shipments are held up in customs. In truth, schedule execution as per plans generated by supply chain planning is just a myth. Significant efforts are expended to expedite orders, to check order status at frequent intervals, to deploy inventory *just-in-case* and to add safety margins to lead times. Supply chain execution thus becomes a very important step. Currently, not much attention is being paid to this step. Monitoring the goods flow from origin to destination and making decisions to counter events that cause disruptions such as truck failures, customs payments or driver ill-health to maintain the commitments to the customers are functions of the execution team normally handled through call centers.

1.1.6 *Focus over the last two decades*

In the early 1990s, companies were proud of their supply chains. Over the previous two decades, they had worked hard to reduce costs in all the three business processes — procurement, manufacturing, and distribution — using techniques such as the lean production, just-in-time manufacturing, single-source suppliers, and outsourcing. The biggest supply chain issue has been supply-demand matching, i.e. reducing obsolescent inventory, loss of sales, and improving customer satisfaction. Accordingly, academics and researchers have complemented with rich literature on supply chain management as an influential research topic in operations research and management science, focusing on problems related to planning and operations in supply-demand matching:

- Supplier/vendor selection; Order allocation;
- Facility location; Network design;
- Production planning; Hierarchical planning and scheduling;
- Inventory management; Pricing;
- Logistics and transportation.

The research on global supply chains continued to evolve in the predictable direction of including globalization-related issues to the above problems. Facility location and logistics considered costs related to international taxation, import and export duties, and constraints imposed by custom regulations. However, the evolution of global supply chains in physical realm has turned out to be more complex with unforeseen issues in addition to the supply-demand matching. This book focuses on these issues and proposes a unified framework for studying supply chains.

1.2 Global Supply Chain Proliferation

Global supply chain networks have emerged as a tremendous source of value creation. The fortunes of companies still rise or fall based on their own earnings and stock performance, not the strength of their networks, although networks are playing an increasing role in their performance. Investors still buy stock in companies, but the extraordinary valuation of a company such as Google depends in large part on the network in which it is embedded. Companies such as eBay, Google, Facebook, Li & Fung, have become major players based primarily on the power of their networks. Established corporations such as Procter & Gamble and Toyota are harnessing networks to tap into new sources of innovation around the globe. The modern equivalent of Smiths pin factory is Li & Fung in Hong Kong. The company produces products for some of the world's leading brands without owning any manufacturing plants but orchestrating a network of 7,500 partner organizations in 37 countries. Its competencies are not in manufacturing but in designing and managing the overall supply chain network.

The migration of sourcing, manufacturing, R&D, and service operations from high cost countries to low cost countries has accelerated. There is an upsurge of outsourcing to India and China. Availability of excellent infrastructure, skilled and educated manpower at low wages enable companies in these countries to deliver high quality products on time. Most countries where businesses are migrating have made investments in infrastructure and also adopted favorable economic policies. Supply chain networks with suppliers located in North America, Europe, and China; customers in the U.S., Europe, and Japan; factories in Asia Pacific, Brazil, Europe, and North America; and development engineers in Europe, India, and North America are common now. A product, either physical or digital, that is made entirely in any one country by any one company is a rarity now.

Globalization is, however, acting as two-edged swords for many business organizations. On one hand, the global networks enable companies with attractive vistas of wide new sourcing horizons i.e. to be able to source from the very best suppliers and fresh market opportunities i.e. to sell into every potential market. On the other hand, companies are exposed to challenges and disturbances globally.

1.2.1 *Institutional innovations and threats*

In 2010, the Canadian company Research in Motion (RIM) found its Blackberry in trouble over new security requirements by governments in the Middle East and in India. The Middle Eastern and Indian governments have lately realized that the tight security provided by Blackberry is taken advantage of by various anti-social elements for subversion. RIM was asked to drastically change the security functionalities of Blackberry, on the threat of being banned. Blackberry being a global product, RIM has to take into account every requirement or change that comes its way from anywhere in the globe.

Institutional threats can also be non-governmental and equally a menace to domestic supply chains. The Tata's ambitious Nano car project in India was launched in Singur, but was later withdrawn with a huge loss due to pressure from the farmers who felt victimized by the acquisition of land over which the manufacturing facility was constructed. Special economic zones, infrastructure development, amending constitutional laws favoring industrialization and foreign direct investment are institutional innovations aimed at leveraging growth fueled by globalization. However, such innovations and changes equally attract opposition and resistance, especially in democratic countries like India. Several special economic zones and infrastructure projects in India are delayed or abandoned due to social pressures. More than any other time in history, supply chains are vulnerable to institutions, both formal and informal.

1.2.2 *Resources and distributed risk sources*

The resources such as suppliers, financial institutions, industry clusters, educational institutions, trained personnel, and utilities play a crucial role in managing the three flows (materials, finance, and information) and the three business processes (procurement, manufacturing, and distribution). On the other hand, their failure or malfunctioning will have disastrous consequences. An example is the devastating earthquake and tsunami that stuck northeastern Japan in March, 2011. The destructive effects of the disasters, compounded by the related nuclear crisis that arose from them, severely disrupted the operations of many Japanese parts suppliers. As a result, the global supply chains of many companies are unexpectedly affected by this shortage of parts. Also, the collapse of U.S. subprime mortgage markets led to a ripple of effects across all sectors of the U.S. economy, necessitating the rescue of Bear Stearns, Fannie Mae and Freddie Mac, and insurer AIG. This further resulted in credit squeeze and trade collapse during the last quarter of 2008 and the first quarter of 2009.

The network challenge can also be seen in the Chinese *toxic-milk scandal.* But a series of problems, including tainted pet foods, recalls of toxic toys, and the spreading scandal of tainted milk powder in China, have revealed the hidden risks of global supply chain networks and difficulties in governance of global networks The sheer complexity of uncovering and recalling all potentially contaminated products that have been shipped globally is formidable. The economic damage to the reputation of China's food industry will be staggering as the scandal has heightened concerns in the United States and Europe about the quality of Chinese products.

1.2.3 *Delivery services and failure to deliver*

The delivery services play an important role in the efficiency of the supply chains. The practices such as telepresence, telemedicine, home delivery, and online sales have significant impact on customer satisfaction. The delivery business models such as prepaid simcards in telecom industry in India have tripled the tele-density. The same channels can be used by the terrorist groups for malicious actions.

1.2.4 *Need for a unified framework for studying supply chains*

Thus we see that the supply chain's performance is very much affected by the governments, social groups, resources and their availability and also the delivery service models. Indeed they are an integral part of the supply chain functioning and they have tremendous influence. It is our aim here to develop a framework that takes into account all the above three factors in the supply chain design and analysis. In other words, our supply chain performance evaluation takes into account all the above three factors. Our risk analysis and risk mitigation will consider the risks that emanate from resources, governments, social groups, delivery mechanisms etc. The design of supply chain in terms of facility location should also take into account investment climate, regulations, social conditions, etc. The innovations that influence the supply chain industry could come from deregulations, reduction of tariffs, creating clusters, providing alternate reliable energy source, financial mobility or through new business models for delivery. In summary, the framework that is proposed below explains the forms of network collaboration, the advantages, the new supply chain formation process, and the new rules of engagement required in global supply chains. As the framework should consist of entities that influence the constituent companies in the supply chain, we use the notion of biological ecosystem to holistically study the new-age supply chains.

In spite of the importance of the subject, there is very little attention by the academic community to develop a unified framework that explains the performance, risks and innovations in current day developed or developing markets. Abonyi and Slyke (2010); Gai and Kapadia (2010) are a few works that have addressed some of the above issues.

1.3   Supply Chain Ecosystem

A biological ecosystem is an environment consisting of the living organisms inhabited in an area, as well as the non-living physical and chemical components of the environments with which the organisms interact. The interaction makes the ecosystem as a functional unit with all its constituents linked together through the flow of energy and nutrient cycles. We extend the concept of biological ecosystem to study the supply chains. A supply chain ecosystem consists of the corresponding supply chain and the other entities with which it interacts. The interaction includes the three traditional flows — goods, information, and finance — and the entities that influence the flows through regulations, technology, management, etc.

Accordingly, the supply chain ecosystem comprises of:

- networks of companies directly and indirectly part of the supply chain;
- countries of operations/presence and their governments;
- industrial, social and political organizations;
- logistics and information technology services infrastructure;
- the third party service providers that connect the companies and the countries to the external economic and social environment;
- resources including natural, financial and human resources with talent, connections and knowledge of the industrial environment;

- industry clusters, universities, etc interacting together with the landscape (horizontal and vertical) and climate (economic and social).

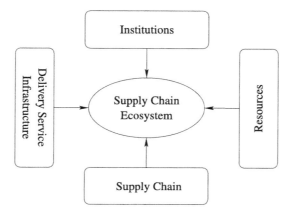

Fig. 1.2   The supply chain ecosystem

We categorize the above entities into the following four categories:

- Supply chain
- Institutions
- Resources and management
- Delivery mechanisms and infrastructure

Figure 1.2 shows the supply chain ecosystem with the above categorization. The ecosystem mapping is equally applicable to services. Recent years have shown a growing interdependence between services and manufacturing industries. The share of services activities that is necessary for or complementary to manufacturing production has increased. Thus, one can have a similar ecosystem mapping for services as well with the appropriate service chain and the other entities defined.

1.4   GRIP: Drivers and Levers of Supply Chain Ecosystem

The drivers of the supply chains are facilities, inventory, transportation, information, sourcing, and pricing [Chopra and Meindl (2007)]. The drivers interact with each other influencing the functioning of the supply chains and hence are used in design, planning, and operation of supply chains. Similar to the drivers of the supply chain, we define drivers and levers for the supply chain ecosystem that interact with each other in synergistic fashion influencing the design, planning, and operation of the supply chain, and as well the ecosystem. Acronymed as GRIP Methodology, it comprises of four factors: Governance, Risks, Innovations, and Performance.

1.4.1 *Governance*

Given the de-verticalization happening at global scale, it is challenging for the diverse interest groups within the network to align themselves with the global objectives of the supply chain and the end-customer. Supply chain governance and leadership are critical for achieving competitiveness. Technological, institutional, and organizational innovations, as well as changes in regulatory environments, transform the structures of industries. Governance structures in supply chains evolve in conjunction with the forces that shape industry structures. We study the forms of governing structure for high-performance supply chains in Chap. 6.

1.4.2 *Risks*

The vertical disintegration and globalization necessitates logistics links, information backbones, and financial gateways connecting all the network entities. These connections are main sources of risk. Risks can also emanate from non-supply chain related factors: protective actions of the very governments that have encouraged the companies to set up shops in their countries, increase in the commodity prices or delivery costs, etc. We consider the risk that arises from the entire ecosystem rather than just the supply chain in the design of the supply chain. The risks in the supply chain ecosystem are discussed in Chap. 4.

1.4.3 *Innovation*

There are two types of innovations: new to the world and new to the market. In the emerging market context, we need new-to-market innovations that can result in blockbuster industries for producing affordable products and delivering them at places accessible to the populations. This kind of blockbuster industries can only result from co-evolution of simultaneous innovations in four distinct forces which make up the supply chain ecosystem: Supply Chains, Institutions, Resources and finally Delivery Services Infrastructure. We focus on such innovations in Chap. 5.

1.4.4 *Performance*

The performance analysis of global supply chains depends on several factors beyond the elements of the supply chain and the traditional metrics such as inventory and production lead times. The performance is affected by the supply chain innovations such as modularization, coordination, visibility, etc.; resources such as clusters; government regulations, tariffs and free trade agreements; and the delivery mechanisms and services such as trade facilitation and other soft infrastructures. Ecosystem-based performance analysis is discussed in Chap. 3.

Performance and risk are drivers with metrics to measure and make judicious decisions. Governance and innovations are more of levers that can be leveraged to determine alternate supply chain and ecosystem configurations. The four factors of the GRIP methodology complement the ecosystem perspective in creating a framework to design and analyze supply chains and as well the ecosystem that contains the supply chain.

1.5 How Can We Use the Ecosystem Framework?

The all-encompassing ecosystem framework can be used not only by businesses but by other stakeholders in the ecosystem.

1.5.1 *Business stakeholders*

The straightforward application is the design of supply chains. Supply chain design includes network design, selection of partners, distribution strategies, etc. As a strategic decision problem, supply chain design incurs majority of the cost and has been extensively studied by researchers and academicians as an application in operations research and management science. For the practitioners and decision makers, there are off-the-shelf commercial software from leading companies like IBM (ILOG LogicNet Plus) and JDA. In addition to traditional metrics of cost and lead time, several new-age parameters like carbon footprint are used by these commercial engines. Powered by mathematical programming techniques and simulation, the commercial solutions are quantitative in nature and are used as computational aids in measuring and comparing alternate supply chain designs. The ecosystem-aware design of supply chains takes into account several non-supply chain related factors particularly of interest to global supply chains and emerging markets. Chapter 7 describes in detail a step-by-step procedure that utilizes the ecosystem framework for designing supply chains. The other business stakeholders in the supply chain — suppliers, service providers, and original equipment manufacturers — can use the ecosystem framework to align the strategies to increase their competitive advantage in the ecosystem.

Moving up the value chain Suppliers and service providers can upgrade or expand their business by identifying opportunities using the ecosystem perspective.

New business models The vertically disintegrated supply chains require new service delivery businesses to seamlessly connect the gaps and ease the frictions due to disintegration. In Chap. 6, we outline governance as a new business model and showcase its application for small and medium enterprises in emerging markets.

1.5.2 *Institutional stakeholders*

The rationale for using the ecosystem framework is to shift the perspective from supply chains to the supply chain ecosystem. As one can design, upgrade, modify, and analyze supply chains, similar things should be done for the ecosystem as well. Institutional stakeholders like policy makers and governments can use the ecosystem framework in designing ecosystems that can attract and sustain businesses of interest. We outline here a few applications:

- **Improving the investment climate**   The notion of investment climate is the ability of a location to attract business. Institutions, resources, and delivery mechanisms constitute the investment climate. It is obvious that the investment climate required for a food processing plant is very different from that of an auto manufacturing facility. However, current investment climate studies are only location-specific and not vertical-dependent. Ecosystem framework is both location- and vertical-specific. In Chap. 8, we describe location analysis using ecosystem framework and how it can be used for improving vertical-specific investment climate.
- **Institutional innovations**   Identify institutional innovations such as strategic de-regulations that attract businesses to co-evolve and create blockbuster industries. We show in Chap. 5 the case of the Indian telecom industry which was a successful outcome of de-regulations.
- Initiate appropriate education, training, and research programs to create the necessary talent and workforce.
- Develop inclusive growth strategies for economically deprived business partners like farmers.
- Devise solutions for wicked problems that cause social and economic divide in emerging markets due to rapid industrialization (refer to Chap. 4 on the case of Tata Motors in Singur).
- Plan and build integrated service systems or systems of systems such as special economic zones.

1.6   Organization of the Book

This book has two parts. Part 1 has seven chapters including this chapter. In Chap. 2, we provide an introduction to the supply chain ecosystem and its four elements: *supply chain, resources, institutions* and the *delivery mechanisms*. We provide examples which illustrate mapping of the supply chain and the various conclusions that can be drawn. A case study of CEMEX, a Mexican Cement Giant, is used as an illustrative example. In this chapter, we also illustrate how the four important issues *governance, risk, innovation,* and *performance* (GRIP) can be studied using the ecosystem framework. In the subsequent four chapters 3–6, we study in detail the GRIP using the ecosystem framework.

In Chap. 3, we study how the four ecosystem elements affect the lead time and cost in detail, while Chap. 4 details how each of the four elements contribute to the collapse of the supply chain and the business in which the supply chain is embedded. Generally researchers consider only partner risk, failures of equipment and how to mitigate them. Chapter 4 shows how the ecosystem framework explains all the risks the supply chain faces and the strategies to be followed. Chapter 5 deals with innovations. Normally people consider only new-to-the-world product or process innovations and how to commercialize them. Our approach considers all the disruptive, radical and small-change innovations in all the four parameters of the ecosystem that can create a blockbuster industry. We consider deregulations, free trade agreements, special economic zones, trade facilitation, speedy delivery, and infrastructure that enables local and global business transport as innovations that can contribute to the rapid industrial growth. Chapter 6 deals with the governance, coordination, and control. It is important to determine who does what and when and also deliver to whom at what price. Selection of partners, keeping in touch with them, delivering to the customers on time and taking care of any malfunctions is an important function. We deal with these very important functions in this chapter. We present an important governance mechanism called orchestration and present the example of Li & Fung, a highly successful Hong Kong trader. In Chap. 7, we present a four-step systematic procedure for supply chain redesign consisting of supply chain formation, project planning, supply chain planning and governance, coordination and control. We illustrate the procedure using an example of food security in emerging markets.

Part 1 of the book covers the concepts to design fundamentals. At the end of Part 1, the reader can, for any industry supply chain, map the ecosystem consisting of various network partners (including manufacturing, logistics, and IT), their (country and regional) locations, risks that the ecosystem faces, and finally the innovations (product, process, business model) needed to make it big in the industry, the value chain architecture with outsourced and ownership details, as well as the organization structure to deliver the product on time.

Part 2 of the book has three chapters: Chapter 8 on location selection based on the ecosystem parameters, Chap. 9 on the design of green supply chain networks, and Chap. 10 on the design of smart villages and cities. The last chapter (Epilogue) shows that the ecosystem framework is a versatile one and can be applied to the design of regions, verticals, villages, cities and countries.

Chapter 2

The Supply Chain Ecosystem Framework

2.1 Introduction

The production process of many industries has gone through a fundamental transformation over the past three decades. Prior to the 1980s, the industry was dominated by large, vertically integrated firms (e.g., GM, GE, IBM, DEC, Fujitsu and Hitachi) that produced most parts and components within their country and firm boundaries using proprietary architecture. Today, industries have increasingly become vertically segmented into various stages and each stage is managed by a different company perhaps in a different country. Each stage in the value chain involves significant competition. The value lies in the standards that create intellectual property based monopolies (Intel chips, Windows OS, auto components) and these component manufacturers wield market power via these standards. This has led to a growing proportion of international trade occurring in components and other intermediate goods and thus the growing integration of world markets and also increasing the service component (logistics, customs clearance) in the production of the final product. The strategic weapon for assemblers (Dell, GM, and Nokia) has moved from factory to managing and governing the global supply chain.

Partnerships between the supply chain players in the emerging markets with US giants coupled with surging local and international demand lead to the ability to invest in better processes and technologies, which in turn leads to higher quality products and the ability to manufacture at lower cost and higher margins. This reinforcing positive feedback cycle results in the strengthening of the supply chain partnerships and partially explains the outsourcing and/or offshoring phenomena that we are observing.

Many of the organizations that fall outside the traditional value chain of suppliers and distributors, and many disciplines outside of manufacturing and production, contribute to the creation and delivery of a product or service and affect the final outcome of the business. We need a more comprehensive way of studying the supply chain networks from location, country of origin of all the partners, cross-border tariffs, customs, and resource acquisition and delivery mechanisms issues. Innovation, Risk, Performance, and Governance should be studied from the entire ecosystem viewpoint since each of these is influenced by occurrences beyond the conventional supply chain.

In this chapter, we develop a supply chain ecosystem framework dealing with supply chain network design and analysis which takes into account the role of the government policies and regulations and the pressures from the social groups, the delivery infrastructure for product and service delivery, and also the human, natural and financial resources and their quality.

2.2   Supply Chain Ecosystem

We define the supply chain ecosystem as follows: An ecosystem comprises of networks of Companies, Countries and their Governments; Other Industrial, Social and Political Organizations; Logistics and Information Technology Services Infrastructure and the third party service providers that connect the companies and the countries to the external economic and social environment; and Resources including natural, financial and human resources with talent, connections and knowledge of the industrial environment, Industry clusters, Universities, etc interacting together with the Landscape (space or vertical) and Climate (economic and social).

The Resources, Institutions and the Delivery service infrastructure together define the investment climate of a region or country. We connect with the World Bank studies on investment climate using our ecosystem approach. In the World Bank studies, the investment climate is defined for a region or country, but our definition is for an industry vertical characterized by the supply chain. It is obvious that the delivery mechanisms for an oil and gas vertical are different from those of an auto or electronic vertical. Similarly, the regulations are not uniform but are vertical dependent.

Supply chain ecosystem can be divided into four distinct mechanisms:

- Global supply/service chains producing standardized products/services;
- Delivery mechanisms such as logistics and IT infrastructure and value-added services for goods and services movement and delivery;
- Institutions involving governments and social groups that determine the trade and economic policies of all countries touching the supply chain network;
- Natural, financial, human and industrial resources.

The ecosystem mapping of supply chains in the above four categories is given in Fig. 2.1. One can possibly categorize the essential entities in different ways. In this chapter, we describe the rationale for the choice of the above four. It is based on our perspective of emergence of global supply chains. In particular, we show that the enablers of globalization of supply chains are closely related to the above four categories. This is not to say that the ecosystem framework is only applicable to global supply chains. Indeed the framework is generic to be applicable to domestic as well as fragmented rural supply chains. However, our perspective of emergence of global supply chains identifies the individual roles of each of the above categories and their interplay in contributing to the governance, risk, innovations, and performance of any supply or service chain.

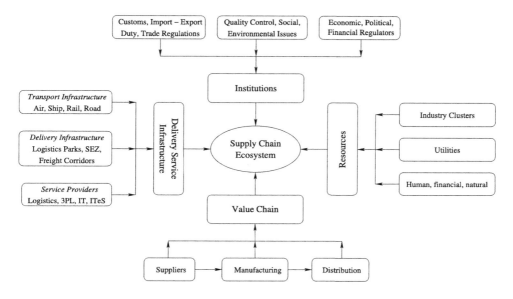

Fig. 2.1 The supply chain ecosystem

2.3 The Ecosystem Elements as Enablers of Globalization

As seen from the discussions above, globalization has moved from import/export of finished goods to multi-company multi-country production environment. Modularization of products and processes enables a single finished product to be composed of various sub-products that are manufactured in a geographically dispersed manner. International trade involves different countries and regions within countries that require appropriate institutional arrangements for legal movements of goods and the supporting financial transactions. Institutions include laws, contracts, labor regulations, import/export restrictions, free trade agreements, customs duties, patent and legal systems, and trade facilitation. Production of goods or service require resources — human, capital, inputs, and utilities. With various activities separated in space and time, logistics and IT delivery infrastructure is required for the flow of physical goods and information.

It is easy to see that the above four are enablers for global supply chains. Without modularization, offshore or outsourcing is not possible physically. Legally, institutions should allow dispersed production of goods and services. Such a dispersed production is feasible only if appropriate resources are available. Transportation of goods and timely coordination of information is essential for successful execution.

The above four enablers are not independent entities that led to a planned development of global supply chains. Rather, globalization of supply chains co-evolved with modularization, institutional arrangements, resource management, and delivery infrastructure. Innovations in one led to innovations in the other, and their synergic emergence resulted in globalization of manufacturing and services. In the following, we look at each of the above factors in detail and their contribution to global supply chains.

2.4   Supply Chain De-Verticalization, Modularization, and Outsourcing

Modularization refers to a product architecture where different functions of a product are implemented by different and relatively independent physical components whose interfaces are defined by a set of interface standards in a way that allow substitutability of components. In integral design strategy, each component may implement many functions and each function is implemented by many different components. Some define modules as sub-systems within a product that are bundled as a unit, and which serve identifiable functions. In other words, modules are units in a larger system where they are structurally independent of one another, but work together. Modularity is an attribute of a complex system that advocates designing structures based on minimizing interdependence between modules and maximizing interdependence within them that can be mixed and matched in order to obtain new configurations without loss of the system's functionality or performance. In a modular system, each module communicates and interacts with the others via standardized interfaces that allow modules decoupling.

Product modularity has two characteristics: similarity between the physical and functional architecture of the design, and minimization of the degree of interaction between physical components. A complete set of design rules would fully address the following categories of design information:

- **Architecture**   What modules will be part of the system, and what their roles will be;
- **Interfaces**   Detailed descriptions of how the different modules will interact, including how they will fit together, connect, and communicate.

Integration protocols and testing standards, that is, procedures that will allow designers to assemble the system and determine how well it works, whether a particular module conforms to the design rules, and how one version of a module performs relative to another. In the product design context, modular design structures are favored over integrated ones when flexibility and rapid innovation are more important than overall performance. Modularization, if carried out properly, is expected to accelerate product innovation primarily through two mechanisms: autonomous (within component) and modular (mix and match of modules) innovation. In an organizational context, it is argued that modularization of product designs can pave the way for similar modularization of organization designs, thus facilitating coordination of activities via coordination structure rather than managerial authority or hierarchy. Modular designs facilitate outsourcing via contracts and/or alliances of non-critical components or modules and thereby reduce the scope of activities that firms need to pursue in-house.

Progress in the division of labor in design (technical modularity) has created opportunities for vertical specialization in project execution, enabling firms to disintegrate the value chain as well as to disperse it geographically. Increasingly this process has taken on a global dimension, giving rise first to offshore assembly in a wide range of industries (both traditional ones like garments and recent innovative industries like semiconductors or mobile phones), and later on to outsourcing to global contract manufacturers. More recently, modular design has also provided ample opportunities for vertical specialization in the production of knowledge intensive services, such as software, information services, engineering and R&D.

2.4.1 *Organizational modularity*

Modularization of product designs paves the way for similar modularization of organization designs facilitating coordination of activities via an information structure rather than managerial authority or hierarchy The codification of knowledge and market-led standardization (through technical standards and design rules) of the interfaces between organizationally separate stages of production has made vertical specialization (*organizational modularity*) the industry's defining characteristic in place of vertical integration. Codification, together with shared interface standards and design rules, reduces the volume of information and hence the amount of knowledge sharing that is required for inter-firm coordination.

The computer industry is frequently cited as an important breeding ground for this new industrial organization model. IBM personified vertical integration within a multi-divisional firm: almost all ingredients necessary to design, produce and commercialize computers remained internal to the firm. This was true for semiconductors, hardware, operating systems, application software, and sales and distribution. Since then, modular design, based on standard interchangeable components as well as the widely shared Wintel architecture, has rapidly eroded the economic rationale for vertical integration. This, it is argued, has made vertical specialization (*organizational modularity*) the industry's defining characteristic.

2.4.2 *Supply chain trends: Modularity and outsourcing*

Modular products with standardized interfaces have led to fragmented yet standardized production processes which could be outsourced. This is the generalized global division of labor resulting in loosely coupled production systems distributed over many countries and we can call them modular supply chains. They are a collection of globally dispersed standardized production processes for manufacturing modular sub-assemblies. Standardized component manufacturers have IP monopoly and wield global market power with components such as Intel chips, Windows OS, Auto components etc. The products themselves have become commodities with codifiable and easily replicable knowledge about assembling the final product. Standardized assembly plants for finished goods and distribution centers are organized nearer to the customer locations.

The strategic competitive advantage for assemblers (Dell, GM, and Nokia) moves from factory to managing the global supply chain. Developments in modular supply chains and efforts of WTO for free trade have resulted in increased Manufacturing Outsourcing and Services Trade. This has also changed the nature of competition between companies. Earlier firms gained market share by building large productive assets specific to their product, thus creating entry barriers. Now, everyone can tap into the same modular supply base and thus gain access to leading-edge production capacity. The barriers to entry are lowered. Thus, competition between lead firms becomes more tightly tied to product-level innovation and global supply chain management.

Large vertically integrated corporations adapted to strategic outsourcing to remain competitive in highly contested and fast moving markets. They focus on product innovation, marketing and other activities related to brand development — areas that provide competitive advantage — and rely on specialized suppliers for providing best-in-class production services to quickly reap value from innovations, and also spread the risk in volatile markets by reducing fixed investments in manufacturing assets. The OEMs can also ramp the output up and down according to changes in regional demand since contract manufacturers have global presence.

2.4.3   *De-verticalization of electronics firms*

During the 1990s, traditional electronics firms sold off many of their domestic and offshore production facilities to the large contract manufacturers such as Solectron, Celestica, Flextronics, and Jabil Circuit. Strategic outsourcing by groups of lead firms has, over time, led to the rise of a shared supplier network, called the contract manufacturers' one that can be accessed by the industry as a whole, even by lead firms that compete head-to-head in final product markets. This has resulted in exponential growth of the outsourcing of electronics production and the concomitant rise of highly competent contract manufacturers based in the United States and Taiwan.

There are three business segments that became popular: *Contract Manufacturing* (CM), *Contract Design and Manufacturing* (CDM) and *Original Design and Manufacturing* (ODM) [Huckman and Pisano (2003)]. CM are EMS firms that just do manufacturing and packaging against the design received from the OEMs and all the component suppliers are typically those specified by the OEM. The CDM firms provide the product design, logistics and engineering services in addition to the contract manufacturing.

2.4.4 *De-verticalization of apparel firms*

Similar to the electronic firms, even the apparel firms have also evolved into four categories with various capabilities. We present them in detail below [Cattaneo *et al.* (2010)]:

Assembly/CMT This is a form of subcontracting in which garment sewing plants are provided with imported inputs for assembly, most commonly in export processing zones (EPZs). CMT, that is, cut, make, and trim, or CM (cut and make), is a system whereby a manufacturer produces garments by cutting fabric provided by the customer and sewing the cut fabric into garments for delivery to the customer in accordance with his or her specifications. In general, companies operating on a CMT basis do not become involved in the design of the garment, just the manufacture.

Original equipment manufacturing (OEM)/FOB/package contractor
OEM is a business model that focuses on the manufacturing process. The contractor is capable of sourcing and financing piece goods (fabric) and trim, and providing all production services, finishing, and packaging for delivery to the retail outlet. In the clothing industry, OEMs typically manufacture according to customer specifications and design, in many cases using raw materials specified by the customer. Free-on-board (FOB) is a common term used in industry to describe this type of contract manufacturer. However, it is technically an international trade term in which, for the quoted price, goods are delivered onboard a ship or to another carrier at no cost to the buyer.

Original design manufacturing (ODM)/full package This is a business model that focuses on design rather than on branding or manufacturing. A full package garment supplier carries out all steps involved in the production of a finished garment, including design, fabric purchasing, cutting, sewing, trimming, packaging, and distribution. Typically, a full-package supplier will organize and coordinate the design of the product; the approval of samples; the selection, purchasing, and production of materials; the completion of production; and, in some cases, the delivery of the finished product to the final customer.

Original brand manufacturing (OBM) OBM is a business model that focuses on branding rather than design or manufacturing; this is a form of upgrading to move into the sale of the customer's *own brand* products. For many firms in developing countries, this marks the beginning of brand development for products sold in the home country or its neighbors.

2.5   Role of Institutions

Institutions are the written and unwritten rules, norms and constraints that humans devise to reduce uncertainty and control their environment. These include:

(i) written rules and agreements that govern contractual relations and corporate governance;
(ii) constitutions, laws and rules that govern politics, government, finance, and society more broadly; and
(iii) unwritten codes of conduct, norms of behavior, and beliefs.

Institutional quality and institutional homogeneity play a major role for the intensity of bilateral trade [de Groot *et al.* (2004)]. A better quality of the institutional framework reduces uncertainty about contract enforcement and general economic governance. This reduces transaction costs directly, by increasing the security of property, as well as indirectly, by increasing the level of trust in the process of economic transactions. Homogeneity in the perceived quality of institutions may give rise to similar norms of behavior (conventions, business practices) and similar levels of trust in doing business. Institutional homogeneity leads to familiarity with each other's formal procedures and with the informal conventions and habits developed to deal with the governance situation. If traders in both countries experience similar levels of institutional effectiveness, they are better equipped to use each other's institutions, to operate in each other's institutional environment. This reduces adjustment costs and lowers the insecurity related to transaction contingencies in trade.

Kaufmann *et al.* (2002) constructed six indicators of perceived institutional quality. Each indicator captures some related aspects of the quality of governance. They reflect either the political process, the quality of the state apparatus and its policies, or the success of governance.

(1) **Voice and accountability** reflects the extent to which citizens can participate in selecting government and hold her accountable for the actions taken. This score includes various characteristics of the political process as well as assessments of the independence of the media. It reflects whether citizens and business can prevent arbitrariness in the behaviour of government and enforce good governance when needed.
(2) **Political stability** refers to the perceived likelihood of the government being destabilized or overthrown by unconstitutional interference or excesses of violence against persons and possessions. These factors are highly detrimental for the continuity of policy and the stability of the economic environment.

(3) **Government effectiveness** is a measure for the quality of government inputs. It represents, amongst others, the perceived quality and independence
of the bureaucracy. This indicates the ability of government to formulate and
implement good policies.

(4) **Regulatory quality** is directly focused on the quality of implemented policies.
It includes the perceived incidence of policies that inhibit the market mechanism, and excessive regulation of foreign trade and business development, and
as such closely reflects the transaction costs that result from policy intrusion
by the state in private trade.

(5) **Rule of law** indicates the quality of the legal system. It indicates society's
perceived success in upholding fair and predictable rules for social and economic
interaction. Essentially, it focuses on the quality of the legal system and the
enforceability of contracts.

(6) **Control of corruption** represents the extent of *lawless* or unfair behaviour in
public-private interactions. It complements regulatory quality and rule of law
indicators, pointing at the impact of bad governance on economic interaction.
Corruption, like regulatory intrusion, affects transaction costs by adding a *third-
party* involvement to private transaction. An added component of corruption
to trading costs is its arbitrary, uncertain nature.

2.5.1 *Economic, regulatory and trade-related innovations*

These are mainly country-related and are policies of the Government. Removing
the trade barriers, reducing or increasing the import or export duties, signing FTAs
with the neighbors, allowing FDI etc are the regulatory measures governments use
to enhance global trade. Creating instruments such as Free trade zones, Special
economic zones, software technology parks, Bonded warehouses etc are economy-
related innovations. Planning and building Logistics infrastructure such as logistics
parks, Freight corridors, Roads, Soft infrastructure (customs, trade facilitation) to
speed up the trade at borders, etc and also the rural infrastructure such as roads,
warehouses and also social infrastructure and financing of these through public-
private partnerships are logistics innovations.

2.5.2 *Institutions and supply chains*

The globalization of value chains has been driven by a number of factors: search
for efficiency, entry into new markets and access to strategic assets. Global supply chains or service chains pass through several countries, and entry and exit
from each country through the ports and airports or in the cyberspace need to
be managed effectively to minimize the lead times and the inventory costs. Soft
infrastructure such as trade facilitation, online customs clearance, trade policies
made by the Governments such as free trade agreements, customs duties, restrictions on entrance of foreign companies, business friendliness and enabling attitude

and economic diplomacy of the Governments, social factors such as labor unions, industry associations and other communities are important for the foreign companies to establish their businesses quickly and also in registering superior performance months or years later. Trade and FDI are thus influenced by quality of the institutions and their governance. Ultimately the functioning of the institutions and the laws affect the products and services used by the people and also their living conditions. It is argued that a favorable institutional environment reduces transaction costs, encourages skill formation and innovation, supports capital formation and capital mobility, and allows risks to be priced and shared, all of which positively influence economic growth.

The availability, price and quality of the products and services that people use are affected by the Government and Institutional policies. Behind every product or service there is a supply chain or service chain and the interaction between the Government policy and the service/supply chain performance is of great interest. Many successful services companies owe their existence and success to the opening up of markets. Companies such as Airtel, Jet Airways in India and South West, E-bay and others in USA owe their existence to policy shift in the government. The opening up of markets has enabled these new entrants to succeed through innovation either in terms of processes or products or new business models or through convergence with IT or logistics. It will be good to investigate the role of policy on the supply chains and, conversely, how companies strategically navigate themselves to make profits while following the regulations and laws. Successful company innovations in this category include strategic reverse outsourcing by Airtel or use of flying direct model by South West (rather than following the established hub-and-spoke network model).

2.6   Resources and Management

Resources for supply chains can be categorized as follows:

- Natural (mines, coast lines, fertile lands, rivers);
- Human (skilled, technical, managerial, scientific);
- Financial (banks, insurance, venture capitalists, supply chain financing, letters of credit);
- Industry inputs (clusters, utilities, land, water).

It is observed that the possession of oil, natural gas, or other valuable mineral deposits or natural resources does not necessarily confer economic growth. Many African countries such as Angola, Nigeria, Sudan, and the Congo are rich in oil, diamonds, or other minerals, and yet their peoples continue to experience low per capita income and low quality of life. In East Asia, the countries with few raw materials (Hong Kong, Singapore, South Korea, and Taiwan) have done even better than the resource-rich ones (Indonesia, Malaysia, and Thailand). The supply chains using these oil and mining resources are capital and engineering equipment intensive although the labor force need not be highly educated. Good governance at the country level is crucial to transform natural resource wealth into good economic performance; otherwise, resources can turn as a curse.

2.6.1 *Clusters*

Clustering among firms in the same industry is driven by common needs for inputs and access to markets, industry-specific knowledge flows and the need for specialized skills [Porter (1998b)]. One potential advantage of clustering is information spillovers, such as the sharing of technological or marketing knowledge. Another type of knowledge that may spread more easily within an agglomeration of similar firms is knowledge of improved management techniques. Learning effects may be easier to achieve when firms are located together. When firms in the same industry are located close to each other, it is easier to monitor what the neighbors do and learn from their successes and mistakes, and competitive pressures may lead to innovation and increase productivity. Clusters may also attract traders and reduce the costs for firms to market their goods. Clusters are geographic concentrations of interconnected companies, specialized suppliers, service providers, and associated institutions in a particular field that are present in a nation or region.

   Clusters arise because they increase the productivity with which companies can compete. The development and upgrading of clusters is an important agenda for governments, companies, and other institutions. Clusters also often extend downstream to channels and customers and laterally to manufacturers of complementary products and to companies in industries related by skills, technologies, or common inputs. Clusters also include institutions such as universities, think tanks, and vocational training providers. There are several clusters around the world and some of them have excellence in improving the competitiveness of the industry they represent and also the country in which they are located. A cluster of independent and informally linked companies and institutions represents a robust organizational form that offers advantages in efficiency, effectiveness, and flexibility. Compared with market transactions among dispersed and distant buyers and sellers, the proximity of companies and institutions in one location fosters better coordination and trust.

   An excellent example is the California wine cluster with a large cluster of commercial wineries as well as several thousand independent wine grape growers. An extensive complement of industries supporting both wine making and grape growing exists, including suppliers of grape stock, irrigation and harvesting equipment, barrels, and labels; specialized public relations and advertising firms; and numerous wine publications aimed at consumer and trade audiences. A host of local institutions is involved with wine, such as the world-renowned viticulture and enology program at the University of California at Davis, the Wine Institute, and special committees of the California senate and assembly.

Clusters affect the community in several ways. Being part of a cluster allows companies to operate more productively in sourcing inputs; accessing information, technology, and needed institutions; coordinating with related companies; and measuring and motivating improvement. Companies in clusters can tap into the vast pool of employees, thereby lowering their search and transaction costs in recruiting. A cluster will have a well-developed supplier base making possible sourcing locally instead of from distant suppliers, thus lowering the transaction costs and minimizing the inventory, importing costs and delays. Local outsourcing with informal relationships is a better alternative to vertical integration not only in component production but also in services such as training. Also, cluster members have access to extensive market, technical, and competitive information. In addition, personal relationships and community ties foster trust and facilitate the flow of information.

A host of linkages among cluster members results in a whole greater than the sum of its parts. In a typical tourism cluster, for example, the quality of a visitor's experience depends not only on the appeal of the primary attraction but also on the quality and efficiency of complementary businesses such as hotels, restaurants, shopping outlets, and transportation facilities. Because members of the cluster are mutually dependent, good performance by one can boost the success of the others. Investments by companies in training programs, infrastructure, quality centers, testing laboratories, and so on, also contribute to increased productivity. Such private investments are often made collectively because cluster participants recognize the potential for collective benefits. They must ensure the supply of high quality inputs such as educated citizens and physical infrastructure. They must set the rules of competition by protecting intellectual property and enforcing antitrust laws, for example, so that productivity and innovation will govern success in the economy. Finally, governments should promote cluster formation and upgrading and the buildup of public or quasi-public goods that have a significant impact on many linked businesses. A vibrant cluster can help any company in any industry compete in the most sophisticated ways, using the most advanced, relevant skills and technologies. Promoting clusters in a country means starting at the most basic level. Policymakers must first address the foundations: improving education and skill levels, building capacity in technology, opening access to capital markets, and improving institutions. Over time, additional investment in more cluster-specific assets is necessary.

To integrate themselves into the global value chains, the cluster members should be capable of delivering specified products, in the right quantity, with the required quality and at the right time. They have to meet the global standards dealing with quality, labor conditions, and the environment. They also have to be ready to upgrade or innovate and add value over time by moving up the value chain. The enterprises should be able to manage the process of identifying, mastering, adapting, and innovating the activities, skills, and technologies that are essential for competitive performance of the global supply chains.

The governments where the clusters are located should provide a hospitable and sustainable business environment. For example, the government actions should take the form of streamlining import and export procedures, providing efficient inter-firm logistics systems, or encouraging the enterprise cooperation and partnerships, such as enterprise clusters.

Governments have an important role to play in facilitating learning and capacity building so that the enterprises can enter and compete effectively within the global supply chains. This facilitating role is different for different supply chains. For example, helping to strengthen the capabilities of farmers to meet global standards for organic fruit and vegetables is very different from supporting auto parts manufacturers to upgrade skills needed for new types of hybrid fuel cars. Similarly, the logistics systems and the import-export procedures for delivering products within and across borders is very different for firms in electronics, automotive parts, garments, and fresh fruit and vegetables. A wide variety of government initiatives may be found throughout the world with programs aimed at raising the technical and managerial skills of enterprises to increase their prospects to be competitive suppliers in global supply chains and to upgrade within networks.

2.7   Delivery Infrastructure: Logistics, Communication, IT, and ITeS

Delivery infrastructure of various forms is the enabler and facilitator of globalization. It is the fundamental force in shaping the pattern of transformation of economies. The transportation and communication technologies have shrunk the world dramatically. Transportation systems for moving goods have several innovations during the last few decades including the commercial jet aircraft to container shipping. The new transmission channels such as the satellites and the optical fibres have revolutionized the global communications. The Internet is the real innovation facilitating instantaneous communication and low-cost information search as well as information delivery. The recent innovations such as wireless and RFID will further create efficiencies in the supply chain communications, visibility, and real-time coordination.

2.7.1   *Logistics*

Logistics is defined as the broad range of activities concerned with effective and efficient movement of semi-finished or finished goods from one business to another and from manufacturers/distributors/retailers to the end consumers. The Council of Logistics Management (CLM) has formulated the following definition of logistics with a flow and process orientation: The process of planning, implementing, and controlling the efficient, cost-effective flow and storage of raw materials, in-process inventory, finished goods, and related information and financials from point of origin to point of consumption for the purpose of conforming to customer require-ments. The activities within the sphere of logistics include freight transportation, warehousing, material handling, protective packaging, inventory control; order pro-cessing, marketing, forecasting, and customer service. Thus, Logistics is that part of the supply chain process that plans, implements, and controls the efficient, effective flow and storage of goods, services, and related information from the point of origin to the point of consumption in order to meet customers' requirements (Council of Logistics Management).

The above definition gives the impression that logistics is concerned only with the manufacturing sector, from the raw material suppliers to the end consumers. But logistics is also important in two other sectors of the economy: agriculture and also in the service industry. The logistics market is huge. It amounts to 10–15% of every product produced and is estimated to be at US$2 trillion worldwide. North America has the largest global market share for logistics services ($1,137.10 bn), with the U.S accounting for $947.10 bn, compared with Europe ($870.10 bn), Asia ($824.00 bn), South America ($94.10 bn) and Africa ($13.10 bn). The competitive-ness of the economies can be enhanced by adopting promising new technologies and next generation logistics thinking. We also underline the importance of logistics in the face of current trends such as the increasing outsourcing of manufacturing, R&D, and service operations from high cost countries to low cost countries.

Types of logistics

We can classify logistics into three categories: Business-to-Business logistics and Business-to-Consumer logistics, and Service logistics. The B2B logistics is very important and forms about 80% of total logistical activity and is again divided into four distinct categories: Manufacturing logistics, which refers to the movement of materials from machine to machine in a factory environment; Inbound logis-tics, which refers to the management of material movement and integration from component suppliers to a manufacturer/assembler; Outbound logistics, which is the management of movement of final products from a manufacturer/assembler to the distributors and retailers; and finally, Spare part logistics, which moves spare parts from the manufacturers to the service centres or dealers. B2C logistics can be divided into two categories: Retail logistics, which is the management of goods delivery from manufacturers, distributors or retailers to the end consumers; and Reverse logistics, which involves movement of used goods from consumer to the manufacturers for service or refurbishment. Finally, Service logistics is logistics in the service industry such as in construction industry, health care, etc.

We thus see that logistics is product dependent and the requirements are differ-ent for each stage of the product life cycle. The logistics requirements of packaging, warehousing and transport are different for Oil and Petrochemical, Pharmaceutical,

Electronics, Auto, Fruit and Vegetables, Flowers, Meat, etc. Also, for new products, the inbound and outbound logistics play a significant role. For mature products, reverse logistics is crucial. Spare part logistics is a big market in life critical applications such as IT servers in banking applications. The profit margins also vary; spare part logistics is more profitable than the inbound or outbound logistics involved with the new products. Also, the profits from maintenance contracts of equipment and software far outweigh those of direct equipment or software sales.

The logistics function is to ensure the availability of right product at the right place, in right quantities and right condition at the right time and right cost for the right customer. To achieve the above objective, integration and synchronization of material, information and financial flows across supplier, manufacturer and logistics organizations is needed. Trading partner integration at the application software and also at the busines process level is important. The important point to note is that, in world-class supply chains, the movement of components, final products, information and funds is not governed by discrete functions, but by a single integrated process, the goal of which is tight management of deliveries, inventories, and costs.

Logistics providers

Most manufacturers handle all logistics functions including trucking and warehousing through their own logistics or transportation departments. In fact in the US, the outsourcing of logistics activities is increasing only now. It is between 8–10% of the total market of approximately 1 Trillion dollars. The second party logistics providers (2PLs) are basic transportation and storage providers such as truck owners, the rail operators, the shipping companies, the airlines, the freight forwarders, the warehousing companies, and the packaging and distribution companies who have high levels of asset intensity but low barriers to entry. Airports and Seaports as capacity providers are also categorized as 2PLs. These companies are now changing their traditional business models and moving up the value chain. They now want to be *one-stop total end-to-end logistics solutions providers* offering multi-modal cargo carriers, trade documentation, financial support such as insurance, customs clearance and a host of other things. They are labelled as integrated third party logistics (3PL) company or a lead logistics provider (LLP), or an integrated express logistics company, or as a 4PL consultant.

Total logistics solution providers offer custom and semi-custom supply chain and logistics solutions to targeted industries through integration and management of services provided by multiple focused service providers. Examples of solutions offered include inbound materials logistics and sequencing for the auto industry, supplier hubs for the high tech industry, spare parts management, and e-fulfillment for retailers. These solution providers provide value through economies of scale/scope achieved by providing similar solutions to multiple clients against customization of solutions to individual clients, and through relationship management. On the information technology implementation side, the shippers are demanding greater visibility of the shipments through improved tracking and tracing capabilities and also higher logistics performance in terms of lead time reliability and on-time delivery.

Trade logistics

The quality and performance of logistics services differ markedly across countries. In Kazakhstan it takes 93 days to export a 20-foot full container load (FCL) container of cotton apparel and in Mali 67 days, while in Sweden it takes only 6 days. In Namibia the costs of all trade-related transactions for a 20-foot FCL container, including inland transport from the ocean vessel to the factory gate, amount to slightly more than $3,000, and in Georgia to slightly less than $3,000. In Germany these costs amount to only $813 and in Sweden to a little more than $500. These variations in time and cost across countries stem from differences in the quality and cost of infrastructure services as well as differences in policies, procedures, and institutions. They have a significant effect on trade competitiveness.

Studies find that differences in logistics performance are driven only in part by poor quality of physical infrastructure services such as road, rail, waterways, port services, and interfaces. Instead, the inadequacies often are caused by (non-tariff) policy and institutional constraints such as procedural red tape, inadequate enforcement of contracts, poor definition and enforcement of rules of engagement, delays in customs, delays at ports and border crossings, pilferage in transit, and highly restrictive protocols on movement of cargo. Efficient logistics services play an essential role in the worldwide flow of goods and services and in the ability of countries to attract and sustain investment.

The Logistics provider generally transports material from the suppliers to the manufacturer i.e. in procurement, or from manufacturers to the distributors and retailers i.e. outbound logistics. The value chain map is shown in Fig. 2.1. The resources in terms of warehouses, fleet of vehicles, containers, the financial institutions including foreign exchange, insurance, manpower training centers for skill development and also for research in new business models, optimal location of warehouses, truck services and maintenance are essential for creating a brand for the Logistics provider. The place in logistics parks, connections with the airport, seaports will help in customs clearance. The logistics provider needs to tread carefully with the regulations and also interface with the truck manufacturers, warehouses, builders, etc.

Transport costs affect growth rates

Shipping costs can affect economic growth in several ways. First, higher transport costs reduce rents earned from the exports of primary products, lowering an economy's savings available for investments. They push up import prices of capital goods, directly reducing real investments. Second, all things being equal, countries with higher transport costs are likely to devote a smaller share of their output to trade. Those countries are also less likely to attract export-oriented foreign direct investment (FDI). Since trade and FDI are key channels of international knowledge diffusion, higher transport costs may lead an economy to be farther removed from the world technology frontier and slow its rate of productivity growth. Third, transport costs determine a country's selection. The strength of world trade and the shift in trade patterns can also be seen in global shipping freight rates, as shipping still accounts for around two-thirds of the value of all international goods transportation. The Baltic Dry Index (BDI), which tracks freight prices for dry bulk goods, has soared to unprecedented levels over the past two years. Unsurprisingly, the pick-up in freight rates has been especially concentrated on trade routes to Asia, and the ports along these routes have become increasingly congested. The BDI provides an assessment of the price of moving major raw materials by sea. Since the goods being shipped in constructing the index are inputs to the production process, as opposed to finished goods, the BDI is seen as providing a good indication of future economic growth. Since peaking at around 11,000 in November 2007, the BDI has fallen over 37%.

We have seen above that the supply chain networks studies need to be conducted taking into account all the four elements of the ecosystem. In Part 2 of the book we present detailed application studies of the above ecosystem framework. In this chapter we give some academic examples as to how to use the ecosystem framework in practical applications.

2.8 How Can We Use the Ecosystem Framework?

The ecosystem framework is fundamental and can be used for a variety of applications. We mention a few of them here:

- Mapping the ecosystem of a supply chain (Auto vertical).
- Mapping the ecosystem of a service chain (Inbound logistics).
- Benchmarking an industry vertical (Food supply chain).
- Analyzing a company with ecosystem framework (CEMEX).
- Improving the investment climate that enables business growth.
- Planning and building integrated service systems or systems of systems such as smart cities, special economic zones, and villages.

We consider each of them below.

2.8.1 *Mapping the ecosystem of a supply chain: Auto vertical*

The Ecosystem approach is comprehensive and integrated and depicts all the stakeholders involved with the vertical on a single platform and involves analysis that

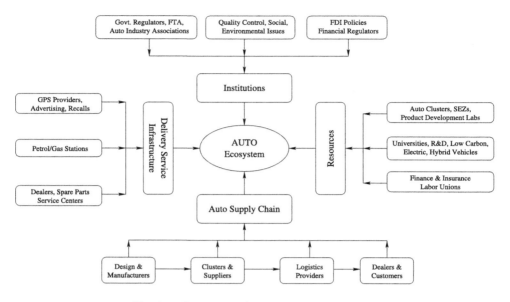

Fig. 2.2   Ecosystem of automobile supply chain

looks at the location, planning, performance, risk, governance and innovation from a systemic viewpoint. Figure 2.2 shows the ecosystem map of automobile supply chain. The resources arm includes clusters for collaboration and partnership, universities for workforce, R&D labs for innovation, FII for financing, letter of credit (LC) etc, labor unions and problems, land acquisition and the risks. They also include the resources such as mines, land, water and management skills. The delivery service infrastructure is very important for on-time delivery. The logistics and IT infrastructure, the availability of logistics service providers and software developers, soft infrastructure at ports and airports, and data banks form the parts of delivery service infrastructure. Customs, Trade, Tax Policies, Industry and FDI incentives, Labor Unions, Foreign exchange, and Legal enforcement form the government side of the Institutions. Government policies that directly affect global economic competitiveness also need to be studied. The social groups, farmers and their welfare, NGOs all form the societal side of the Institutions. We present other examples of mapping the ecosystem in future chapters.

2.8.2   *Mapping the ecosystem of a service chain: Inbound logistics*

Inbound logistics refers to the management of material movement and integration from component suppliers to a manufacturer/assembler. This is a part of the procurement function which has in recent times gone global. The inbound logistics function therefore includes warehousing at the supplier and manufacturer; transportation from supplier to warehouse and to international transport via sea or air.

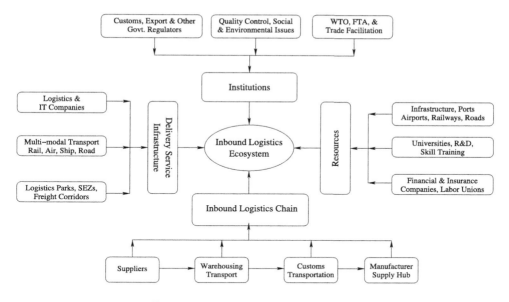

Fig. 2.3   Ecosystem of inbound logistics

It is an important function that affects the inventory held and the timeliness of the manufacturer's schedules.

The ecosystem (see Fig. 2.3) shows all the actors influencing the effectiveness and efficiency of the inbound logistics function. The institutions play a significant role while the freight is crossing the borders. The port and airport infrastructure, the availability of the software and other logistics players also are factors for the efficient functioning of inbound logistics vertical. The logistics function is executed by the third party logistics companies. Some companies own their own logistics departments. There were several innovations such as supply hubs, where the component or sub-assembly inventory is held by a third party at the supplier's cost nearer to the assembler site.

2.8.3   *Benchmarking the food supply chain in India*

With food safety assuming growing importance in world markets, much of India's success in doing business will depend on its ability to meet the increasingly stringent food safety standards imposed in developed countries.

The food supply chain

India has one of the most fragmented produce-supply chains in the world. Lack of adequate cold chain infrastructure and a supportive food processing industry leads to wastage of about 30 per cent of all foods produced. Conservative estimates put

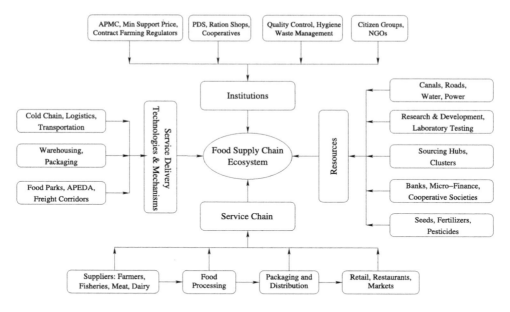

Fig. 2.4   Food supply chain ecosystem

processing levels in the fruit and vegetable sector at 2 per cent, meat and poultry at 2 per cent, milk at 14 per cent, fish at 4 per cent, while bulk meat de-boning is to the tune of 21 per cent. As of now, the food processing sector constitutes only 14 per cent of the manufacturing GDP. The ecosystem mapping for the food supply chain is shown in Fig. 2.4.

Resources and management

In India, 52% of total land is cultivable as against 11% in the world. All 15 major climates of the world, snow bound Himalayas to hot humid southern peninsula. Sunshine hours and day length are ideally suited for round-the-year cultivation of crops. In spite of the vast natural resources and abundant agricultural produce, India ranks below 10th in the export of food products. Compared to other countries the land productivity in India is low. Even within the country, there are tremendous variations among the states in terms of farm productivity. There is a tremendous scope for increasing the farm outputs using state of the art pre-harvest technologies and harvesting techniques. Pre-cooling, cold chain, packaging, transport using totes or small containers are all absent, resulting in substandard delivery of groceries and enormous amounts of wastage. Research should be initiated to develop indigenous packaging materials, machines and laboratories for developing new food products and more importantly protocols for storage and processing raw food materials.

Institutions

In India, there are several regulatory measures handled by a multitude of departments divided between the state and central governments. While some of this is inevitable, streamlining the process would be extremely productive. The APMC Act in most states of India requires all agricultural products to be sold only in government-regulated markets. These markets impose substantial taxes on buyers, in addition to commissions and fees taken by middlemen. Under the present Act, the processing industry cannot buy directly from farmers. The farmer is also restricted from entering into direct contract with any manufacturer because the produce is required to be channelized through regulated markets A key impact of this regulation is the inability of private sector processors and retailers to integrate their enterprises directly with farmers or other sellers, eliminating middlemen in the process. Farmers also are unable to legally enter into contracts with buyers.

Delivery service mechanisms

The food supply chain is temperature-sensitive and manual handling reduces the product quality and life. India does not have a comprehensive cold-chain network. Even the few existing cold storages are found to be under-utilized. The farmers use mostly open trucks to send their produces to the mandis at a high percentage loss, probably because of the high cost of refrigerated transport. This is a big opportunity for infrastructure builders, cold chain operators, logistics companies and food manufacturers both from inside and outside of India for investment. The service providers can also adopt state-of-the-art techniques such as cross-docking that will reduce transit times and cut down on inventory. In India, there is no real channel master managing the supply-demand situation and coordinating the supply chain and managing the logistics. This provides a tremendous opportunity for players to enter the growing retailing market.

The food service chain ecosystem above presents a holistic picture of all the elements that affect it and solutions can be found to make it globally competitive. A detailed design of food supply chain to address the food security in India is discussed in Chap. 7.

2.8.4 *GRIP analysis*

GRIP (governance, risk, innovation, and performance) analysis, outlined in Section 1.4, is useful for studying the supply chain ecosystems.

Governance

The global supply chain is fragmented, it is challenging for the diverse interest groups within the network to align themselves with the global objectives of the supply chain and the end-customer. Supply chain governance and leadership are critical for achieving competitiveness. Technological, institutional, and organizational in-novations, as well as changes in regulatory environments, transform the structures of industries. Governance structures in global value chains evolve in conjunction with the forces that shape industry structures. We study the forms of governing structure for high-performance supply chains in Chap. 6.

Risk

The global supply chains are highly connected logistically, informationaly, and fi-nancially. These connections can become sources of risk. Risk in global supply chains can emanate from several sources including the supply chain and its part-ners, and several other non-supply chain related factors such as: protective actions of the very governments that have encouraged the companies to set up shops in their countries, increase in the commodity prices and hence the delivery costs, etc. We consider the risk that arises from the entire ecosystem rather than just the supply chain in the design of the supply chain (Chap. 4).

Innovation

There are two types of innovations: new to the world and new to the market. In the emerging market context, we need new-to-market innovations that can result in blockbuster industries for producing affordable products and delivering them at places accessible to the populations. This kind of blockbuster industries can only result from co-evolution of simultaneous innovations in four distinct forces which make up the supply chain ecosystem: Supply Chains, Institutions, Resources and finally Delivery Services Infrastructure. We focus on such innovations in Chap. 5.

Performance

The performance analysis of global supply chains depends on several factors beyond the elements of the supply chain and the properties such as inventory and production lead times. The performance is affected by the supply chain innovations such as modularization, coordination, visibility, etc.; resources such as clusters; government regulations, tariffs and free trade agreements; and the delivery mechanisms and services such as trade facilitation and other soft infrastructures. We study this in Chap. 3.

2.8.5 Smartening the players in the industry vertical

In any industry vertical the manufacturing and service processes are intermingled. Services such as construction, power networks, water networks, education were de-signed almost a century ago. These services can be designed smart and more efficient now. Some of the services have gone digital and they can be accessed more easily on the internet. Library services, media, reservations are today accessed in much different ways than a decade ago. Also the industry can strategically position itself for rapid growth by following new business models depending on the current and future regulations. There should be a review of all the services in both public sector and private sector such as Banking, Retail, Procurement, Legal, Health care, Judiciary, Construction, Power, Water, Education etc that affect the Industry vertical and investigate the regulations and their relevance. It is also prudent to investigate how the use of computing, communication and ITeS can be used to modernize the services as well as manufacturing. For example, in auto industry, procurement services as well as the monitoring and execution of delivery of the components from suppliers to Detroit are all outsourced to a BPO service provider in India. This improves the delivery reliability. Education, in general, and higher education, in particular, plays a key role in the realization of the potential of the industry vertical. Vocational training centers and also the graduate programs in engineering, manufacturing and services such as accounting, law and logistics are very important apart from high quality research.

Integrated system design and implementation taking into account the entire ecosystem involving several technologies such as sensor networks, smart instrumentation, cloud computing, smart meters, data mining and manipulation are needed in addition to coordinated decision-making, involving both state and central governments. Better planning, selection of contractors, monitoring and execution are the answers to improve the situation. Use of IT, standardization of procurement and other processes, monitoring and execution using call center based decision support systems, use of supply hubs, automation of financial and other government clearance processes are solutions that can be followed.

2.8.6 *Improving the investment climate for industry growth in India*

Investment climate is determined by the political, economic, resources, logistical and IT infrastructure, human resources, trade regulations and industry clusters. For services growth and also to attract foreign direct investment it is important to have the proper investment climate. For example, for IT services, the Indian government has given tax breaks, created SEZs and software technology parks, opened more IITs for generating manpower, encouraged creation of IT training centers awarding certificate courses and launched NASCOM as a representative organization for the IT industry.

In India, opportunities for investment exist in all the 28 states and 7 Union territories. Some states have more advanced infrastructure. Maharashtra, Delhi, Tamil Nadu, Karnataka, Gujarat and Andhra Pradesh are the top six attractive FDI destinations. Mumbai, Chennai, Kolkata, Cochin, Visakhapatnam and Ahmadabad are favored locations for industries requiring sea transport. Delhi has good air transport facilities. However, there are large numbers of manufacturing and service industries already in operation in those cities and they are already very congested. Among other states, West Bengal and Orissa have recently seen some investment activity over the last few years. Nagpur is going to be a highly attractive regional multi-modal hub of the future. It is a virtuous spiral or a vicious spiral: crowded cities attract companies for setting up operations in the name of backward-forward linkages, human and financial resource availability.

What is needed is a study on the investment climate in each state and every city in the state, listing the industries that can be nurtured in that state. Based on this information, investors can plan on the human resource training centers such as polytechnics and universities, improve the logistic and IT infrastructure etc and also make attempts to attract PPP investments in industrial clusters. Also there should be a well-orchestrated strategy of both *people moving to jobs* and *jobs moving to states*. The current modes of planning and resource allocation should be replaced by innovative and newer strategy, planning, resource allocation, orchestration and execution.

2.8.7 *Design of smart cities*

A Smart City is a bundle of dozens of services delivered effectively to the residents and businesses in an efficient manner. The investment climate of the city is assessed first and this gives the information regarding the people and their professional levels, the occupation of people (agriculture or tourism, big industries or the SMEs (Small and Medium Enterprises)) in manufacturing and services that can be nurtured. The City should provide all the necessary services such as utilities, affordable housing, transportation, retail, healthcare, elementary and high schools, universities, and access to vocational training centers.

Some of these services could be location-specific depending on the demography of the city or village and occupations of the residents. This requires strategy, integrated planning and above all monitoring and execution of the activities using appropriate governance models.

2.8.8 *Ecosystem-based analysis of CEMEX*

In this section, we show an ecosystem-based analysis of CEMEX. For more details on CEMEX, see Hoyt and Lee (2003). Founded in Mexico in 1906, CEMEX grew from a small local player to one of the leading global building solutions companies. With headquarters in Monterrey in the north of the country, CEMEX expanded throughout Mexico in the 1960s and 1970s through both acquisition and construction of new plants. The company went public in 1976. In 1989, CEMEX acquired the country's second largest cement maker, thus becoming the largest Mexican cement producer. In 1992, CEMEX expanded outside of Mexico, buying the two largest Spanish cement companies. In the next few years, CEMEX bought the largest cement company in Venezuela, cement companies in Panama, the Dominican Republic, Colombia, and a Texas plant — making it the world's third-largest cement maker in 1996.

The company continued its geographic expansion, buying the second largest U.S. cement producer (Southdown) in 2000 as well as companies in Asia and elsewhere throughout the world. CEMEX made its largest acquisition in March 2005, when it purchased U.K.-based RMC for a total price of $5.8 billion. Overall, CEMEX acquired 16 companies (either wholly or in part) from the time Zambrano became CEO. By the end of 2003, the company's 54 cement plants worldwide had an annual capacity of about 81.5 million tons. It had 466 ready-mix plants, 191 distribution centers, and 60 maritime terminals, and employed over 25,900 people. In September 2004, the company announced its largest acquisition ever: the purchase of the British cement company RMC Group plc for $5.8 billion. The acquisition increased the company's geographic diversification, adding substantial business in Northern and Eastern Europe, and increasing its presence in the United States. The acquisition of RMC was completed in March 2005.

The major cement MNEs typically entered new markets by acquiring existing capacity, often during local economic downturns, instead of adding new capacity. This mode of expansion narrows the scope for MNEs to achieve competitive advantage versus local firms by operating more efficient physical assets. The pattern of multinationalization in the cement industry is that the presence of the Big 6 firms is agglomerated or bunched. That is, the largest MNEs have a tendency to locate in the same country markets probably because of large number of common market attractors, or factors that make a country appear attractive to all potential MNE entrants, and Mimicry or strategic convergence or imitation herding so as to appear with-it or so as to avoid standing out. CEMEX was extremely successful in integrating its acquired companies by using technological and managerial processes that it developed and proved in Mexico to drive down costs, improve operational efficiency, improve customer service, and establish the company's brands in a commodity market. CEMEX was also broadening its product line, adding other building materials needed by its existing customers.

What are CEMEX's offerings to its customers?

Lorenzo Zambrano, CEMEX CEO 2001, says that customers need construction solutions (Service), not Cement. Accordingly, we need to supply not only cement but also a broad range of other building materials leveraging our world-class logistics and distribution capabilities to help our customers succeed. Thus, CEMEX is a growing global building-solutions company that provides products of consistently high quality and reliable service to customers and communities in the Americas,

Europe, Africa, the Middle East, and Asia. Its operations network produces, distributes, and markets cement, ready-mix concrete, aggregates, and related building materials to customers in over 50 countries. The ecosystem of CEMEX is mapped in Fig. 2.5.

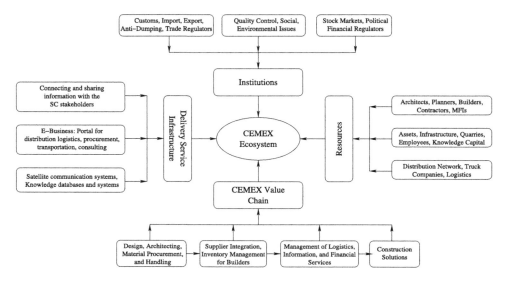

Fig. 2.5   Ecosystem of CEMEX

Who are CEMEX's customers?

We depict the governance structure of CEMEX in Fig. 2.6 (Chap. 6 discusses governance in detail). CEMEX has various categories of customers. They include Distributors, Small house constructors, Ready-mix concrete dealers, value-added transformation companies (slabs, pre-fabricated concrete blocks), and finally Large infrastructure projects such as airports, roads, housing complexes, etc. For each of these customer groups, CEMEX sells not products but the entire value chain. For example, for its Distributor customers, CEMEX manages a multi-product building material supply chain, helps with inventory control, logistics, marketing strategy, product line expansion, and with the store building its look and logos. It also provides computers, training for its personnel and courses on store management. These distributors are now a part of large national professional network Construrama and get benefits of large size and now are able to face competition from large well-managed stores such as Home Depot.

For Small house constructors, CEMEX offers Construcard — a credit card in partnership with GE capital accepted by Construrama stores which offers credit with weekly payment schedule; Patrimonio Hoy — a micro lending program like a kitty party in which participants were organized into groups; and

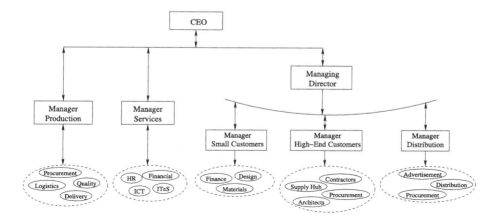

Fig. 2.6   Governance structure of CEMEX

Construmex — a program where CEMEX received money in the USA and provide families with construction materials and technical advice and sometimes a completed house.

For Builders of large house projects, CEMEX manages inventories with an on-site warehouse. The material is owned by CEMEX until drawn by the builder. CEMEX did the material planning and all the back-office tracking and scheduling. This saves the storage, working capital and provides security and single window on-site delivery system for the builders. In return, CEMEX received from the large construction project owners such as hotels contracts for design, architecture and material procurement. The contract assignment is based then on value-added service and includes cement purchase.

Delivery service infrastructure

Freight management   CEMEX uses trucks, ships and trains to transport building materials as well as fuel for the plants. i2 and ERP software packages are used for planning the materials procurement and also the deliveries. Complete visibility of all orders. Truckers, shippers and customers are all available on the same communication platform. CEMEX has a logistics department and a logistics University.

IT capabilities   CEMEX built an IT infrastructure to facilitate the collection and sharing of information to enable the company to offer excellent customer service and drive costs down. Two breakthrough investments were in a satellite telecommunications system in 1988 and in the Executive Information System in 1990. Leveraging on its information capabilities, CEMEX started experimenting with e-business initiatives. e-Enabling consists of three major areas:

(1) **e-selling**   Using Internet technology to enrich customer relationships by means of an electronic storefront that delivers customized online services to customers.

(2) **e-procurement**   An initiative that reorganized CEMEX's purchasing process for more simplicity and efficiency; it allows employees to purchase supplies online based on their exact requirements.
(3) **e-workforce**   An initiative that aims at connecting CEMEX employees globally; promoting greater knowledge sharing among employees by means of a corporate Intranet.

The CEMEX way

In 2000 CEMEX also initiated The CEMEX Way [Marchand *et al.* (2002)], an information system and process standardization program to incorporate best practices developed by various CEMEX units around the world into the standard platforms. The CEMEX Way is the core set of best business practices with which CEMEX conducts its business throughout all of its locations. This program allowed knowledge sharing and the development of better information processes as well as more information-oriented employees on a global basis. Such development allowed CEMEX to ride the wave of change in its industry. The approach was instituted in recognition of the need to build *one CEMEX* that is more flexible in response to rapid growth and maintains a consistent customer focus worldwide. CEMEX was extremely successful in integrating its acquired companies by using technological and managerial processes that it developed and proved in Mexico to drive down costs, improve operational efficiency, improve customer service, and establish the company's brands in a commodity market so as to integrate acquisitions quickly and achieve optimal operating standards. Toward this end, CEMEX has implemented several standardized platforms to reduce our costs, streamline our processes, and extract synergies from our global operations. With each international acquisition, they further refined the technological and managerial processes required to integrate acquisitions into our corporate structure. Consequently, they have been able to consolidate acquisitions more quickly, smoothly, and effectively.

2.9   Conclusions

This chapter outlined the ecosystem framework that aptly explains the properties of the global supply chain networks. We showed with illustrative examples how the ecosystem framework can be used for growth by business, policymakers, and institutions. Finally, we have, through the example of CEMEX, illustrated the use of ecosystem for strategic and operational analysis. The following Chapters 3–6 will focus on the GRIP methodology, that comprises of the drivers and levers of the supply chain ecosystem.

Chapter 3

Performance Analysis

3.1 Introduction

In global supply chain networks, products and services pass through several countries and companies multiple times, as imports and exports, before they reach the final customers. The barriers to efficient supply chain management, in addition to those faced by domestic supply chains, include time-zone differences, country borders, logistics infrastructure such as warehousing, transportation and transport infrastructure such as roads, airports and seaports, organizational silos, cultural diversities and distinct corporate objectives. In global supply chains, companies need to work more closely with supply chain partners and customers who are geographically dispersed. However, the supply chain researchers and software package providers still think of supply chains as simple linear processes of goods passing though an efficient logistics or IT pipeline and concentrate only on that part of the pipe directly controlled by them or at best by their customers and suppliers. Further, the performance measures are still company-oriented, not end-to-end supply chain oriented. For example, delivery times of computers are measured from online order to home delivery which could be a few days. But if you take into account the suppliers to consumer lead times, they could be of the order of months.

The global supply chains visit a number of ports and airports and several manufacturing facilities and assembly stations with the help of several logistics players. The most important performance measures are lead time, cost and quality. These are directly influenced by the supply chain and delivery mechanisms and services, and indirectly by the human resources, natural resources such as oil and coal and infrastructure, governmental regulations and practices and social pressures for local sourcing and employment creation. The indirect influences are somewhat longer term and are taken into consideration periodically. The inbound and outbound logistics i.e. delivery mechanisms are very important factors determining the day-to-day performance. The decisions of goods and information movement in manufacturing and logistics are important in daily operations.

Over the past decade, globalization has helped many companies and countries to improve their competitive positions. Organizations that pushed their supply chains to emerging markets were often rewarded with lower input costs and increased sales. However, their supply chains have become longer. But today, growth in many global economies has slowed, Oil prices and thus transport costs have increased and the economic prosperity of the past several years is being replaced by uncertainty. This reversal of fortune is placing downward pressure on business, causing corporations to seek savings and improved efficiencies. Since a large portion of a company's revenues and expenses flows through its global supply chain, managements are expecting their supply chains to increase efficiencies. Thus, performance analysis of global supply chains is becoming very important. The performance analysis has several angles to it.

3.1.1   *Business metrics*

The business success angle concerning the goods, information and financial flows and the performance issues are the end-to-end lead times, total cost of delivery, quality, and flexibility. Large emerging markets such as India and China have two or three supply chains with widely different customer base, the so-called middle class and the below the poverty line. Such emerging economy supply chains need to produce products and services for consumption by their populations. For the businesses to succeed, the manufacturers should take care of the cultural fit of the product designs and also the affordability (price) and the ease of access (delivery) at the place of consumption. Some decisions such as modularization, supplier selection, and location for assembly are made at the design stage and their impact will be felt throughout the life cycle.

3.1.2   *Societal and environmental concerns*

Rapid industrialization of the emerging economies also brings in the societal and environmental concerns and these should be addressed as a part of the integrated supply chain design. Important issues based societal angle include local indus-trialization and job creation, use of local suppliers, participation in local welfare programs, etc. Industrialization and job creation, however, should not be at the expense of the environment. From an environmental angle, going green i.e. mov-ing to more sustainable business practices is becoming a regulatory mandate from several governments.

3.1.3   *Political issues*

Also, political issues are becoming as important as the business issues in recent times. Coordination of the industry activity with the city, state, and central gov-ernments needs attention. Also, in the developing world, counterfeit networks thrive in creative, auto and pharmaceutical industries accessing the same IT and logistics networks and creating substitute products.

Our performance analysis of the supply chain is based on the supply chain ecosystem earlier in Chap. 2 comprising of the four elements: The Supply chain network; Resources including the human, financial and natural resources; Institutions i.e. the Government regulations on imports and exports and social and industrial organizations; and finally the Delivery mechanisms and services including logistics and IT.

In this chapter, we concentrate on the conventional performance analysis of global supply chains from the business angle and consider the lead time and cost. We also analyze briefly the effects of supply chain innovations such as modularization, coordination, visibility, etc.; resources such as clusters; government regulations and cooperation such as free trade agreements; and the delivery mechanisms and services such as trade facilitation and other soft infrastructures. Our analysis is elaborate and needs understanding of the effects of globalization.

3.2 Performance Measures

In this chapter, we consider the following four performance measures for global supply chain networks [see Viswanadham (1999) for more details].

3.2.1 *Lead time*

The lead time of a business process is the interval between the start and end of the process. It is the concept-to-market time in the case of the product development process and the time elapsed from raw material ordering until the final assembly reaching the retailer or the end consumer in the case of the supply chain process. In the case of global supply chains, consisting of companies which are globally dispersed and are under different ownerships, lead times are higher and include the sourcing times, manufacturing times, transport times, customs processing times, financial flow delays, coordination delays and host of others. Streamlining the flows of goods to reduce the lead times is a big challenge. Lead time reduction by removing non-value-adding activities; using smart technologies such as IT, mobility, sensor networks; and effectively coordinating the interfaces with suppliers, manufacturing, logistics, and distributors is an important exercise. Lead time management helps in the delivery of the desired products to the customer at the right time, right place and in right quantities. It is essential to identify the customer chain, their expectations on performance and activities that add value to them.

3.2.2 *Cost*

The total cost of delivery includes the unit cost, negotiations, inspection and co-ordination costs, margins, costs involved insurance, customs duties and transport, and finally costs due to obsolescence, wastage and theft. Thus, there are several fixed and operational costs associated with the product delivery in a supply chain network. Both the lead time and the total cost of delivery provide tremendous insights into process problems and inefficiencies.

3.2.3   *Flexibility*

Flexibility is the ability to meet customer requirements under various environmental uncertainties in various dimensions such as delivery time, schedules, design and demand changes, etc. Flexibility of business processes is closely related to product structure and to the technology. Modular designs and automation technologies enhance the ability of the company to meet the customer preferences. It is measured in terms of product variety manufactured and delivered, changeover times between products, and time interval between successive new product introductions.

3.2.4   *Quality*

Quality is management of all the work processes so that they are on design target with low variation. This goal is achieved through monitoring the performance for defects, conducting root-cause analysis of defects, and eliminating the sources of defects.

3.3   Performance Analysis

The global supply chain is an inter-organizational, inter-continental process touching several countries and organizations and several functions within each organization. These include suppliers, manufacturing, distribution, and retailers in the countries it visits. For effective supply chain management, one has to coordinate the goods flow across boundaries of countries and companies and reduce the variations in the lead times along the supply chain. A perfect delivery requires that all sub-processes in the supply chain such as purchasing, suppliers, logistics, manufacturing, and distribution act in cohesion without errors or defects from one end to the other.

3.4   Lead Time

Lead time is the interval between start and end of a delivery process. As mentioned before, the supply chain network is a collection of large number of globally dispersed companies crossing several warehouses and ports. The goods flow using logistics providers and cash flows using international banks. The total lead time should include:

Procurement lead time The time required for supplier selection based on various time, cost and priority considerations.

The supplier lead time The time elapsed from the time the order is received till the component is ready for delivery at the supplier.

Inbound logistics delivery time The time required for the components or sub-assemblies to reach the supply hub near the factory. It is the maximum of the delivery times from various suppliers and includes the passage through international ports.

Assembly time The time required for assembly, testing and packaging for final delivery to the distributor.

Customs and trade facilitation Time taken by the customs for processing the shipment at various ports that the components and final product visits.

Outbound logistics delivery time Time required for various sub-assemblies to reach the consumer site and customizing it for use.

Coordination time Time required for choosing the partners for particular order and for quality and exception management.

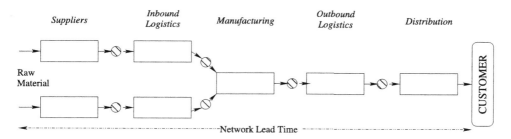

Fig. 3.1   End-to-end lead time

The lead times are destined to be longer in global supply chains particularly because of the transport delays and the customs procedures at international ports. Reducing lead time will eliminate all non-value-adding activities and free resources, reduce cost, and improve quality [Pyke (2007)].

The time required to export and import a good is an important measure of effectiveness of trade. In particular, there are two aspects of time that represent a cost for trade. One is the lead time, that is, the length of time between placement of an order and receipt of the goods. This depends on the distance between customers and suppliers, the speed of the mode of transport chosen, the type of product, the management of the supply chain and the logistics as well as the type of administrative procedures related to exporting or importing, waiting time for shipment and delays related to testing and certification of goods. A long lead time represents a cost and therefore an obstacle to trade because it raises the costs of uncertainty and variation in demand for the final products. If, for example, future demand for a fashion product has been underestimated, the seller may run out of stock. This has costs in terms of foregone sales and the possibility of losing customers.

Product value often declines with time while in transit. For perishable products, spoilage or wastage may increase with transit time. Electronic products with time-sensitive components decline sharply in value. Seasonal and fashion apparel has similar time sensitivity. These costs can also reflect lost opportunities, as when critical inputs cannot reach manufacturing plants in time or perishable commodities cannot reach markets in time or when production plants must hold higher-than-optimal levels of raw material inventories to cover for logistics delays.

The other aspect of time is the variability of delivery time. Process variation is common and is the tendency of the process to produce different results under the same given set of conditions. For example, a truck takes different times between two destinations. An assembly station may take different times to assemble parts. The more variable the delivery time is, the greater the buffer stocks needed to face demand. High variability of delivery time would make it very hard to organize *just-in-time* delivery, where inventories are kept to a bare minimum and inputs arrive at the factory only when they enter the production process. In cases where just-in-time methodology is followed, a delayed delivery of a component can hold up the entire production and cause costs that are much higher than the market price of the delayed component.

Location of facilities in several countries will certainly increase the complexity of coordination, scheduling, transportation, and in-transit inventory. Uncertain lead times will increase the inventory levels. Political uncertainties and differences in culture further exacerbate the problems.

3.5   Total Landed Cost

A supply chain network has a large number of facilities connected by transportation and communication operations through which the products move. Each firm in the supply network may have multiple vendors, multiple manufacturing facilities, several distribution centres, and multiple logistics providers. There are several fixed and operational costs associated with the supply chain network. We enumerate the important costs below. It is necessary to streamline the supply chain to keep the costs low. Total landed cost model should include:

Cost of components   Many companies are able to capture significantly lower raw materials and component costs by buying from low cost countries.

Inbound logistics cost   The logistics cost is the cost of moving materials and components to the factory site from the suppliers located in different countries. Factories that are close to raw materials or supplier clusters will have cost advantage.

Assembly cost   This includes the labor, assembly and equipment costs (such as molds or other asset-specific investments), and also the quality costs due to low yield rates, setup times, and costs.

Customs, duties, and taxes   These figures clearly change over time as nations modify their trade relations. Plant location can make a difference if there are special short- or long-term tax advantages to certain regions so it is important to involve accountants, lawyers, and tax experts.

Inventory costs   Raw materials, work in process and finished goods inventories cost a lot of money. It is important to consider issues such as who owns the inventory, how much is required to meet the throughput needs, and the associated costs.

Outbound logistics cost   The transportation issues involved include: supplier in LCC to the port, LCC port to domestic port, Domestic port to distribution centers, Pick and pack operations at the distribution centers (and plants, if appropriate), Distribution centers to customers. One needs to consider the costs and lead times for all these segments and add them to get the final outbound logistics cost and lead time.

Coordination costs   The managers need to visit suppliers and inspect the performance and quality. The time and cost associated with creating a country brand, managing relationships with companies in different time zones, culture and language can be significantly higher than managing a domestic supplier. This also needs to include the costs associated with information technology infrastructure, communications, administrative and legal functions.

For many firms, even after accounting for all these costs, LCC sourcing is significantly cheaper than their current domestic source. We group the total landed cost into the following components: Product cost, Transport (shipping) cost, Trade-related costs (processing, customs clearance, port operations, and the like), Inventory holding cost for pipeline (in-transit) inventory, and Inventory holding cost for safety stock inventory. If a particular country has highly variable processing times for port operations, supply chain managers need to hold additional safety stock to maintain desired customer service levels in the face of increased supply uncertainty [see Pyke (2007) for more details].

3.6   Performance Measures and Ecosystem Components

Table 3.1 summarizes the effect of ecosystem components of a global supply chain on the performance measures. For example, in the supply chain context, product

Table 3.1   Performance measures and supply chain ecosystem components

	Supply chain	**Resources**	**Institutions**	**Delivery mechanisms**
Enablers	*Modularization, Standardization, Collaboration, SC Visibility*	*Natural, Human, Financial Resources, Clusters, R&D Institutions, Roads, Ports, Airports*	*Trade FTAs, IP, Legal, Customs, Labour, Social issues*	*3PLs, IT, Software vendors, Soft infrastructure, Trade facilitation*
Lead time	Reduced with practices like supply hubs	Streamlined resource availability; Reduces time taken	Trade relationships; no corruption; reduces lead time	Standardized procedures result in predictable waiting times
Cost	High product design cost low assembling cost: outsourcing	Low factor costs and good external linkages	Low tariffs, streamlined customs, good labor relations	Low transportation and inventory costs, and predictable lead times
Quality	High quality standard products	Training standard practices; Mobility	Good institutions enhance service levels	High service levels and market reach
Flexibility	Limited product configurations	Multinational sourcing	Choice of countries depending on friendly policies	Standardized Delivery to global customers

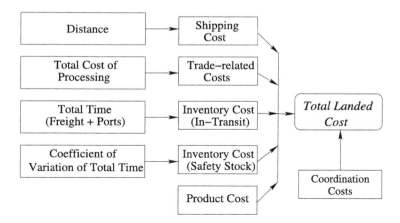

Fig. 3.2   Effect of transit on supply chain cost

modularization, process standardization, collaboration with partners and the supply chain visibility using sensor networks, call centres and Internet, late customization and use of supply hubs will certainly reduce the lead time and increase the efficiencies and product flexibility but may increase the cost of production. The total landed cost to the consumer could be less, however.

Availability of Natural, Human and Financial Resources, Clusters and R&D Institutions will reduce cost and improve the lead times. Needless to say, good logistics infrastructure such as Ports, Roads is essential for good performance; a favorable institutional framework will improve the trade, international relationships, multinational sourcing and service levels. 3PLs, IT, Software vendors, Soft infrastructure, and Trade facilitation will result in low transportation and inventory costs and predictable lead times and Standardized Delivery to global customers.

Since the logistics plays a very important role in global supply chains, we consider in this section the global logistics performance which is a result of the actions of the multiple governments and their agencies and also the delivery services business models and infrastructure. We consider below the important issues concerning the global logistics performance.

3.6.1   *Global logistics performance*

Government agencies and the private sector in a country can collaborate to improve indicators of logistics performance. The distance between two countries cannot be changed. But the freight costs could be reduced by, for example, deregulating transportation, expanding ports to increase capacity, and promoting the growth of the third-party logistics industry to allow more consolidation of cargo flows. Trade-related processing time and cost can be improved by reengineering processes to eliminate unnecessary steps and streamline others, introducing advanced information technologies such as electronic customs clearance and documentation flows, using data mining and screening methods to identify only high-risk containers for security inspections, and adopting advanced scanning technologies to shorten cargo inspection times. The development of logistics parks — such as the Suzhou Park in China, which includes free trade zones with special transport routes to ports and streamlined customs processes — can also help reduce time and cost. All these improvements can also help reduce bottlenecks in the process and eliminate unnecessary waiting times and therefore reduce the variation in the processing time.

The logistics performance index (LPI) defined in the World Bank report [World-Bank-2010 (2010)] is a composite index based on proxy measures for transport and information infrastructure, supply chain management (SCM) and trade facilitation capabilities, which are calculated based on a world survey of international freight forwarders and express carriers. The LPI is based on seven underlying factors of logistics performance:

(1) efficiency of the clearance process by customs and other border agencies;
(2) quality of transport and information technology infrastructure for logistics;
(3) ease and affordability of arranging international shipments;
(4) competence of the local logistics industry;
(5) ability to track and trace international shipments;
(6) domestic logistics costs; and
(7) timeliness of shipments in reaching destination.

Building the capacity to connect firms, suppliers and consumers, is the key in a world where predictability and reliability are becoming even more important than costs. The references Dollar *et al.* (2004), Hausman *et al.* (2005), Hummels (2007), World-Trade-Report-2008 (2008), World-Trade-Report-2010 (2010), World-Bank-2010 (2010) contain more details. We summarize their contributions in our context. We consider three of these measures below and more details can be obtained from the above references.

3.6.2 *Hard infrastructure*

The relevance of transport infrastructure for logistics costs is high. Poor transport infrastructure results in high transportation costs (because of higher fuel consumption and maintenance), large inventories and inventory costs, long and uncertain delivery times and congestion in port areas, where in many cases manufacturing is expanding faster than infrastructure capacity. Inventory holdings in manufacturing were found to be two to five times higher in developing countries than in the United States because of poor infrastructure. If these inventories were halved, they could cut unit production costs by 20% [Guasch and Kogan (2003)].

3.6.3 *Quality of logistics services*

The most important driving factor of logistics performance is reliability of delivery, measured by the predictability of the clearance process, the timely delivery of shipments, and by the quality of logistics services. Quality of logistic services depends on the availability and quality of inter-modal transport services, freight forwarding, third party logistics/fourth party logistics. More number of companies offering inter-modal transport services, freight forwarding, and 3PL/4PL services indicate higher quality. Undeveloped market, the absence of competition and inadequate market regulations often lead to corruption or to poor quality of logistics services.

3.6.4 *Trade facilitation*

Cumbersome customs procedures, long clearance times for goods at customs, excessive and unnecessary data and documentation requirements, and lack of co-ordination between customs and certification organizations are also important determining factors of transaction and logistics costs. Longer time requirements for border crossings may cause higher inventory holding and red tape, adding more costs to already high logistics costs in developing countries. These inefficiencies can be greater barriers to trade than tariff barriers.

Rules, procedures and mechanisms that help to simplify and standardize customs procedures and make the information flows associated with the import and export of goods easier (also referred to as trade facilitation) can help cut transit times and red tape, and thus improve transparency. Trade facilitation is an important issue for small- and medium-sized enterprises (SMEs) because they are often not equipped to cope with non-standardized customs procedures and intermediaries, and for exporters in landlocked countries, because they have to transit several countries to reach their export markets. Trade facilitation diminishes the discretionary (sometimes arbitrary) power of customs officials and therefore cuts the scope of corruption. It also contributes to security through more effective customs controls and to government revenues, which in some cases make up around 50 per cent of government income. Revenue loss from inefficient border procedures in some developing countries may exceed 5 per cent of GDP.

In a globalized economy, trade facilitation and efficient regulations directly contribute to enhancing linkages of local supply chain with the global value chains. Some studies point out that substantial differences across countries in the quality of trade facilitation, including port infrastructure, e-commerce use, customs clearance, and regulatory administrations, are related to the differences in the quality of trade performances. Trade facilitation is defined by a wide range of rules, procedures, and mechanisms that can help the simplification, harmonization, automation and speeding up of the goods and information flows across the borders. Its effectiveness is measured by: Customs clearance time, Raw material stocks in comparison with developed countries as percentage of GDP, Utilization rate of trucks, Charging/discharging costs in ports in developing and developed countries for each unit of homogenous good, and finally delay times in delivery.

Thus, we see that performance of the global supply chain networks is not just dependent on the supply chain configuration but on all the other three elements of the ecosystem as well. Some decisions such as modularization, supplier selection, and location for assembly are made at the design stage and their impact will be felt throughout the life cycle. The decisions of goods and information movement in manufacturing and logistics are important in daily operations.

3.7 Conclusions

In this chapter, we have studied the conventional performance measures of lead time, total cost, quality etc. in the supply chain ecosystem framework. Looking at the influence of the four elements to evaluate the performance measures brings to focus several important issues. From Table 3.1, we see that the lead times and cost are also dependent on other ecosystem parameters. Quantitative performance analysis of global supply chains can be done using Markov chains, queuing networks and Petri nets by modelling them as discrete event systems. Discrete event simulation can have detailed models of all the entities involved in the GSN and can evaluate the lead times.

The performance of the supply chain is vertical dependent. Countries may have good infrastructure for oil and gas but may not for electronic components. Countries need to focus on their competitive products and develop infrastructure accordingly. Most developing nations expand the hard infrastructure — airports, highways, ports, etc. — overlooking other network components such as efficient customs clearance and quality trucking services. When countries specialize in stages of production and trade intermediate goods, the inventory-holding and depreciation costs for early-stage value-added accrue throughout the duration of the production chain. Balance between brick-and-mortar facilities and policies, regulations, and their enforcement results in consistent processing times and reduction of inventory levels. The emerging markets need to improve the logistics infrastructure selectively for the verticals they want to nurture so that both lead time and landed cost are improved.

Chapter 4

Supply Chain Risk

4.1 Introduction

The supply chain encompasses the full product life cycle and includes design, development, system integration, system operation in its environment, and disposal. People, processes, services that support the products and the political and social factors that make up the economic and geographical environment wholly impact the supply chain. Identifying, assessing, mitigating and managing risk in the supply chain is the core of business behavior.

In the early 1990s, companies were proud of their supply chains. Over the previous two decades, they had worked hard to reduce costs from the mechanisms and processes by which they got components and inputs to the right places at the right times. Companies have also perfected global delivery of goods from their low cost production centres to the customer sites. They had done this by implementing techniques such as the lean production, just-in-time manufacturing, single-source suppliers, and global outsourcing from low cost countries. The biggest supply chain risk in those days was either obsolescent inventory or loss of sales and customer confidence.

But more recent events such as terrorist strikes on ships, political instability in several natural resource-rich countries, oil price and currency fluctuations, protectionist policies of the governments during global financial crisis, labor unrest and shutdown of shipping docks, financial institution (bank) failures and natural disasters, etc have added to supply chain risks, some of which have been the consequence of the very actions companies had taken to drive costs out of their supply chains. Many of the key risk factors have developed from the ways to enhance productivity, eliminate waste, remove supply chain duplication, protect the intellectual property, and drive for cost improvement. Single-mindedly pursuing reduction of costs, as in chasing low-cost labor anywhere in the world, without sufficient regard for the many risks it creates, made the supply chain more brittle. Every actor in the supply chain operates more leanly today to achieve efficiencies at low cost, but this makes the cost of a supply chain disruption greater.

For example, companies go for a single supplier to ensure protection of the company's intellectual property, but have to be aware of risks of single point failure. Cheaper manufacturing located further away from a company's distribution centers is offset by higher transport costs, and companies may seek to move production closer to customers. For instance, a US company which previously outsourced to China might see Mexico as more attractive. In other words, the supply chain configuration needs to change adaptively depending on the changes in the environment, for the companies to make profits.

Since the global supply chain is a complex network of suppliers, customers and third party service providers, the inter-organizational coordination of risk mitigation is a critical requirement. In addition, the leaner and more integrated supply chains become, the more likely it is that uncertainties, dynamics, and accidents in one link will affect other links in the chain. Given the interdependencies between organizations and their supply chains, it is true that the business is at risk from its supply chain and vice versa, i.e., the supply chain is at risk from the business environments.

4.1.1   *Risks due to high connectedness*

In the dynamic highly connected world, all industries in all countries are affected by incidents in all corners of the world. In this sense, some parts of all the supply chains are affected every day. In today's global environment, transnational security challenges pose serious and dynamic challenges to national and international stability. Stated more directly, many of today's dangers are qualitatively different from classical security threats of overt military aggression stemming from a clearly defined sovereign source. Rather, security, conflict, and general threat definition have become far more opaque, diffuse, and amorphous. It is no longer apparent exactly who can do what to whom and with what means. Over time, designers have to make them resilient to the risks that affect the partners of the networks, the industry and the environment. To clearly see these in the context of Global logistics and supply chain networks, we consider the following examples.

The recent home loan crisis and the resulting financial failures are being felt all over the world. The resulting credit squeeze has led to the global trade collapse. The global container-shipping offers terrorists a viable logistical conduit for facilitating the covert movement of weapons and personnel. The maritime trading system creates a plethora of openings for terrorist infiltration and opportunities to tamper with boxed crates because of the ineffectiveness of point-of-origin inspections. Piracy, an act of boarding or attempting to board any ship with the intent to commit theft or any other crime, has become very common. A 2008 report published by Peter Chalk for the RAND Corporation, "Piracy at sea: is your supply chain at risk?", states that acts of piracy totaled 2,463 actual or attempted incidents between 2000 and 2006, or 351 per year on average. Indonesia, Bangladesh, Nigeria and Somalia have been the most attacked countries for the past 3 years.

Several sources say that shipping companies are now seriously considering avoiding the Suez Canal and taking the long route around Africa instead. This would further increase the transportation cost. Also, there are mounting social protests against globalization strategies.

At first glance, a thunderstorm or an earthquake in a distant place should not be cause for alarm. Yet in 2000, when a lightning strike from such a storm set off a fire at a microchip plant in New Mexico, it damaged millions of chips slated for use in mobile phones from a number of manufacturers. Some of the manufacturers quickly shifted their sourcing to different US and Japanese suppliers, but others could not and lost hundreds of millions of dollars in sales. More recently, though few companies felt threatened by severe acute respiratory syndrome (SARS), its combined effects are reported to have decreased the GDPs of East Asian nations by 2 percent in the second quarter of 2003. Very recently, in the wake of the devastating March 11, 2011 earthquake, tsunami, and consequent nuclear crisis in Japan, several supply chain verticals from automobiles to semiconductors were affected. Several management philosophies that have created the industry norms such as lean and just-in-time are now being questioned. Manufacturers are starting to diversify their sources of supply away from Japan, both as an immediate and as a longer-term exercise.

While any future predictions are to be taken with care and caution, there could be some disasters that can strike resulting in world situations that could make all predictions irrelevant. These are events such as tsunami, global warming, increases in oil prices, new cold war with new players, nuclear disasters, SARS, changes in the political scenarios such as break up of countries or continents, etc. Although these disruptions may affect only parts of the world and may not have the power to change the entire living world drastically, they will have their ripple effects all over. Suddenly your supply chain is full of weak links — everything from outsourcing to currency fluctuations to dock strikes to terrorism to political instability. The Japanese tsunami disaster brings to focus some of these issues.

4.1.2 *Risk transmission and amplification*

Any risk of the types mentioned above will not limit itself but will propagate if not immediately addressed. Sometimes, like the earthquake-tsunami connection, the effect may be very rapid and automatic bringing devastation to the supply chain stakeholders. As we will see in cases of Phillips and Land Rover, early remedial action would save companies. Sometimes the ripple effects may not be easily seen as in the case of the recent global trade collapse.

The cause of the global crisis is clearly financial, but the global productive networks served both as transmission and amplification channels [Escaith (2009)]. While the crisis spread initially to all developed countries through toxic assets and exposure to the US financial market and seemed to spare the developing economies,

Table 4.1   Japan's disasters cause global supply chain turmoil

Supply chains today are attenuated and extremely vulnerable to repercussions from events far outside the control of those who manage and rely on them. The devastating March 11, 2011 earthquake, tsunami, and consequent nuclear crisis in Japan caused plant shutdowns in Japan shutting supplies to manufacturers across the globe of items from semiconductors to car parts. The damage to factories and suppliers in quake-hit north-eastern Japan and the fuel shortages nationwide and power outages in the Tokyo area are affecting production, distribution and the ability of staff to get to work.

Japanese-made equipment and materials play a key production role in many of the region's main industries, from automobiles in Thailand to semiconductors in the Philippines. Manufacturers may be able to shift to chip suppliers outside Japan. But that can be difficult if product specifications call for a particular brand. Boeing faces new delays in the delivery of the Dreamliner. GM slows or shutdown production in U.S. factories due to a shortage of parts. Key parts of Apple's iPad 2 suddenly became difficult to find. Toyota factories were shuttered. Apple relies heavily on Japanese partners for critical components for its iPhone and iPad. Some of these components require lead times of 6–18 months, and alternate sources cannot simply be brought on line in a matter of days. And consumers might not want to wait that long.

The numbers are simply shocking: Toyota Motor Corp. reported that Japan production in April fell 74.5 percent to 79,341 vehicles while its global production declined 48 percent to 346,297 vehicles. Meanwhile, Honda's production in Japan nose-dived 81.0 percent in April to 14,168 vehicles, while its worldwide production declined 52.9 percent to 138,498. At Nissan, Japan production declined 48.7 percent to 44,193 vehicles, and global production slipped 22.4 percent to 248,024 vehicles.

Lean may not be an industry norm anymore but certainly won't be dead. No one will ever go back to the days of bloated inventories. We will, however, see the practice of safety stock and holding inventory against commodity price fluctuation and supply chain disruption to provide relief from the fragility of the supply chain. Companies will choose to invest wisely, moving from *just-in-time* to *just-in-case* for materials that are critical.

Source:

http://www.amptevents.com/Japan_Earthquake-Related_Industry_News_update.pdf

the premise of the North-South *decoupling* disappeared quickly. International supply chains were rapidly identified as one of the main factors for the synchronized trade collapse.

There is now growing evidence that the financial crisis caused financial institutions to cutback in trade finance to exporting firms. Trade finance is not just letters of credits but guarantees, financing for shipping and insurance, temporary loans against the collateral of goods and loans for working capital etc. The costs of trade credits jumped up in 2008 and 2009 compared with 2007. Credit crunch has affected trade finance, and hence trade volumes in almost all the countries have declined sharply during the downturn.

Trade barriers normally escalate during economic downturns. This results in preference for sourcing from domestic suppliers because of trust or financing problems and countries' protectionist policies. Protectionism does not seem to have played a significant role in the trade collapse.

4.1.3 *Inventory effects*

In geographically fragmented networks, each company needs to maintain a minimum level of buffer stocks in order to face the usual risks attached to international transportation. Large players keep low inventories and force their suppliers to maintain supply hubs. Thus for the suppliers, a sudden collapse in customer demand results in a slowdown or stoppage of the production and reduction of the labour force.

In a 2009 Economic Intelligence Unit survey, the CEOs felt recession-related supply-chain disruptions have increased. The survey shows that disruptions associated with the effects of the recession have had the most impact on supply chains in the years following the recession. The downturn has led governments to consider a raft of measures designed to protect domestic business interests, including bail-outs, state aid, tariffs, and trade defense measures.

The very instruments that were created to make the supply chains more efficient and lean have become sources of risk that can destroy the supply chains. Risk can emanate from several sources including the supply chain and its partners, and several other non-supply chain related factors such as: protective actions of the very governments that have encouraged the companies to set up shops in their countries, increase in the commodity prices and hence the delivery costs, etc. It is important to consider the risk that arises from the entire ecosystem rather than just the supply chain. The four distinct risk sources in manufacturing and service supply chain networks include:

- Supply chain network;
- Institutions: Governmental and Social;
- Resources including Human, Natural, Financial and Industrial (Clusters);
- Delivery service mechanisms.

4.2 Supply Chain Risk Management

Supply chain risk Any changes in the information, material and financial flows of the supply chain network — deviation, disruption, disaster — due to events anywhere in its path or its network partners or in the industry vertical or in the economic environment.

Supply chain risk management Supply chain risk management is the identification and management of risks within the supply-chain or external to it, through a coordinated approach amongst supply-chain members, to reduce supply-chain vulnerability as a whole. The above definitions are taken from Gaonkar and Viswanadham (2007). Events in the ecosystem affect the supply chain functioning, efficiency and output. These changes create mismatch between supply and demand and also cost or quality problems. To prevent these problems one needs to build *resilient supply chains.* Resilience is the ability to resume and restore operations after a disruption.

4.2.1   *Supply chain risk in the ecosystem framework*

Usual supply chain risk studies consider only supply failures, partner risks, logistics failures, sharp fall in demand etc. Risks for the supply chain can arise from all the four elements of the ecosystem rather than the supply chain alone. They can arise from political agenda during election times (outsourcing is the theme during US elections), foreign exchange fluctuations, WTO regulations, entry of competitor country into WTO, quota removal by WTO, credit freeze by banks in the supplier's country, resource shortage such as oil, minerals, food etc, labour productivity, labour unrest, social unrest against land acquisition or wholesale markets, delivery failure due to piracy and terrorist attacks and several others. Thus we see the risks include those from Governments, political and social networks, resources and delivery systems such as logistics and IT. These changes create mismatch between supply and demand, affect the supply chain functioning, efficiency and output, and sometimes may result in company closure. Risk mitigation or avoidance strategies should include all the ecosystem entities and plan the strategies accordingly. Planning multisourcing from various markets taking into account the taxes, logistics costs, country stability, possible natural disasters, war or infectious disease scenarios, etc is one of the risk mitigation strategies.

4.2.2   *Risk sources in the ecosystem*

Risk sources are the following uncertainties that impact the supply chain outcomes. From the above discussion we can classify the risks into four different categories:

- Supply chains;
- Institutions: Political and Social;
- Resources: Financial, natural, human and industry inputs;
- Delivery service mechanisms.

Table 4.2 lists the risks that a supply chain faces under the four ecosystem elements.

Risk sources in supply chains

Companies worked hard to reduce the procurement costs to get components and inputs to the right places at the right times. They had done this by implementing techniques such as the lean production, just-in-time manufacturing, single-source suppliers, efficient logistics and trade facilitation and global outsourcing from low cost countries. Countries have created industrial clusters which are independent

Table 4.2   Risks in the ecosystem

Supply Chain related risks
Location risk from natural disasters such as earthquakes, hurricanes for all stakeholders
Community risk: Wars
Outsourcing risk: Partner Risk, Breach of trust, IP theft
Design and/or Manufacturing defects, Counterfeit, Inventory deficit
Supplier failures
Sudden loss of demand due to economic downturn, company bankruptcies, war
Breakdown of facilities (Fabs, machine shops), loss of power or water

Resource related risks
Logistics Infrastructure deficit, Industry Clusters' quality and accident vulnerability
Energy & Water shortage
Credit squeeze
Social unrest, labor unions
Raw material: Price increase, Disease in live stock, Contamination
Talent shortage for supply chain execution

Institutional risks
Regulatory risk: FE, IP, Customs delays, Antidumping, Taxes, Trade agreements
Protectionism, VAT, Voluntary export restrictions
Political: Govt. changes, Center-state relations, Environmental issues
Labor Unions, NGOs, Social interest groups, Industry associations

Risks due to delivery infrastructure
Hardware or software failures or virus attacks affecting the information and communication infrastructure and the supply chain visibility
Inbound and Outbound logistics failures
Piracy and terrorist attacks, Insurance cost increase

and loosely coupled companies offering advantages in efficiency, effectiveness, and flexibility. Companies in clusters can tap into the vast pool of employees, thereby lowering their search and transaction costs. Logistics networks and Internet have made possible efficient and secure transfer of goods, information and funds across continents. Globalization and outsourcing have improved the connectedness between people, companies, and countries. Universities and other knowledge centers were developed to help train manpower and also help in product development.

On the supply side, the risk could be due to either design or manufacturing defects resulting in product recalls. There could be delay or unavailability of materials from suppliers or there can be a total failure of suppliers. On the demand side, sudden loss of demand due to economic downturn, company bankruptcies, war, etc is a possible risk.

Globalization and outsourcing may lead to unknown risks. In fact, global supply chains are riskier than local supply chains as they need to deal with poor logistics infrastructure and intellectual property issues. Breaches in freight or partnerships, and violation of the integrity of cargoes, products (can be due either to theft or tampering with criminal purpose, e.g. smuggling weapons inside containers) or company proprietary information could be another issue. There are top contributing regions with several risks, including intellectual property infringement, supplier and internal product quality failure, and security breaches.

An OEM can reduce its labor costs, free up capital, and improve worker productivity by outsourcing all the manufacturing of a product. The company can then concentrate on value-adding activities: R&D, product design, and marketing. The double-edged relationships between OEMs and their CMs need to be carefully monitored and managed.

High performance design makes supply chains very fragile and they get severely affected by disruptions to transport, communications, raw material inputs, etc. We illustrate in Table 4.2 some of the risks faced by some actors through real examples.

Institutional risks

The businesses are embedded in an institutional setting. The Institutions such as constitutions, laws, contracts, and regulations like the labour laws and import and export restrictions affect the supply chain performance. Also important are informal institutions including NGOs, social activists, farmers' unions, trade associations such as Chambers of commerce etc which wield political clout. The social and governmental institutions of the countries which the supply chain crosses, the direct and the indirect barriers of trade such as protectionism, sourcing from local companies, raising the tariffs, lack of laws to protect intellectual property, corruption, etc can pose severe financial losses.

The social, economic and political organizations can create risks of various kinds. These risks are high in emerging markets or countries where politics matters as much as economics. In developed countries, the financial crisis has created a situation of oversight by the government. Social unrest and regulatory risks are high in emerging markets.

The economic and political related uncertainties affect businesses across all industries and they include Economic factors such as economic slowdown, country policies and ratings, foreign exchange, interest rates, and Political issues such as war, country-to-country relationships, changes in governments, and uncertainty in trade agreements (Anti-dumping, Voluntary export restrictions). Government policies can change such as price controls, free trade zones, inadequate public services, nationalization, barriers to repatriation of earning or Security-related such as terrorist attacks, virus, piracy, etc.

Government regulatory risk   The most pervasive and subtle forms of discrimination against the MNCs is regulatory discrimination such as anti-dumping, continuously changing rules and regulations particularly in taxes and tariffs, foreign exchange regulations, corruption, inspections, site visits, delayed payments, Local company preference for indirect materials for Govt. contracts. These measures are sometimes intended to shield uncompetitive locals and also to protect natural resources. Walmart could not enter Indian retail market and MCC was vandalized. Offshoring also presents IP risks. The Chinese government, for example, is already cavalier about intellectual property rights and shows signs of becoming more so. Companies moving manufacturing and other functions there may be hard-pressed to protect some of their most valuable intellectual assets.

Patent laws Before 2005, India protected only process patents, not product patents, for drugs. Indian companies can produce the drug if the chemical synthesis of the manufacturing process differed from the patented one. Ranbaxy has set up sophisticated laboratories with hundreds of world-class chemists and also invested in state-of-the-art factories. Ranbaxy has become one of the world's top ten generic manufacturers to synthesize drugs that were going off patent. In 2005, under WTO pressure, India adapted product patents which require drug discovery, clinical trials and drug certification and approval. The talent required is researchers and the whole process is highly risk prone. Companies suffer disabilities due to the patent change.

The changed nature of war In the 20th century the world was confronted by adversaries who were stationary, observable, and conventional. The enemies' weapons of choice were tanks, planes, bombs, ships, and so on; and an individual soldier was not a significant threat to any nation's security. The adversary today is agile, unconventional, and stealthy. His weapons are software virus, hacking, suicide vests, machetes, AK47s, and roadside bombs. These have created the so-called "super-powered individual" that can inflict significant harm to any nation. Nation-states have benefited from the information revolution, stronger political and economic linkages, and the shrinking importance of geographic distance. Unfortunately, criminal networks have benefited even more.

Sustainable development for a business enterprise Sustainable development means adopting business strategies and activities that meet the needs of the enterprise and its stakeholders today while protecting, sustaining and enhancing the human and natural resources of the future. The companies look for favorable infrastructure for making their products, while the state and central governments would like industrialization for economic progress of the state and also for creating jobs for its people and thus provide several benefits for location in the state to the companies. The customers could be in far-off locations and transporting final product takes time and causes pollution. The economic, social and environmental issues facing the governments could be in conflict. The focus area should be the one that meets all the three objectives of economic progress, social well-being and environmental protection.

Social or community risk   In the past couple of years India has seen several companies abandoning half-done projects due to social or government pressures. They include: Tata Singur, Nandigram, Vedanta mining Orissa, Posco in Orissa, Goa SEZ, MCC Bangalore, and Reliance fresh banned in several states. The reason for the failure is partly change of position by the government and partly the ineffectiveness of the government to implement the Promised Land deals. There is a palpable opposition in the East and West to the globalization of many multinational companies. French farmers demonstrating against McDonald's as a symbol of American cultural hegemony garnered widespread support despite the company's claim that 80 percent of the products they served were made in France. Similarly, Metro Cash and Carry had to face demonstrations in Bangalore, India despite the fact that it followed the B2B business model that helps the small shop owners to access high quality goods at wholesale prices.

Risk due to resource failure

The resources that we consider are the natural, human, financial and industry resources. In the human resources arena there are skills shortages and employee attrition at one end, communicable diseases affecting the number of effective working days and strikes which lead to stoppage of production. There is also possible opportunistic behavior by the managers and staff such as theft of intellectual property. The input material shortages such as grains, fruits and vegetables, live stock, quality problems due to diseases such as mad cow disease, chicken flu, price fluctuations such as Oil prices, foreign currency fluctuations all affect the supply chain effectiveness. Equipment failures, failure of power or water resources can lead to unavailability of plants, warehouses and office buildings. Power shortages, unavailability of spare parts are also issues that need attention. Availability of quality producer services such as accounting, management consulting, advertising, venture funding etc is essential for strategy formulation.

Clustering and concentration   Global pressures in some industries encouraged the search for efficiency through larger scale and a high degree of concentration as in, for e.g., super-aero planes and gigantic dam projects, Giant firms such as DHL, Flextronics etc., mergers and acquisitions, and geographical concentration (e.g. low-cost manufacturing in China, IT clusters in India, auto or pharmaceutical industrial clusters). Damage due to an accident is higher for a concentration rather than for separate owners in several locations (bird flu effect on China in early years of this decade).

Risk failures of delivery service infrastructure

Delay or unavailability of either inbound or outbound transportation to move goods due to carrier breakdown or weather problems will cause the supply-demand matching problem. Failure of information and communication infrastructure due to line, computer hardware or software failures or virus attacks, will lead to the inability to coordinate operations and execute transactions. While the physical supply chain handles the movement of documents data and physical goods, the financial supply chain handles the movement of documents data and money. Thus, any credit squeeze by the financial institutions will affect the supply chain. The letters of credit will also become more expensive.

Pirates have expanded over the years 2006–2010. Many of the world's most powerful navies are involved: US, EU, India, Malaysia, Indonesia and South Africa. The Japanese and South Koreans send warships to protect ships carrying cars. It is still cheaper and convenient to pay higher insurance fees and take the risk of being attacked by pirates than to incur the extra cost of diverting vessels around the Cape of Good Hope.

Connectedness Connectedness makes individuals and organizations accessible over distance. On the positive side, victims of disasters are easier to reach, and emergency rescues can be organized more efficiently using Satellites and Wireless based monitoring and warning systems. On the negative side, connectedness multiplies the channels through which accidents, diseases, or malevolent actions can propagate. Natural disasters at one side of the planet can have substantial economic and financial impacts at the other. Epidemics spread more rapidly due to the international travel and trade and tourism. The terrorist and counterfeit networks are also globally connected and indeed they follow the HR practices of recruitment, training of people and also systematic planning processes for implementing their objectives.

4.3   Risk Propagation

Any risk in any one of the four sectors mentioned above will not limit itself but will propagate if not immediately addressed. Sometimes, like the Earthquake-Tsunami connection, the effect may be very rapid and automatic bringing devastation to the supply chain stakeholders. Early remedial action would save companies. Sometimes the ripple effects may not be easily seen as in the case of the recent global trade collapse.

4.3.1   *Systems of systems, systemic risks, and risk governance*

In a globalized world, the risk for the supply chain could come from three other very important factors which are often ignored:

- Connectedness on a global scale;
- Large-scale concentration for competitive efficiency;
- Lack of governance structures for fast response.

Excellent examples are the Network industries of critical infrastructures — electricity, transport, or communications — that have the features of connectedness, large size, and loose governance structures. These systems of systems are subject to systemic risks.

Risk management needs to be radically modified with the changing role of governments in the economy and dismantling of state-owned monopolies. Public issues related to risks nowadays involve a variety of actors, including corporations, representatives of civil society, non-governmental organizations, and experts. Risk situations might be met with excessive inertia or inappropriate institutional responses, as in 26/11 terrorist attack in Bombay.

4.3.2 *Global risk response strategies*

Design of resilient supply chains is an important topic and should focus on specific vertical. We have discussed above that risk sources can arise from any of the four ecosystem elements. Risk transmission and amplifications are also possible. Also, in globally dispersed supply chains, disruptions occur almost every day in one country or one city or other. Risk mitigation in our opinion should be a part of regular operations rather than after-the-event intervention as is practiced today. The operations manager is familiar with normal conditions and also how abnormality arises and should be tasked to handle the abnormal conditions with the right kind of information and communication tools.

Strategies to reduce overall risk exposure such as mitigating the risk directly by improving flexibility by dual sourcing, adapting to the risk by preparing for its occurrence (e.g. Earthquake-resistant building construction, Quick evacuation in case of floods), or transferring the risk to a third party such as an insurer are frequently followed.

No supply chain strategy will eliminate risk, and if one tries to eliminate it the cost would be too high. The managers can and should excel, however, in identifying, quantifying, and preparing for the new realities of risk. The organization or individual should make provisions to deal with the possible consequences. Determining whether greater resilience is worth the extra cost is part of the new strategic economics.

We believe, however, that alliances may be the safest form of international expansion. Acquiring global assets, which was always risky for operational and cultural reasons, now increases an organization's vulnerability to physical attack as well. A network of alliances, appropriately managed, is potentially more resilient than a collection of global acquisitions. Alliance partners retain local management, eliminating the costs and risks of deploying employees around the globe.

4.4 Case Study: Institutional Risks that Moved Tata from Singur

We have chosen a well-known example of recent times, *Tata Nano Plant at Singur*, as a vehicle to illustrate various concepts discussed. Tata Motors is the largest passenger and commercial vehicle manufacturer of India. It is a part of the Tata Group of Companies which holds ninety-six operating companies in seven business sectors. In 2003 Ratan Tata (Chairman, Tata Group) embarked on his vision to build Nano: a *people's car*, inspired by the people. In his own words, *I observed families riding on two-wheelers, the father driving the scooter, his young kid standing in front of him, his wife seated behind him holding a little baby. It led me to wonder whether one could conceive of a safe, affordable, all-weather form of transportation for such a family. We are happy to present the People's Car to India and we hope it brings joy, pride and the utility of owning a car to the countless families that need personal mobility.*

Priced at just over INR 100000, it happens to be the lowest priced car in the world. Naturally, most states across India offered to host the first Nano plant of Tata Motors. In addition to the potential boost to the industrial growth and the economy of the state, there would also be the prestige of hosting such a unique venture, along with the media coverage and attendant visibility. After a series of negotiations on 18 May 2006, Tata Motors announced the location of its first Nano plant: Singur, West Bengal.

The government in West Bengal succeeded in convincing Tata Motors to locate the Nano automobile complex in West Bengal and offered subsidies to the company. The government offered the highly fertile land in Singur, and invoked the Land Acquisition Act, thereby compelling landowners to surrender their land at a low price. Our study here primarily looks at the lacuna in project planning in these kinds of problems. We also recognize that these kinds of problems are wicked problems and that they require special skills to deal with them.

The state of West Bengal offered Tata Motors a host of incentives. It offered 997 acres of land, out of which 647 acres was for the Nano plant, 290 acres for ancillary units and 60 acres for the government-run Industrial Development Corporation. The Singur farmers opposed the handover of their lands to Tata, converting this once-peaceful village into a war-zone with round-the-clock presence of armed police providing protection to the Tata Motors site and its workers. The state government, supported by a High Court ruling in January 2008, declared that the land had been legally acquired for public interest through the Land Acquisition Act, and urged all farmers to accept the compensation package offered by the state. But soon after the project commenced, land prices in surrounding areas increased, and hence farmers who had already received compensation were unhappy with the rate of payment made to them.

Gradually the spate of agitations intensified to such an extent that the inventory in the Nano plant was damaged, factory gates were not allowed to be opened, and employees of the Nano plant were assaulted. Distressed at the violence and time spent on the issue, the Tatas started negotiating with other prospective states that expressed an interest in this project and finally moved out of Singur to Sanand in Gujarat.

In Tata Singur case, though the supply chain was meticulously planned in co-locating the vendors, auxiliary units and proximity of the plant to the Durgapur highway etc, there were a few gaps in project planning. The land acquisition procedure and social unrest was not seriously taken up by the Tatas and they relied on the Government of West Bengal to look into the land proceedings. In the meantime they started headlong into the construction of the plant and installation of the machinery to commence operations at the earliest. Though this is a small factor in the backdrop of the project at large, it finally caused a big blow in the later stages resulting in abandoning the operations at that site. Hence, project planning is of a very prime concern for all kinds of projects.

4.4.1 *Wicked problems*

Some of the project planning problems like location selection, land acquisition problems, labor issues, culture and social issues during outsourcing/mergers and acquisitions in other countries, environmental risks etc that arise in social context are wicked problems. The concept of wicked problems was first introduced by Horst Rittel and Melvin M. Webber in their work *Dilemmas in General Theory of Planning*. *Wicked problem* is a phrase used in social planning to describe a problem that is difficult or impossible to solve because of incomplete, contradictory, and changing requirements that are often difficult to recognize. Moreover, because of complex interdependencies, the effort to solve one aspect of a wicked problem may reveal or create other problems. A wicked problem has innumerable causes, is tough to describe, and doesn't have a right answer. Environmental degradation, communism, and poverty — these are classic examples of wicked problems.

The characteristics of wicked problems as identified by Rittel and Webber (1984) are:

(1) The problem involves many stakeholders with different values and priorities.
(2) The problem is difficult to come to grips with, changes with every attempt to address it.
(3) The issue's roots are complex and tangled.
(4) Every implemented solution to the problem has consequences.
(5) There is no right answer to the problem.
(6) There is no definitive formulation of the problem.
(7) These problems have no stopping rule.
(8) There is no immediate and no ultimate test of a solution to the problem.
(9) Every problem is essentially unique.
(10) The problem has no precedence.

4.4.2 *Tata Singur as a wicked problem*

We have elaborated here two characteristics of how Tata Singur is a wicked problem. The other characteristics of wicked problems can also be interpreted in a similar way for the Tata Singur case.

The problem involves many stakeholders with different values and priorities. While the direct stakeholders were the Tatas (the project owners) and the farmers to whom the land belonged, numerous other stakeholders were watching nervously the Tata Singur Episode: employees and trade unions; shareholders, investors and creditors; suppliers and joint venture partners who already made a huge investment of about $150 million at the project site; competitors who were the manufacturers of low-price cars like Maruti Suzuki, Reva, Renault Yeni, Ajanta Group's Oreva Super; the other state governments looking for luring the factory to their home states such as Maharashtra, Karnataka, Andhra Pradesh; several companies from the U.S. and other nations who want to enter India. The West Bengal government had a lot of stake in keeping the Tatas within Singur in order to improve the economy of the state. The whole country and other companies were watching this episode. In fact, after the Tatas moved out, several companies have cancelled their plans to set up shops in WB. Tata's predicament has been the most closely watched, because the $2,500 Nano mini-car has been touted around the world as revolutionary, and Tata is known as one of India's most powerful, yet socially responsible, employers. Not only direct stakeholders, many others across the industry were also interested in the project.

The problem is difficult to come to grips with and changes with every attempt to address it. In the wake of increasing protests by farmers over forcible acquisition of their lands, a petition was filed against the project in the WB High Court. The High Court ruled that there was no procedural infirmity in the land acquisition proceeding. Instead of allaying the agitations, this verdict of the West Bengal High Court added further fuel to the fire. The protests became more aggressive and showed no signs of relenting.

The protests continued and even aggravated over time. They rose to such an extent that the employees of the Nano plant and their families were attacked. In the meantime, the other state governments in India which were keen on industrialization were making overtures, inviting the Tatas to visit their states and offering land and other infrastructure facilities at subsidized prices. Even the Tatas could not wait for the agitations to subside. Worried about the prolonged agitations against the project and the security of its employees, Tata finally pulled out of Singur. This problem has changed with every attempt to address it and finally the project has been abandoned in that region.

4.4.3 *Aftermath of Tata Singur episode*

Even after the Tatas abandoned all their operations in Singur and moved to Sanand in Gujarat, controversy still persisted over what needed to be done with that project site for about two years. The verdict on 22 June, 2011 by the High Court for the case filed by Tata Motors challenging the Singur Act, revoked the lease agreement for 997 acres, asking Tata to vacate the site, ending politically in a blame game.

After this entire issue, if we look back into the problem, analyse it and deliberate over the question as to who has benefited out of this — the Tatas certainly did not benefit because they had to relocate the entire plant to Gujarat which cost them an enormous amount and delayed the launch of the most awaited car; Government of West Bengal also did not benefit as it could neither convince the opposition party to not raise any issues nor the Tatas to wait until the talks materialized; the farmers obviously did not benefit because those who protested to get their land back did not get it and the land lay abandoned after Tata pulled away. So ultimately, the project did not serve the purpose it was intended to.

Moreover this incident has impacted further investments in West Bengal. Many companies that were interested in starting their operations in West Bengal eventually reconsidered their earlier decisions after this incident. This fiasco is a major blow not only to Tata Motors and West Bengal government but also to all the *prospective investors* like FIIs who have an eye on West Bengal.

4.4.4 *Decision-making strategies for wicked problems*

Lack of decision-making is the radical cause of the deadlock situation in a wicked problem. There is no systematic procedure to solve wicked problems. These wicked problems are different from hard mathematical programming problems (such as NP complete) for which approximate solutions are possible. Adopting the conventional problem-solving approaches like sequential waterfall approach, algorithms, mathematical models to tackle wicked problems can only aggravate the problem further. A variety of methods have been developed to help tackle these messy wicked problems; collectively they are known as *soft operations research, soft systems* or *problem-structuring approaches.*

Traditional problem-solving techniques were primarily Operations Research techniques. Operations research, also known as operational research, is an interdisciplinary branch of applied mathematics and formal science that uses advanced analytical methods such as mathematical modelling, statistical analysis, and mathematical optimization to arrive at optimal or near-optimal solutions to complex decision-making problems. In recent years, doubts have been raised over the value of traditional OR. These doubts have not been related to the correctness or validity of the techniques employed, but rather their applicability to certain problems; problems that have become increasingly difficult to model mathematically. Critics argue that OR practice has been considerably more diverse; that problems have become increasingly complex; and that standard formulations of OR methodology cannot cope with these less well-behaved situations. It was in their ability to address these increasingly complex problems that Soft OR methods gained credence. As opposed to the traditional or hard methods, soft OR employs predominantly qualitative, rational, interpretative and structured techniques to interpret, define, and explore various perspectives of the problems under scrutiny. Soft OR includes methods such as Checkland's Soft Systems Methodology, Cognitive Mapping, Scenario Planning and Strategic Options Development and Analysis. Such methods generate debate, learning, and understanding, and use this understanding to progress through complex problems.

After identifying a problem as wicked, all the risks that are associated with the problem must be analysed and corresponding mitigation measures must be designed during the planning phase itself. Then, we must have the right kind of people, who are proficient in soft skills involving Soft OR techniques and who are accomplished in facilitating negotiations effectively, to analyse the situation. *Once a clear understanding of the problem is achieved using the soft OR techniques, strategies like authoritative strategy, cooperative strategy and collaborative strategy can be adopted in decision making depending upon the kind of situation* (Conklin, 2001).

4.5 Our Solution: The Supply Chain Redesign

The global supply chain designs are mimics of the local designs mostly from the advanced countries for the situation when all the partners are in the same country; resources are utilized in the same country using the same currency. Now the world is logistically and informationally and financially well-connected, technology development and adoption are very rapid and foreign exchange trade and fluctuations are very volatile. The current problems we encounter are due to the bad designs of the supply chain as a chain linking individual companies but not as a chain linking networks of companies spanning the globe. While one cannot eliminate risk whatever be the design, the ecosystem approach will create risk awareness and mitigation approaches. We present an ecosystem-aware supply chain design methodology in Chap. 7 that takes into account risks from the entire ecosystem.

4.6 Conclusions

Risk management as discussed in this chapter is an important subject in the current scenario where every product or service has a global footprint. The supply chain is affected by all the ecosystem elements. Proactive risk management is essential for avoiding catastrophic failures of companies involved in the supply chain. Developing analytical models to assess the probability of occurrence of bad events and advanced thinking on the mitigation strategies is an essential part of mitigation exercise. A lot of analytical and data-intensive work needs to be done to create resilient supply chains of the future.

Chapter 5

Innovation

5.1 Introduction

In this chapter, we focus on supply chain ecosystem based innovations in emerging markets; in particular, we focus on India. Generally, product or process innovations are studied in the literature. We have seen earlier that innovations can occur in creation of resources such as solar energy, search engine such as Google, in Government actions such as deregulation, changing the patent laws, signing trade agreements with other countries and also by innovating alternate delivery mechanisms such as containerization, online sales, webinars, telemedicine, etc. We need the holistic supply chain eco-systemic view of things particularly in emerging markets where policies are being changed, mobility of foreign capital is important, and infrastructure development needs both financial and technology investments.

5.1.1 *What are emerging markets?*

Emerging markets are countries having increasing disposable incomes, large young populations and markets with characteristics as high-growth, high-potential, and high-risk, a consequence of economic liberalization. Most of these economies were protected for decades. Earlier, their Governments followed import substitution policies and were trying to reinvent everything within. In recent times, many Governments liberalized their economies and started initiatives such as public-private partnerships (PPP) and special economic zones (SEZ) to attract foreign investments in manufacturing, services, and Infrastructure and also to facilitate global trade. These Initiatives were introduced with lots of incentives to the public, private, or foreign enterprises. This has led to the growth of cities, regions, and countries across the developing world.

Most emerging economies present a dualistic picture with urban-rural divide, industrialized vs. not so industrialized regions. Most populations in emerging economies like India live in rural areas with poorer connectivity than their urban counterparts. Rural development is largely in the hands of the government.

The governments introduce lots of schemes to ensure food security and education to their populations. Politics and social issues are very important for businesses. More information is available in Deloitte (2008) and Lorentz *et al.* (2009).

5.1.2   *Innovation in emerging markets*

The emerging market countries have many disadvantages such as primitive industry presence, weak infrastructure and research institutions, not so sophisticated banking, and other soft infrastructure. But the big advantage is that they do not have the legacy infrastructures of the developed world, which were built when global connectivity technologies for goods, information and funds flows were just developing and also when smart technologies were not available for network industries. If the emerging market countries have the talent and political will, they need not follow the same path as the developed countries but could actually jump ahead of them with breakthrough innovations.

There are two types of innovations: *new to the world* or *new to the market*. In the emerging market context, the new-to-market innovations can result in blockbuster industries if quality products affordable by the populations are produced and made easily accessible to them. Emerging markets are thus becoming centers of innovation in fields like nutritious food, low-cost health-care devices, carbon sequestration, solar and wind power, bio-fuels, distributed power generation, batteries, water desalination, microfinance, electric cars, and even ultra-low-cost homes. To further these opportunities, emerging market companies must learn reverse innovation: develop products in their home country and then distributing them globally. The BCG Study report shows that the future belongs to them [Bailey *et al.* (2009)].

Generally the focus of most innovation studies is design of products or services and commercializing them. There are reasons why this mindset may not always work. Having a good product does not always guarantee business success. The availability, accessibility, affordability, price, and quality of the products and services and the talent working to make these happen are necessary to make the product a great success. In essence, the business success is affected by the supply chain efficiencies and in turn the supply chain efficiencies are affected by the ecosystem parameters such as Government and Institutional policies, logistics infrastructure, resources such as clusters, venture capital firms and host of others including availability of natural and industrial resources. Thus, behind every product or service there is a supply chain or service chain, and the interaction between the ecosystem elements such as the Government and Institutional policies and the service/supply chain performance is of great interest.

Several innovations such as the opening up of the markets by the countries have resulted in many successful services companies [Erocal (2005)]. Companies such as Airtel, Jet Airways in India, and South West, e-Bay and others in USA owe their existence to policy shift in the governments. Choice of the business models such as doing it in-house or outsourcing to low cost countries can be classified as business model innovations. Business models such as prepaid simcards, sell direct, packaging in small quantities have sometimes led to blockbuster industry growth. Some innovations are integrative; meaning that the effect of innovations in individual supply chain elements such as suppliers, distribution and retail is less effective than following an integrated supply chain ecosystem approach. There is also the phenomenon called the co-evolution of innovations, responsible for creating blockbuster industries. In the context of global supply chains, co-evolution takes place between organizations that are interconnected and thus have an effect on each other in a mutually beneficial way. Innovations in sectors such as Internet, mobile phones, search engines, e-mail, internet banking, e-reservations, Telemedicine, and thousands of other innovations which have contributed to the quality of life on this planet are results of co-evolution. To capture all the innovations that would lead to growth in the industry, one needs to consider all the possible innovations in the supply chain ecosystem elements and innovate again to integrate the innovations to create industry growth. The aim of this chapter is to formulate precisely such strategies through some examples.

This chapter is organized as follows: In the following section, we introduce the supply chain ecosystem concept and describe its features. We also discuss the innovations in institutions and management that affect the supply chains. We list all the possible innovations in the supply chains in Table 5.1. We also discuss innovations in Indian Telecom, Indian auto industry, and also the new governance model of an orchestrator. Finally, we apply the innovations to two examples in India: the fragmented Indian logistics industry, and orchestrating the same to a successful industry model. We provide an integrated supply chain network solution by combining innovations in public distribution, warehousing, and distribution for food items and using the midday meal and hawkers as the final food retailers in Chap. 7. The job security schemes of the Government are used for vocational training of the hawkers, midday meal cooks and distributors, distribution and food retailing and also in warehousing and public distribution system (PDS). The entire food security network can be wired up with GPS, mobile phones and sensor networks and can be monitored using a call center. The innovation framework developed in this chapter is a general one and can be applied to any company, industry vertical, or country intending to move up the value chain.

5.2 Supply Chain Innovations

We have described above that the global supply chain formation is the result of co-evolution of four distinct forces and corresponding innovations in manufacturing and service sectors. They include the supply chains; both governmental and social institutions; human, natural, financial and industrial (clusters) resources; and finally delivery services (logistics, IT) infrastructure.

Traditional service innovation is rooted on a standard and well-accepted model characterized by heavy investments in the discovery processes and invention followed by commercialization in the form of new processes and products. The new-to-the-world inventions are characterized as innovation. A standard three-step procedure followed across the world is to incentivize and boost the levels of R&D spending by Corporate and Universities; increase the number of people skilled in science, technology, engineering, or mathematics (STEM) by nurturing top-tier universities and R&D laboratories; and improve the knowledge transfer from universities and laboratories to businesses. Wider innovation Science policy which includes both the new-to-the-market as well as new-to-the-world innovations is critical to India's future economic success and should be recognized as part of a full innovation policy. Non-science-based forms of innovation such as prepaid simcards, opening up cyber cafes to provide internet connectivity on a pay per use basis or social innovation like mid-day meal program to attract children below the poverty line to schools in India are important innovations helpful for growth of the country. In fact, lots of laws made by commerce ministries across the world have positive or negative effect on the supply chain efficiencies or industry growth, although there is little realization of the fact that such laws which are innovations in their own right can be used to trigger growth (Co-evolution or Integrative innovation) by making changes/innovations in other ecosystem elements.

There are examples of several product and process innovations in terms of low-cost cars such as Nano, TVs, Video Games, Cell phones, Search engines, IPod, IPad and also business model innovations such as outsourcing, call centre based execution, etc. This linear model cannot capture several innovations that created blockbuster industries in recent times such as:

- **Government regulations**   Patent law; Deregulation of telecom and airlines; Value-added tax; Free trade agreements; WTO; New labor laws.
- **New business models**   Outsourcing; FDI; Sell direct; e-Business; Cloud computing; Orchestration; Social networks; Public-private partnerships.
- **New technology solutions**   Redesign of basic services such as water, power, gas, construction, banks, healthcare and education to be intelligent and smart.
- **Resources**   Industrial clusters; Special economic zones.

Services innovation is about creativity, technology, R&D, and entrepreneurship and new ways of doing business and interacting with society. Broadband, mobile and wireless networks, devices and services allow for richer services: communication, commerce, media, health, marketing and security. The global service platforms such as Internet, Facebook, YouTube, Wikipedia, Telemedicine, Suez and Panama canals etc provide the key to open the doors for integration and betterment of the world economy. The supply chain or service chains consist of global partners collaborating in serving the customers who are also globally dispersed. We provide the list of innovations that can lead to blockbuster industries or high growth in Table 5.1.

Table 5.1   Innovations in supply chain ecosystem

Supply Chains
Low-cost high-quality blockbuster products: Nano, Video Games, Cell phones,
IPod, Search engines, Wikipedia
Designing products for efficient logistics: Modularization, Process Standardization
Distributed manufacturing, JIT, TQM, Procurement
New technology solutions: Redesign services (water, power, gas, construction,
banks, education) to be intelligent and smart, UID, e-health records, Clouds
Market Channel Innovation: Supply chain visibility, Joint inventory management,
CPFR, RFID, Direct to customer, Home delivery, e-retail, International markets
through JVs, Packaging for all sections of populations
New business models: Outsourcing, BPOs, FDI, Sell direct, e-retail, PPP

Institutions
Government regulations: Process or Product patent, Deregulation of service
industry (Telecom & Airlines), VAT, Free trade agreements, WTO, New labour
laws, Competition Act, Land Acquisition Act, etc
Green, Customs for perishable goods, Trade, Hygiene, Regulations on packaging,
formulations, pricing, procurement like APMC Act, Essential Commodities Act,
Minimum support price for PDS
Social factors, Labor unions, NGOs

Delivery Services Infrastructure
Supply hubs, Cross-docks, Postponement, Product recalls
Shared services: Containerization, ATMs, Clouds, Orchestration, e-bay, Amazon;
social networking: Facebook, Linked in, Twitter; Canals: Suez, Panama
Cold chain, Packaging, Sensor networks for visibility, Delivery with bad
infrastructure, Distribution backbone, Linking Ports and airports into the global
transportation network
Soft Infrastructure: Trade facilitation, e-approval, e-letter of credits

Resources
Water, Power, Financial Institutions, Research institutions & Universities, Product
development and Testing laboratories, Creating new industrial clusters, Special
economic zones, Talent
New technology solutions for redesign of services (water, power, gas, construction,
banks, education) to be intelligent and smart, UID, e-health records, land records

5.2.1   *Innovations in regulations*

After independence in 1947, India followed inward-looking and state-interventionist
policies that shackled the economy through regulations and severely restricted trade
and economic freedom. The result was decades of low growth termed pejoratively
the Hindu rate of growth. Reforms beginning in 1991 gradually removed obstacles
to economic freedom, and India has begun to play catch-up, steadily re-integrating
into the global economy. The reforms are the best things that have happened to
India and they are major regulatory innovations.

Government policies have in many respects been salutary. There has been
a co-evolution of public policy and firm strategy. The growth of the Indian

pharmaceutical over the last four decades owes a lot to the 1970 Patent Act, which allowed the domestic marketing of patented products without a license. During the process patent regime, Indian firms developed competence in applied research for developing production process technologies, particularly for synthetic bulk drugs. The production of drugs increased many folds between the early 1970s and the 1990s. India has achieved global recognition as a low-cost producer and supplier of quality bulk drugs and formulations to the world. Similar is the case with telecom industry. The liberalization, entry of private operators, FDI in phone manufacturing have all made telecom a blockbuster industry. The distribution landscape, the retail operations are all dependent on the innovations that the Government has to make. The resource availability in the form of logistics, IT, Clusters, Universities, Financial Institutions, Power, Water, all will determine the service chain competitiveness. Thus, deregulation of telecom industry, allowing foreign players in auto industry, following the process patent in the pharmaceutical industry, attracting FDI through special economic zones, reducing tariffs, streamlining ports using trade facilitation software — all these regulatory innovations have contributed to or created blockbuster industries in their landscape.

5.2.2   *Co-evolution of innovations*

There is also an important phenomenon called the co-evolution of innovations, responsible for creating blockbuster industries. In the context of global supply chains, co-evolution takes place between organizations that are interconnected and thus have an effect on each other in a mutually beneficial way. For example, modularization of products and standardization of sub-modules has led to outsourcing to low-cost countries and this has forced or prompted countries like China and India and other countries to liberalize their economies and reduce the trade barriers. This in turn has increased the need for global services such as logistics, management consulting, accounting etc and the services trade has skyrocketed. RFID and GPS have improved the supply chain visibility and increased the trade efficiency. Ports, airports were developed to cater to the increases in the cargo and passenger traffic. This in turn has led to increased outsourcing. Although the outsourcing first started with the electronic industry, other sectors followed the path and outsourcing has become a competitive strategy. Similar is the story with the software industry. The creation of software technology parks, the tax breaks offered, introduction of University curricula in IT and allowing foreign companies to operate in the IT sector has created an IT economy in India with tremendous impact on social, economic and family sectors. You can also see this in India becoming a small car hub, a power house in the pharmaceutical industry, a back-office IT hub. Also, the rise of countries such as Singapore, Hong Kong, and China can be attributed to co-evolution of innovations in products, services and regulations. Mutualistic co-evolution, a relationship between two organizations of different verticals that benefits both and harms neither, may be observed when countries develop infrastructure such as roads, ports, airports, power plants, reduce tariffs and introduce trade facilitation methods for faster customs clearance to complement logistics company's capabilities for faster transportation and supply chain visibility and the manufacturing company's abilities for low-cost production. We have shown above the virtuous circle of co-evolution. On the other hand, Institutions can play a negative role.

5.2.3 *Our approach*

Our purpose here is to take a strategic and growth-oriented approach to the new-to-the-market innovation. Here the products and processes already exist and have been successful in different economic and social settings. The big question is how do you make them succeed in emerging markets?

We would like to formulate an integrative, co-evolutionary innovation strategy that would lead to high industry growth or excellent service quality by working with innovations in several of the ecosystem elements and also their convergences to provide easy access to quality products at affordable cost to the people. The example could be cell phones, small cars, affordable housing, vocational training, midday meal scheme, etc and their convergence for welfare of the citizens. We should not forget that the integration of services such as logistics, finance, trade and government policy with manufacturing and agriculture has been the basis for several iconic global manufacturing and service industries. Similar success stories can result in emerging market studies.

The converse questions are also very important. Given the government regulations, the investment climate and the vertical space, the company has to tread carefully with right products, services, planning strategies such as location and partnership decisions and business models to succeed. For example, the growth of the Indian pharmaceutical over the last four decades owes a lot to the 1970 Patent Act, and the co-evolution of public policy and firm strategy. The Government of India has adopted product patent law as of 2005 and this has taken the pharma industry through turmoil. Competencies such as contract manufacturing and reverse engineering that make you succeed in process patent environment need to be replaced with competencies in drug discovery and commercialization. Similarly the VAT regulations are going to bring big changes in the logistics and warehousing industry.

As we have argued above, regulatory innovations are more strategic and need to be done with thought and care. Currently these are done without much research following the success stories on other countries. Special economic zones were highly successful in China, US and other countries, but in India they were very badly implemented and they did not serve the purpose except in the case of software technology parks. Similar is the case with private-public partnerships in airports, roads and also in privatizing the public sector undertakings. While it may not always be possible to make correct predictions in all aspects of the regulations, the pros and cons as well as the actions to prevent any major occurrences can be thought through via simulations and mathematical modeling techniques.

As one moves forward, there is word of caution of the risks of implementation of these huge initiatives. India had to industrialize to realize its destiny and this requires acquisition of conversion of agricultural land from farmers to set up factories. Also India needs to create zones to attract foreign companies where the infrastructure is world-class with water, power, connectivity to global markets and with attractive tax and tariff benefits. This requires again land acquisition in the urban areas. Similar is the case with infrastructure development like roads, ports, etc. The real issue is the terms on which the land is acquired. It should not be acquired at prices with which the farmers are dissatisfied and with the possibility of creating social unrest. Power requirements multiply; coal usage and lack of environmental consciousness among industries will create problems to the environment. Labour productivity and their unionization could create problems. The governments should plan the activities which involve land acquisition, pollution and people migration with care showing benefits to the stakeholders. It should not appear as though the Government is colluding with the industry against the people. The problems such as these are called wicked problems and can easily lead to long, drawn unsolvable situations.

5.2.4 *Public sector innovation*

The public sector is by far the dominant service provider in the emerging economies particularly with respect to health, education, infrastructure, social insurance, culture, defense, security and justice. Yet its innovation record is often weak and its innovation practices are regularly dysfunctional. The government is the biggest customer in the Indian economy, and consequently has the power to demand the production of innovative products and services. For example, if the government decided that all new buildings should be carbon neutral, the scale of the subsequent procurement would immediately stimulate firms to develop and supply environmentally-friendly construction techniques. With the current terrorist attacks on civilian targets, government can direct business and publicly funded R&D towards major policy challenges such as network security and intelligent transport systems. Also, new ways of management, use of technologies to better execute the processes and use of just-in-time and supply hub kind of techniques which drove high efficiencies in manufacturing in public sector procurement are innovations that should be adapted. In the public sector, innovation can mean many different things. It can mean new ways of organizing things (like Public-Private Partnerships), new ways of rewarding people (like performance-related pay) or new ways of communicating (like ministerial blogs). Policy or regulatory innovations like e-voting, UID, creation of a national public health service, or the move to a low carbon economy can have tremendous impact on the businesses and citizens. The government should start a Center for Judicial Innovation which helps develop, test out and appraise new approaches such as specific courts for dowry offences and domestic violence, and a Center for Administrative Innovation which can try administrative reforms.

Public sector innovation matters for two broad reasons. First, the public sector is a significant component of all economic activity. The innovation performance of this sector significantly impacts the entire economy. Second, public policy innovation is a basic route to maintain relevance with the business and economic evolution of the private sector. In the absence of this, the public sector becomes increasingly a drag on the private sector through outdated regulatory and policy settings. We present some examples below.

5.3 Some Examples

In this section, we give three examples: one from service industry, the Indian telecom; the other from Nano, a small car project which is yet to be proven a success; and the third one a business or governance model called the orchestrator model, which we feel is the right model for some Indian sectors.

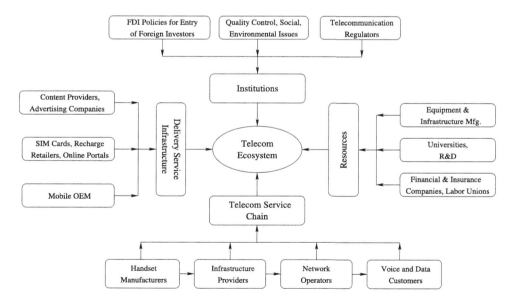

Fig. 5.1   The Indian telecom ecosystem

5.3.1   *The Indian mobile telecom industry: The success story*

The wireless industry revolution is the result of several innovations across several dimensions which converged into a massive manufacturing and service industry. The prolific growth in the usage of mobile phones is one of the most remarkable infrastructure stories of the past decade.

The telecommunications industry is a large and vital part of the global economy. From Alexander Graham Bell's initial discovery of the ability to send sound waves over a wire to the inventive engineers at Bell Laboratory that churned out decades of breakthrough inventions that have changed the way we live and work, the industry has a long-standing and impressive tradition of innovation. World growth depends on the telecommunications sector. The telecommunications market is highly concentrated in the developed world.

The telecom vertical's remarkable growth is a classic example to understand how co-evolution of several innovations led to its dramatic success. The government has deregulated the telecom industry. Following this, many positive policies were made by the government. It allowed private and foreign players to set up shops through FDI independently or through joint ventures, allocated spectrum through auctions, created Special Economic Zones to attract equipment and other manufacturers, and allowed foreign players to participate as manufacturing and service providers. The banking industry is the forerunner in starting mobile banking, as is the media industry in focusing on advertising through cell phones.[1,2]

Telecom deregulation

Though the specifics differ by country and region, in large part three common factors drove reforms around the world:

(i) The exceptionally poor performance of state-owned telecom firms generated pressure for reforms. Long waiting periods for telephone connections and the unreliability of those connections generated popular demand, while inefficient operations often requiring large subsidies encouraged governments to divest firms that were draining national treasuries.

(ii) International lending organizations began pressuring countries to divest.

(iii) There was a general worldwide trend towards divestiture, started largely by Britain's Thatcher government in 1979, which coined the term *privatization*.

At the beginning of 2003, more than half of the countries in the world had fully or partly privatized their incumbent telecom operators. The pace of privatization has stalled basically due to poor market conditions and for political reasons. In most cases, privatization faced resistance from labor unions, opposition parties and

---

[1]http://www.ibef.org/industry/telecommunications.aspx
[2]http://www.mit.gov.in/

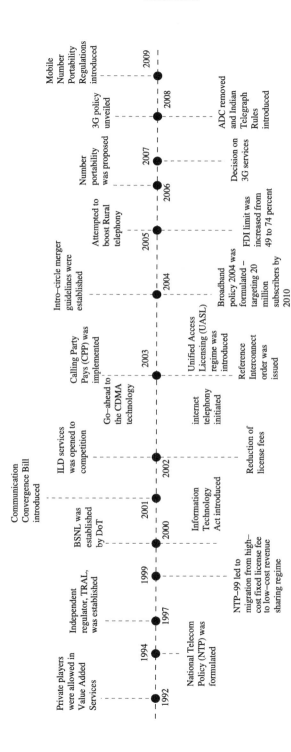

Fig. 5.2   Innovations of the Indian Department of Telecommunications (DoT)

Source: http://www.ibef.org/download/Telecommunications_171109.pdf, slide 26.

armed forces on account of national security concern due to perceived involvement of foreigners in critical telecom sector.

In a landmark pact by the WTO, 68 countries, which control 95% of the world's telecommunications market, have agreed to completely liberalize their telecommunications. Privatization has also been done to meet the WTO obligations. The market barriers are breaking down by lowering costs to consumers through increased competition.

In the developing countries, investment in Telecom infrastructure is considered a necessary foundation for economic growth. Massive investment is required to combat low Tele-density, poor service quality and to introduce modern technologies. Such investments are far beyond the reach of many governments, and telecom modernization needs to attract private sector investment and reduce government involvement to ensure fair competition.

The telecommunications sector is generally touted as one of the most successful examples of market-oriented reform of the Indian public sector. At the same time, the industry is not the exclusive domain of the private sector and market competition because the government continues to play a major role. For example, the public sector continues to be a major telecommunications service provider (through the Bharat Sanchar Nigam Limited, or BSNL). The Ministry of Communications in the Central Government continues to have important (and costly) development and social policy objectives such as rural telephony.

5.3.2 *A success story*

The most remarkable infrastructure story of the past decade is the spread of the mobile phone, which has eclipsed mainline phones around the world. Ten years ago, not many in India would have imagined that one can communicate in real time at affordable rates and do business while traveling on the road, rail or airplane. This has become a reality today. Convergence of several innovations along the four ecosystem dimensions is responsible for the success of the Indian wireless industry.

The Indian telecom growth has been phenomenal. India is the second-largest telecom market in the world with 900 million subscribers as on March 2012, which are estimated to reach approximately 1 billion by 2014. Mobile handsets sales in India are expected to reach 230 million units in 2012. For more than a decade, the sector has witnessed a steady addition in wireless subscribers. India has been adding 15–20 million subscribers every month, making it the world's fastest growing wireless market. The Indian telecom industry can be primarily divided into basic, cellular and internet services. It also has relatively segments such as radio paging services, very small aperture terminals (VSATs), public mobile radio trunked services (PMRTS) and global mobile personal communications by satellite (GMPCS). The subscriber base of wireless services stood at 670.6 million as of August 2010 with tele-density of 72 per cent.

Revenues of the Indian telecom industry are projected to reach US$45 billion by 2012, compared with US$33 billion in 2009. The wireless segment in India is much larger than the wire line segment and is growing steadily due to the convenience and utility it offers. The telecom sector is one of the highest FDI-attracting sectors in India, and has recorded FDI inflow worth more than US$9 billion between 2000 and 2010. Moreover, the rural markets are expected to be the next key growth drivers for the Indian telecom sector, given rural India's growing population and disposable income. See India and FICCI (2010) for India's telecom success story.

Various important regulations and laws have been passed in the Indian telecom industry post-liberalisation era:

Product and value chain innovation The major innovation in this industry came from creating a quality product at an affordable cost, with features for voice, text, picture, games and other video communications. This required a product redesign with standard components and outsourcing innovations in manufacturing, to bring down the cost. As a result, it created the contract manufacturing industry in India with Nokia, Flextronics and the likes playing a key role. Large volumes were essential for low unit costs to create economies of scale. There were marketing innovations such as prepaid, family and corporate connection discounts, etc. that led to obtaining a large share from every customer since customer acquisition and retaining costs are very high. Reliance Infocom, for example, had the boldness of vision in estimating the market when it was in its nascent stages. Reliance asked itself a simple question: *How many people will make a phone call if making a phone call is as cheap as sending a postcard?* They then worked out the scale of operations to make this low cost possible. The innovation principle that comes out of this is that in an emerging market, *Do not ask how large the market is but estimate how large can it be made to be with an appropriate intervention.*

Economic innovation through government regulations The government for its part has deregulated the telecom industry. There were many positive policies made by the government. It allowed private and foreign players to set up shops through FDI independently or through joint ventures, allocated spectrum through auctions, created special economic zones to attract equipment and other manufacturers, and allowed foreign players to participate as manufacturing and service providers, creating a booming industry through FDI.

Resources and resource management Human resources for manufacturing of phones and telecom equipment and for service providers (MRO, Billing, etc.) were readily available with little training. Telecom and other engineers were available through engineering colleges, IITs, etc., while management experts with MBA degrees came from the management training institutes. Financing the ventures was possible through banks and also FDI. This has created a highly lucrative as well as competitive industry attracting many players including large Indian conglomerates like Bharti, Reliance, etc. as well as MNCs like Vodafone.

Delivery service infrastructure — Logistics and IT   Innovation in technology came from service providers to survive the competition. Also, while the Indian mobile industry still uses GSM and CDMA technologies, companies across the board are now investing and rolling out 3G systems. The advancement in systems and freeing up of spectrum has also attracted Mobile Virtual Network Operators (MVNOs) like Virgin that leverages the Tata Teleservices network. Outsourcing within the industry has also matured. For example, Bharti outsourced:

- Call-center operations to 4 BPOs — IBM Daksh, MphasiS, TeleTech and Hinduja TMT — as part of a INR 1000 crore deal;
- Entire cellular network to three existing equipment suppliers — Ericsson, Nokia and Siemens — under a \$725 million three-year deal.

Learnings from this study   The wireless industry revolution is the result of several ecosystem innovations which converged into a massive manufacturing and service industry. A well-articulated industry design could have resulted in faster convergence as well as a more mature industry. A similar model for convergence can also be applied to other industries such as infrastructure, retail, etc. to pinpoint current shortcomings, plug the gaps, and design a roadmap for the future, thus helping decision makers develop far more effective strategies. In India, communications are used for personal communications but the importance of communications goes beyond personal communications. Use of these technologies in business communications as well as in real-time control of networks such as water, power, gas etc to make them smart and also in increasing energy efficiency in homes, buildings, offices etc would lead to more benefits. The communications revolution should go beyond SMSs and advertising to improving systems and also for improving the energy efficiencies.

5.3.3   *The changing face of Indian auto industry*

Nano is a great example of the blue ocean strategy of producing products for emerging market customers at affordable prices. Nano is innovative on multiple levels from its engineering to marketing and to its manufacturing. Tata brought in suppliers such as Bosch, a German maker of appliances and motors, and Delphi, a world leader in automotive parts (and one-time subsidiary of GM), in early-stage design, challenging them to be full partners in the Nano innovation by developing lower-cost components. The Nano shows that a new world order is possible in the auto industry. For information on the Indian auto industry, refer to the recent paper by Ranawat and Tiwari (2009).

During their first 100 years, vehicle manufacturers (VMs) are used to applying a single dominant approach of assembling and selling similar vehicles with the same power trains through remarkably similar franchised dealer networks, with 80 percent of automotive sales and production based in the United States, Europe, and Japan.

Nano is a departure from this approach and shows a glimpse of what is to come. In the future, China and India could become the world's leading producers of small cars and of vehicles that use alternative fuels. The supply chains will be shorter and regional, producing several flexible power-train options: electric in China, ethanol in Brazil, diesel in Russia due to the volatile price of oil, the climate change issues. On the management side, flexible methods of combining efficiencies of lean and resilience of inventory; sourcing from Auto clusters with alternatives in case of wars, natural disasters or terrorist attacks; manufacturing in emerging markets with awareness to risks and mitigation strategies; innovation such as Green Vehicles in the presence of government regulations; and Governance models for event-based supply chain execution of the globally dispersed auto chains, need to be developed. Also, with fast changing technologies, so need be the supply chain networks. See the paper by Sehgal *et al.* (2010) for the full details of Tata Nano.

This requires a new approach for Innovation and Governance which is much different from the existing. Our objective is to develop a methodology for the design of future high-performance auto supply chains using the supply chain ecosystem framework. Similar business models should be adopted in low-cost housing, health care, vocational training, food courts where goods and services are provided at affordable rates while maintaining safety and quality.

5.3.4 *Orchestrator: Innovation in governance models*

Organizations generally follow either the organic expansion and/or acquisition routes to business growth. Upfront investment needs to be made in physical resources like factories or in talent and information infrastructure. The growth strategies of this kind involve capital expenditure and the payoffs may take a long time to come. There is also a risk of technologies getting outdated and obsolescent designs, products and the resources. An alternate growth strategy called leveraged growth strategy, mobilizing others' resources to support your own growth initiatives, involves less risk and has the potential to go to the market quickly. This growth model, called the orchestrator model, allows one to capture the first to the market and the corresponding economic benefits. Here one avoids the burdens of asset ownership and time required for acquisitions and integration or for raising a green field. Orchestrators have been around for quite some time in certain industries. A contractor of a large commercial building construction project orchestrates a broad array of service providers for building construction, electrical wiring and fittings, plumbing, interior decoration, furniture design, etc. Similarly, movie producers orchestrate the complex processes involved in movie production including raising the capital.

Li & Fung has become a popular and powerful example of a new kind of orchestrator coordinating a very broad process network [Fung *et al.* (2007)]. Li & Fung makes no products of its own. Rather, it orchestrates the production of goods by others, drawing on a vast global network of highly focused providers to arrange for private-label manufacturing, primarily on behalf of US and European clothiers. For a specific product or client, Li & Fung assembles a customized set of specialized providers to handle product development to the sourcing of raw materials, production planning and management, and, eventually, shipping. If problems arise at any stage of the process, the company can quickly switch from one provider to another.

Boeing's 777 jet is an assemblage of three million parts from more than 900 suppliers in 17 countries around the world. For its 787 jet, the company is also outsourcing systems for collision avoidance and landing in zero visibility to HCL Technologies. Boeing produces only the wings and fuselage, and assembles the aircraft. Apart from spreading risk, it also helps to make nations have a vested interest and hence in global sales.

There are several other successful orchestrators in today's business world. They do the functions of sourcing and marketing divisions of big retailers or brand manufacturers to attain the scale of operations. The orchestrators also focus on the governance and acquire the required talent with domain knowledge and capabilities for international coordination. There is, however, also a huge risk that the orchestrators face and that is of takeover by the asset owners they do business with.

One can use the orchestrator model to advantage to improve efficiencies in fragmented verticals such as in Indian retail or logistics industries where millions of small stakeholders could benefit with coordination and information visibility. We show in the next section how the Indian logistics sector can benefit from such a model.

5.4   Innovations in the Delivery Infrastructure

Located midway between the Australian, Middle Eastern and European continents, India can play the role of a transshipment hub, a knowledge services hub, and a food hub for the oil-rich Middle Eastern neighbors. Indian organizations can also leverage the geographical position and resources to gain sustainable advantage as a manufacturing hub, education hub, after-sales service hub, etc. to meet local as well as export demands. Several innovations are possible in the delivery infrastructure space. There are wide variety of innovative logistics products that companies can offer such as Containerization, Transshipment, Supply hubs, Cross-docking, Modularization and Standardization for efficient logistics and value-added services such as packaging, late customization, merge in transit; operational innovations such as shared warehouses, outsourcing, sensor networks for visibility, cross-docking, merge in transit; and finally regulatory innovations such as low carbon footprint, green logistics and IT, warehouse locations to suit the VAT regulations, relationship with customs with better knowledge and connections, trade facilitation, etc. There is a tremendous opportunity for building the distribution backbone for the country connecting the various demand points along the path of goods flow which is the future

Table 5.2   Innovations in logistics

Supply Chain Innovation
Heavy vessels, Containerization, Transhipment, Supply hubs, Cross-docking, Outsourcing, Modularization & Standardization
Packaging, late customization, merge in transit, Customs, sensor networks for visibility

Institutions
Green, VAT, Customs, Trade, Knowledge, Connections, Foreign exchange, FTAs & Trade facilitation

Delivery Services Infrastructure
RFID, GPS, 3PLs, 4PLs, Data integration and mining, Remote monitoring and Execution

Resources
Training and other HR approaches, efficient operations with poor industry inputs, Supply Chain Finance, Innovative Governance models

---

railway and roadway corridors such as the golden quadrilateral, freight corridors etc. These will improve the supply chain efficiency in India.

5.4.1   *Indian logistics: Innovation through orchestration*

The logistics industry basically started as a part of procurement division in an enterprise and slowly became an independent function. The companies usually outsource the warehousing and transportation to small players and auctions are a popular way of choosing the transporter. This practice has given rise to second party logistics providers. Warehouse management and transport management software packages have come into existence for managing the end-to-end execution and also for inventory management in the warehouse. The ports, airports, rail freight yards, roadways, are also second party logistics providers facilitating the movement of goods across countries or within a country. Only recently the third party logistics providers such as GATI, TCS, DHL, UPS, TNT, etc, who are experts in end-to-end execution of goods transport, came into existence. They are assisted by various standard and custom-built software packages. The inbound and outbound logistics and the innovations such as containerization, supply hubs, transhipment and supply chain visibility using GPS and wireless were born. There are now fourth party logistics providers emerging connecting the loosely coupled independent logistics players.

The logistics industry moves to modular clusters or stacks populated by specialist firms and infrastructure authorities. The logistics industry stack divides activities into layers that are complementary to each other. Most companies specialize in one or a few layers and rely on other companies to offer complementary components by communicating through standard interfaces. The first layer consists of the infrastructure such as ports, airports, rail and road, inland water transport and free

Owners/ Regulators	OEM	4PL	Consultants	Software providers	BPO	Regulators
Service providers	3PL	Clearing agents	Customs	Trucking companies	Warehouse owners	Call Centers
Software packages	WMS	TMS	Trade Facilitation		GPS	Sensor Networks
Storage	CFS	Warehouse	Transshipment hubs		Supply hubs	Distribution Centers
Carriers	Ships	Aircrafts	Wagons	Trucks	Pipes	Minivans
Infrastructure	Ports	Airports	Rail Freight	Road Freight	Inland Water Transport	Free trade zones

Fig. 5.3   Logistics ecosystem

trade zones. The second and third layers contain the carriers and warehouse and distribution centers. The fourth layer consists of software providers, and the fifth, the third party logistics providers and clearing agents. Sitting on the top are the OEMs, lead logistics providers, BPOs etc who are making decisions and assisting in execution. The organizational structure is chosen to manage the logistics operations by selecting the appropriate players from each order. The orchestrator model can be used to connect all the players to plan and execute the logistics function.

In India there are millions of very small players with one truck and two trucks or a warehouse or a family-owned distribution center. They may not be IT-enabled, but the scenario is changing with wireless technologies. A few large 3PLs such as GATI, TCS, SICAL, etc make things happen in the 3PL space. Most of the shippers do not have logistics connectivity and use private players. The train is cheaper than truck but hauls mostly the government freight such as the iron ore or the food grains.

5.5   Conclusions

In this chapter, we have considered two kinds of innovations: the *new to the world* and the *new to the market* kind of innovations. Our focus is on countries like India which are termed as emerging market countries. These countries have their own peculiarities and require easy access to affordable products and services. Our thesis is that the ecosystem framework should be used to simultaneously innovate in all the four elements of the ecosystem and also look for co-evolution of the innovated products. The new-to-the-market kind of innovations to provide easy access to affordable products will be more useful in the emerging market context.

In the emerging market context, the big challenge is to decide how global leadership in fundamental research and manufacturing and services interacts with leadership in emerging markets to create similar growth in food security, education, and infrastructure for the benefit of mankind below and on the borders of poverty line in the world. We have shown this in the telecom and logistics sectors. In Chap. 7, we show how food security can be achieved using innovations in integrating food supply chain and integrating the supply chain elements using sensor networks, wireless, call centers and other smart technologies to monitor and govern the food distribution. Similar concepts can be applied to education, health care and affordable housing etc. The new-to-the-world kind of innovations are also important and can be the focus of educational institutions and R&D laboratories.

Chapter 6

Governance

6.1 Introduction

Supply chain governance, coordination and control are topics of particular importance in global supply chains. We have seen earlier that the products and services generated by the supply chain or service chain visit several countries, organizations such as ports, customs, distribution centers and the facilities of the stakeholders including suppliers, contract manufacturers, logistics providers and retail shops before finally landing in the customers' hands. Given the fragmented and competitive nature of the global supply chains, it is challenging for the diverse interest groups within the network to align themselves with the objectives of the global supply chain and the end-customer. The movement of goods, information and finances need to be facilitated by someone within these organizations or outside of them. This function involves supply chain governance and is increasingly becoming critical for achieving competitiveness. The following example by Adam Smith emphasizes the importance of governance:

> The woolen coat, for example, which covers the day-labourer, as coarse and rough as it may appear, is the produce of the joint labour of a great multitude of workmen. The shepherd, the sorter of the wool, the wool-comber or carder, the dyer, the scribbler, the spinner, the weaver, the fuller, the dresser, with many others, must all join their different arts in order to complete even this homely production.

Adam Smith (1776)

In this chapter, we deal with this issue of the organization structure for coordinating a globally dispersed supply chain or service chain networks of companies with independent ownership. In such networks, coordination of the managerial processes that help realise the organisational goals such as strategic planning, procurement, global expansion, supply chain execution, etc is a very important function. The governance of loosely coupled companies to achieve the strategic as well as operational objectives is an important subject.

6.2   Types of Governance Structures

Since the supply chain networks and their ecosystems involve companies which are globally distributed and are under independent ownership, the governance involves inter-organizational coordination. The governance of global supply chains requires interaction with several agencies such as resource owners, financial institutions, governments, social institutions, industry organizations, ports, airports, logistics and software providers and several others. Here, we consider two different types of organizations: vertically integrated organizations and globally distributed organizations.

In vertically integrated hierarchical companies, coordination and control of activities along the value chain is managed through ownership and direct managerial oversight. The company, together with subsidiaries, affiliates and joint ventures located in different geographic locations, retains ownership and control of inputs, components and products, as they move along the value chain. The coordination and control of production and related activities is internalized to the firm, though it may stretch across borders. The automobile manufacturers such as Ford and GM provided (until recently) perhaps the clearest examples of such a hierarchy.

In globally networked modular organizations, the codification of knowledge, rapid diffusion of information and communication technologies and standardization of the interfaces between organizationally separate stages of production through technical standards and design rules enabled coordination and control of various processes that run across different companies which are in geographically distant locations under different ownerships. Thus, actors in a global supply chain network are linked through a variety of relationships such as subcontracting, licensing, common technical standards, marketing contracts and shared network product- and process-related standards. While the organization structures of vertically integrated networks are a well-studied subject, the subject is not deeply studied in the case of globally distributed supply chain networks.

Provan and Kenis (2007) identify three types of networks. The network members work together to achieve their own and a collective goal. Either self-initiated by themselves, or mandated or contracted, they form a network. The network governance may be brokered or may follow shared governance i.e. they are governed completely by the organizations that comprise the network. In the shared governance case, every organization would interact with every other organization regarding network governance. Network members may divide governance responsibilities among themselves, with no single organization taking on significant governance tasks. Instead, network governance could occur by and through a single organization, acting as a highly centralized network broker. Also, brokered networks may be participant governed or externally governed. Each governance form is utilized in practice for a variety of reasons and no one model is universally superior to the other.

Governance, coordination and execution are done through a well-defined network organization structure. Organization structure in companies is allocation of work roles and an administrative mechanism that creates a pattern of interrelated work activities and allows the organization to coordinate, conduct, and control its work activities. The organization structure is reflected in the organization chart, which gives each employee his or her place in the organization, tasks and responsibilities, and supervisors. In the case of networks, the network-organization structure may exist formally in case of brokered networks or informally in case of participant-governed networks.

The governance discussed in this chapter has more responsibilities than those that conventional company organization structures deal with. These include relationships with institutions and companies outside of the day-to-day production functions and also the risk identification and mitigation functional groups identified as control room.

Traditionally, network governance has been considered mainly a structural construct, with less emphasis on relational aspects, especially from the management point of view. Ritter *et al.* (2004) point out that the research focus in interorganizational networks is shifting from structures and governance to business models, planning, execution and managing relationships. Networks have now become a strategic option that firms can use to collaborate with partners to enhance the market share. The management function of network governance requires capabilities that enable a firm to identify partners; coordinate the resources, government and social agencies and activities performed by other members of the supply chain network; as well as abilities to plan and control activities at the network level. Accordingly, a well-defined governance structure has the following features:

- Identifies and manages relations with government, trade, social groups, labour, resources and B2B and B2C delivery mechanisms;
- Builds business models and relationships for growth enhancement;
- Identifies and categorises risks that can arise from various ecosystem sources and puts in place risk mitigation strategies in operational readiness based on their severity;
- For every customer order, selects the suppliers and forms the network for the order;
- Describes the allocation of tasks and responsibilities to organizations forming the network;
- Builds systems for effective communication, collaboration and coordination among the network partners;
- Manages a control room for monitoring and execution of the planned activities in a timely and efficient manner under normal as well as severe conditions.

In the rest of this chapter, we first introduce the networked organizations in the current manufacturing and service industries: vertically integrated versus spatially and ownership-wise distributed organizations. We then discuss the governing structures for these organizations.

6.2.1   *Vertically integrated organizations*

These organizations have been in existence for a long time and domestic companies or multinationals setting up shops in another country also follow the same vertical structure. There are several organizational structures followed for vertically integrated enterprises. We discuss some of them below.

6.2.2   *Functional structure*

The distinctive feature of a functional structure is that people and activities are grouped by resources or inputs such as finance, marketing, engineering, research and development, and human resource management, etc. Organizing companies around functions has several advantages. It is a simple, straightforward, and logical way to build departments around basic functions in which the enterprise is engaged. It is the best way when the organizational context stresses specialization, efficiency, and quality. Employees in similar functions adopt similar values, goals, and orientations, which encourages collaboration and makes communication easy. However, if coordination and cooperation across departments is weak, the departments may work in silos.

6.2.3   *Product structure*

The product or multidivisional form is structured according to the outputs such as products, services, programs, and projects. The company creates multiple functional organizations, each with its own product line. Heads of divisions are in charge of self-contained companies. Since the units are small, employees identify themselves more with products than with functions. General Motors is one of the earliest and best-known examples of product structure firm, with separate divisions for Buick, Cadillac, Oldsmobile, Pontiac, Chevrolet, and Trucks. Hewlett-Packard and 3M also followed this structure. The product structure has several strengths. The coordination across functions is excellent because of small size and focused goals. Product structures also have some serious disadvantages. Each division tries to reinvent the wheel, duplicating resources and missing opportunities for resource sharing.

6.2.4   *Customer-based structure*

In customer-based structures, departments are organized to meet the need of groups of customers. General Electric was organized into the aerospace group, appliance group, construction industries group, industrial group, and power generation group. While customer service could be better in this organization structure, there could be duplication of efforts and resources. This structure is popular because large buyers and the big retailers insist on dedicated units to serve their needs. Also, companies organized around customers have superior knowledge about the particular market segment, which provides competitive advantage. The Hong Kong-based Li & Fung is organized according to customer groups.

Organization structures based on customer-based divisions are becoming very popular, since they are compatible with the present day emphasis on customer focus, outsourcing based on core competencies, and competitive advantage through market knowledge and information.

6.2.5 *Matrix structure*

The matrix structure may be the answer when the organization needs both technological expertise within functions and horizontal coordination of the product line for the same departments. The unique characteristic of the matrix organization is that both product and functional structures are implemented simultaneously. The product managers and functional managers are equally powerful, and employees report to both of them. The manager of the project is given authority and responsibility with a separate budget and resources. His manpower resources come from the functions, however.

There are various other organisation structures such as Geographical, Hybrid, Process, etc. There are several leading global players following the above models. We briefly mention four of them: Flextronics, Nokia, Intel and Zara.

6.2.6 *Examples*

Flextronics International Ltd., headquartered in Singapore, offers a model for the integrator role. With revenues of tens of billions of U.S. dollars, it is a leading electronics manufacturing Services Company, operating in 32 countries and five continents. The company provides complete design, engineering and manufacturing services that are vertically integrated with component capabilities to optimize its manufacturing operations and time to market. Flextronics operates several industrial parks in low-cost regions around the world. Each park functions as a manufacturing center, producing all the components needed for the final system assembly. Flextronics' approach is built on controlling the production process and having tight relationships with its corporate customers. Similarly, Nokia does nearly all its manufacturing in-house, designs its own chips, and manages its goods flow of billions of components each year. Design and supply chain assembly are developed as core and highly competitive capabilities by Nokia.

Intel Corporation, too, is an integrator with combination of world-class R&D, massive scale, and extreme standardization, and has achieved extraordinary successes through the do-it-all innovation model. Intel invests in R&D with thousands of researchers around the world pushing for the next advances in semiconductors as well as advanced computing, communications, and wireless technologies. Intel also operates fifteen major manufacturing facilities worldwide. The company believes that if it controls literally every aspect of idea generation, commercialization, and realization, it controls its destiny.

Zara, the fashion retailer, integrates many activities in order to generate new clothing designs, manufacture them, get them to stores and on shelves quickly, and sell as many of them as it can at the highest possible price. Zara collects through various sources the information on what is the latest fashion and what is selling. The designs are shared with a network of Zara factories, which use sophisticated just-in-time systems that enable them to put items into production quickly and produce just the required quantities. All new items are priced and tagged before delivery to the stores. Zara can react swiftly to changing market trends and quickly distribute new products throughout its system. While other companies in the industry take up to nine months to get new product lines into their shops, Zara takes only two to three weeks.

Companies usually choose to integrate to have greater control over costs and timing of product development and commercialization and because they want to avoid risks of partnership such as IP leakage. In the process, the integrator also takes on the major share of the financial risk. We study now the networked organization structures which are followed in most of the global manufacturing and service organizations.

6.3   Networked Organizations

In a network organization, a number of independent companies, each concentrating on its core businesses, form an alliance towards a specific goal. They act together as though they were a single corporation performing activities along an industry's value chain. They are also called the virtual corporation. This approach is the opposite of vertical integration discussed before. The basic organizational or management challenge in such networks is the selection of partners for fulfilling the customer order and then coordination of their activities in sourcing, design, production, distribution and service, and monitoring their performance. Thus, partner selection, coordination and control are of particular importance in global value chains. It refers to how some lead firms determine and coordinate the activities of the actors in the supply chain. This includes selection of suppliers; what will they supply (outputs of suppliers in the network); how it is to be produced (e.g., product tolerances and process standards); assigning the functions to the suppliers and the production and delivery schedules (how much to produce and when); and upgrading of suppliers in terms of equipment, capacity and their moving up the value chain (e.g., moving from manufacturing into design), and others. Also, key production parameters such as the product definition, specification, the production schedule and location, the technology to be used, quality systems, labor standards and environmental standards need to be decided along with the targeted price, and communicated to the chain partners. In addition, Government agencies and international organizations regulate product design and manufacture, keeping in view the consumer safety and market transparency as in the case of food safety standards, children's toys, and motor vehicles. There could be regulation on environment and child and women labor. The broker or lead firm has the responsibility of ensuring that the labor laws are followed and that products follow the environmental standards.

We have mentioned above that global supply chain networks can be classified into two different types: the participant-governed networks, and highly brokered networks. Again in participant-governed networks, there are two types:

Shared participant governance   This is a highly decentralized structure, involving most or all network members interacting on a relatively equal basis in the process of governance. The network acts collectively and no single entity represents the network as a whole.

Lead organization governed structure   Here the network may be highly centralized, governed by and through a lead organization that is also a network member.

Shared governance networks are common in community and human services organizations. Also, agriculture and dairy organizations generally operate through cooperatives. The cooperatives are represented by elected representatives. Lead organization governed networks can be either producer-driven or buyer-driven chains. In producer-driven networks the lead firm, often a large multinational manufacturer, plays a central role in exercising relatively close control in coordinating a geographically distributed network of subsidiaries, affiliates and suppliers. This type of networks is common in capital and technology intensive industries, such as automobiles, electronics, aircraft and electrical machinery. Cisco Systems Inc. and Nike Inc. are examples of lead firms. In buyer-driven networks, large retailers and brands (e.g., Wal-Mart, Carrefour, Levi, etc) play the lead role, sourcing from distributed networks of independent suppliers, defining product and process specifications and standards. This generally happens in labor-intensive, consumer goods industries such as apparel, footwear, agro-industry and consumer electronics. This is a model that often occurs in health and human services where there may be a core provider agency that assumes the role of network leader because of its central position in the flow of clients and key resources. In community health, this may be a hospital or a health clinic.

Networks need governance, which includes partner selection, coordination, and control for their proper functioning. We consider these below.

6.3.1   *Partner selection*

Network governance involves selecting a subset of members, who have persistent business interactions, engaged in creating products or services based on implicit and open-ended contracts to adapt to environmental contingencies. The exchanges are not derived from vertical authority or from legal contracts but rely on coordination and control, social networking and reputations. Thus network governance facilitates integrating multiple autonomous, diversely skilled parties to create complex products or services meeting the time and quality requirements. Hierarchy, where the coordination and control of production and related activities is internalized to the firm, or markets, where company independently produces to the market, are the two governance structures. The third structure is the network structure where the interactions take place through networks of individuals engaged in mutually supportive actions i.e. one party is dependent on the resources controlled by another, and there are gains to be had by the pooling of resources. Network governance constitutes a "distinct form of coordinating economic activity" (Powell, 1990), which contrasts (and competes) with markets and hierarchies.

From the transaction cost perspective, three exchange conditions — *uncertainty*, *asset specificity*, and *frequency* — determine which governance form is more efficient. Asset-specificity involves unique equipment, processes, or knowledge developed by participants to complete exchanges that may not be useful for transactions with other companies.

We interpret the asset specificities using the supply chain ecosystem framework. We have the supply chain specific assets that are concerned with the supplier manufacturing processes such as specialist dies and manufacturing processes. The physical asset specificity and dedicated asset specificity are included under the supply chain assets. There are asset specificities under the resources wing; these include the human, clusters, financial institutions, etc., location-specific infrastructure such as ports and airports which attract the companies to the location. Delivery infrastructure specificity includes customized logistics and IT processes that enable on-time delivery, 3PLs and IT providers, etc. Institutions also create specificities giving companies several benefits in terms of taxes and tariffs with special regulations, creating special economic zones, special universities for training manpower, etc. The ecosystem and the investment climate widen the definition of asset specificity from supplier to buyer to tying the businesses to the location. We thus use the ecosystem framework in the location analysis chapter in Part 2 of this book.

Frequency of interactions between the buyer and supplier is important for reasons of economies of scale for the specialized mechanisms created, for transfer of tacit knowledge in customized exchanges and for establishing relations with network partners. *Environmental uncertainty* can come from suppliers, customers, competitors, regulatory agencies, unions, or financial markets. Understanding the sources of uncertainty is important, since they influence what governance form is used to coordinate and safeguard exchanges.

Even modest levels of supply uncertainty, combined with predictable product demand, entice firms to integrate vertically, whereas demand uncertainty encourages firms to disaggregate into autonomous units, primarily through outsourcing or subcontracting. For example, the network structure of the textile industry in Prato, Italy, enhanced the textile firms' ability to respond quickly to changes in fashion. In Japanese automobile *keiretsu*, decoupling enhanced organizational flexibility as parties learned from one another what reduced lead time and improved quality for new models. In the film industry, structured relations among subcontractors and film studios are based on a division of labor: film studios finance, market, and distribute films, whereas numerous subcontractors with clearly defined roles and professions (e.g., producer, director, cinematographer, and editor) create the film.

6.3.2 *Coordination*

Coordination is to bring different elements of a complex activity or organization into a harmonious or efficient relationship (Oxford Concise Dictionary, 1999). The basic organizational or management challenge in global supply or service chain networks of this kind is the coordination of its activities in sourcing, design, production, distribution and service with spatially distributed, independent actors.

There are several activities that need to be repeatedly performed in a timely and orderly manner end-to-end by the network participants. Key parameters such as the product definition, specification, the technology and the quality systems, labor and environmental standards need to be decided along with the targeted price, and communicated to the chain partners. In addition, Governmental and international organizational regulations on product design and manufacture for ensuring consumer safety (as in the case of food safety standards, children's toys, and motor vehicles) and on environment and child and women labor need to be adhered to by all partners.

More importantly, decisions need to be made on the following:

(1) For every order, selection of suppliers; assigning the functions to them such as what to supply, how is it to be produced (e.g., product tolerances and process standards), the production and delivery schedules (how much to produce and when) and to whom and when to deliver, etc.
(2) Upgrading of suppliers in terms of equipment, capacity and delivery methods to meet the regulations, standards and delivery schedules.

6.3.3 *Control*

This step involves the real-time control of the supply chain execution which involves monitoring the goods flow from origin to destination and making decisions to counter events that cause disruptions such as truck failures, customs payments or driver ill-health to maintain the commitments to the customers. Currently this step is ignored and is done through expediting in case of failures.

We now consider the brokered model in detail.

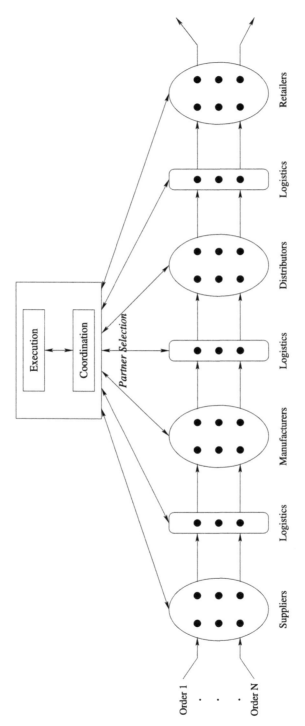

Fig. 6.1   Governance: Partner selection, coordination, and execution

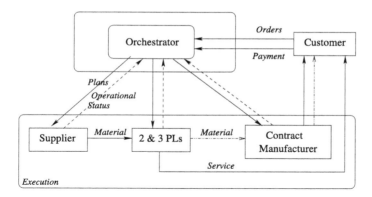

Fig. 6.2   Orchestrator business model

6.4   Orchestrator Governance Model

The other category of network governance is broker-driven governance or network orchestration. In this case, a firm outside the network takes the governance responsibility. The orchestrator firms do not own any production facilities and their basic role involves coordinating and integrating activities along a given value chain. Because they own fewer assets and leverage the resources of partner companies, network orchestrators generally require less capital and often generate higher revenues than traditional firms, in several product markets. We now consider the governance mechanisms in detail.

The traditional routes to business growth — organic expansion or acquisition — share the common requirement of owning proprietary assets. But ownership of assets, whether factories and machinery or intangible assets like information and skills, is what makes traditional growth strategies so risky. But the orchestrator growth strategy or leveraged growth strategy involves substantially less risk and offers the potential of an immediate and sustainable boost in profitability. It is not always necessary to own the assets required for expanding; one can mobilize needed assets existing within other companies, to support their growth initiatives. This way one can capture the economic benefits of growth while avoiding the economic burdens of asset ownership.

Orchestrators have been around for quite some time in certain industries. A contractor of a large commercial building construction project orchestrates a broad array of highly specialized service providers for building construction, electrical wiring and fittings, plumbing, interior decoration, furniture design and security systems. Similarly the cinema producer orchestrates the complex processes required to make a movie. In apparel business, Li & Fung provides a powerful example of a new kind of sophisticated orchestrator coordinating a very broad process network.

6.4.1 *Roles of network orchestrator*

According to Hinterhuber (2002), the network orchestrator has four roles: *network architect, network judge, network developer*, and *charismatic leader*. The task of the network architect is to select member companies that make up the business network and to set objectives. The role of the network judge is to set performance standards to which the member companies of the business network must comply. Performance standards need to be defined individually for each network member in terms of specific capabilities and global performance objectives. Performance standards are then monitored and adapted, again on an individual basis. The reason for this is that *the orchestrator remains the key interface for end customers and is thus fully accountable for the network output*. The third role, network developer, is to develop a network's physical and non-material assets, including knowledge acquisition, knowledge transfer across the member firms and the creation of a strong brand image. Lastly, the role of a network orchestrator is that of a charismatic leader. Orchestrators should create and manage a rich texture of interactions in the network. They also should take a long-term view on the relationship and expect partner companies to do likewise. As central firms, they have the key responsibility of motivating partner firms to collaborate on overall network priorities. Orchestrators should specify the contributions they expect from each partner company, whether as contributions to the orchestrator, or to the network or to other network members. Orchestrators are successful only together with their partners, and the success of partner companies comes with the success of the orchestrator. Orchestrators should therefore make clear this mutual dependence and motivate the partner companies to take on an active role in further developing specific competencies.

6.4.2 *Talents needed for orchestrators*

(1) **Deep Domain Knowledge**: Detailed understanding of practices and processes being coordinated, Intellectual Property relating to Products and Processes.
(2) **Management of** Procurement, Acquisition, Partner selection, Monitoring, Supervision and Visibility across the SCN.
(3) **Relationship Management**: Trusted relationship with Customers, Suppliers, Service Providers, Government, Employees.
(4) **Capabilities** to Identify, Continually Redesign and Manage Processes to changing market needs.
(5) **Human Resources**: Training, Mentoring, Performance evaluation.

Network orchestration has applications across diverse industries and activities from R&D to services. Orchestrators must be adroit at recruiting the right providers, configuring the right modules, and overseeing the performance of the network. Their ability to do so begins and ends with a deep knowledge of the network's operations. Orchestrators are learning organizations with privileged relationships; their employees may never touch a product. Such organizations mobilize other companies' assets and capabilities to deliver value to customers. Orchestration involves more than simply the bringing together of a set of capabilities. It is the assembly and management of a whole range of tangible and intangible elements — design skills, manufacturing capabilities, a workforce, a brand, a distribution system — into a functioning whole. For an Orchestrator, the supply chain formation and execution are the most important steps.

6.4.3   *Orchestration is the riskiest model*

Once a company has chosen to orchestrate, it is difficult (though not impossible) for it to go back and reintegrate. Orchestration can look very tempting and seductively easy: *let your partners do a lot of the hard work while you sit back and reap the rewards*. But there is substantial risk lurking beneath the attractive surface. Unused internal capabilities can quickly atrophy. Collaborators that are meant to facilitate the process can get in the way. Partners may unexpectedly become competitors.

Here is the story of Schwinn, the iconic American bicycle manufacturer, which allowed orchestration to hollow out the core. Schwinn's management felt that the company's legacy of innovation and customer relationships were the most valuable assets, so they outsourced production to a small supplier in Taiwan, Giant Manufacturing Corporation. The supplier gained knowledge and expertise, and cut costs to become a far better bike maker than its partner. Giant is now one of the world's largest bicycle companies.

The governance model for risk mitigation or hollowing out is to get involved in orchestration, keeping some production at home or running it as a joint venture, or keep innovating and make the outsourced model outdated and look for a new partner. Complete hands-off orchestration is certainly a straight road to disaster.

6.5   Orchestration in Logistics

Most manufacturers handle all logistics functions including trucking and warehousing through their own logistics or transportation departments. In fact in the US, the outsourcing of logistics activities is increasing only now. It is between 8–10% of the total market of approximately 1 Trillion dollars. The second party logistics providers (2PLs) are basic transportation and storage providers such as truck owners, the rail operators, the shipping companies, the airlines, the freight forwarders, the warehousing companies, the packaging and distribution companies who have high levels of asset intensity but low barriers to entry. Airports and Seaports as capacity providers are also categorized as 2PLs. These companies are now changing their traditional business models and moving up the value chain. They now want to be *one-stop total end-to-end logistics solutions providers* offering multi-modal cargo carriers, trade documentation, financial support such as insurance, customs clearance and a host of other things. They are labeled as an integrated third party logistics (3PL) company or a lead logistics provider (LLP), or an integrated express logistics company, or as a 4PL consultant.

Total logistics solution providers offer custom and semi-custom supply chain and logistics solutions to targeted industries through integration and management of services provided by multiple focused service providers. Examples of solutions offered include inbound materials logistics and sequencing for the auto industry, supplier hubs for the high tech industry, spare parts management, and E-fulfillment for retailers. These solution providers provide value through economies of scale/scope achieved by providing similar solutions to multiple clients against customization of solutions to individual clients, and through relationship management. On the information technology implementation side, the shippers are demanding greater visibility of the shipments through improved tracking and tracing capabilities and also higher logistics performance in terms of lead time reliability and on-time delivery. Further, since 3PLs work simultaneously with multiple supply chain partners, they can standardize data and processes across firms and provide supply chain visibility beyond the individual firm. In addition to providing standardization and visibility, they can be neutral arbitrators between entities because they are typically unbiased third-parties. 3PLs can serve as change agents, especially in the case of full outsourcing. Finally, because 3PLs can see opportunities for improvement through standardization and visibility and pursue them without being perceived as driving their own agenda, they can often facilitate collaboration much more effectively than a customer, supplier, or competitor within the supply chain. Therefore, what makes a 3PL an orchestrator is the degree to which it can assist a company with standardization, visibility, neutral arbitration, and collaboration.

4PLs can emerge as intermediaries at various stages of the supply chain. On the supply side the IKL can manage inbound shipments, as exemplified by Vector SCM for General Motors and Exel for Ford (in Europe) amongst others. Similarly, there are consumer-centric IKLs such as Amazon.com, UPS and others. At a slightly higher plane, there are IKLs, also known as channel masters, such as Dell and Cisco who manage the entire supply chain network inclusive of the demand, supply and service chains.

IKLs are, typically, dominant players within their supply chain networks, who possess deep domain knowledge and strong influence over other parties in the network. They exploit this clout to coordinate the activities across players within the sub-network and across the entire network. Due to the fact that IKLs leverage upon the complementary capabilities of other parties in the chain as and when needed, their offerings are characterized by a broad scope of multi-modal services, global reach, complex management capabilities, and superior technological systems. Based on customer requirements, an IKL is able to select effective supply chain partners to team the best competencies available that optimally fulfill the requirements. Their ability to coordinate activities is to a large extent determined by their ability to transform their superior information, on the state of the network, into real-time decisions that enhance the performance of the entire network. When these dominant players achieve a high level of proficiency in coordinating the network, they no longer have to hold assets and instead rely on the physical assets of their partners in the network to fulfill market demand, thereby substituting physical assets with dependable relationships. In this manner, new value players such as IKLs dominate the supply chain, outsource non-core capabilities to contract manufacturers and 3PLs, and take control of the supply chain decision process.

6.6 Olam International: Orchestrator of Global Agri-food Networks

Another successful example in the Agri-food area is the Olam International Limited which supplies raw and processed agricultural commodities, grown mainly by small and medium-size producers in developing and emerging countries, to well-established regional and international customers. Olam directly engages in the sourcing, primary processing, transport, warehousing and distribution of a broad range of commodities, including cocoa, rice, timber, cashew nuts, cotton, coffee, sugar, sesame, sheanuts, and spices. From a small Nigerian export company, Olam International has evolved as a global leader in agricultural commodities with its base in Singapore. Olam does not own farms, but instead concentrates on orchestrating a network of many small producers. This global network is geographically dispersed in both sourcing and sales.

Olam is a supplier to many of the world's most prominent brands offering them reliability, consistency, trust, traceability, and other value-added services. Olam manages each activity in the supply chain from origination to processing, logistics, marketing and distribution. The active presence in every link of the supply chain allows Olam to orchestrate the whole supply chain, achieve operational efficiencies, and manage the various risks along the entire supply chain.

6.7 Orchestration of SMEs

Small and Medium Enterprises (SMEs) significantly contribute to economy, poverty alleviation, employment, and availability of products and services at affordable costs. In India, the sector accounts for 45 percent of the manufacturing output and 40 percent of the total export (in terms of value). Further, the sector employs

59.7 million personnel across 26.1 million enterprises. Globally, SMEs account for 99 percent of business numbers and 40 percent to 50 percent of GDP. With low capital investment, SMEs are known for fast decision making, adaptability to change, driving innovation and competition. One of the main issues of concern is integrating the SMEs into the global supply chain. Limited capital, IT resources and technical manpower; Lack of R&D; No visibility into the supply chain activities; Limited exposure to regulations, import-export policies and government incentives and several other factors contribute to their limited growth. Added to all this, SMEs are in low-barrier-for-entry businesses such as toys, leather, apparel, etc. We have seen the example of small logistics companies in India in Chap. 5.

Certainly a lead firm with connections to get orders from reputed retail and manufacturing customers worldwide and with knowledge about the taxes and tariffs and with government connections, can use the services and products of SMEs for mutually beneficial business. There are several very active orchestrators in the world today. Orchestrators such as Olam International and Li & Fung can overcome many of the challenges faced by SMEs in emerging markets in terms of marketing, finance, collaborative networking, government connections, and supply-demand matching, and enable inclusive growth of these small industries in the global markets.

We outline the strategic and operational roles of the orchestrator below. Executing these roles requires continuous and resilient connectivity of the service providers with the orchestrator.

The strategic roles include:

- Develop, maintain, and continuously upgrade the SME network in response to the market requirements;
- Recruit and develop service providers into the SME network;
- Identify the various players in the ecosystem (customers, government, third party providers) and develop strategic relationships;
- Structure appropriate tangible and intangible incentives for SME participants and other players;
- Cultivate a deep understanding of underlying business processes and practices in the vertical;
- Define standards with SMEs for communication, coordination, and execution of constituent services;
- Develop and manage performance feedback loops to facilitate learning about individual SME performance and risk profile.

The operational roles are managing customer orders. Two primary operational roles are planning and execution:

- For a customer demand, unbundle the service and dynamically compose a service chain, involving multiple service providers.

- Identify check points, targets, deadlines, and interfaces for each of the activities in the service chain and monitor at the higher level, whether these are met.
- If there are exceptions, orchestrator should in real time handle the exception, so that the final service delivery is not affected.

We now present the Li & Fung case to illustrate how the above requirements are met and executed in practice.

6.8 Li & Fung

The Li & Fung Group was founded in Guangzhou, China, in 1906 by Victor and William's grandfather, Fung Pak-liu, and his partner, Li To-ming [Fung *et al.* (2007)]. Li & Fung was one of the first exports companies from China. It initially traded largely porcelain and silk before diversifying into bamboo and rattan ware, jade, ivory, handicrafts, and fireworks. Victor and William, the current CEOs, returned to run the family business after finishing their studies in the United States and together with their father worked to modernize and rebuild Li & Fung into a structured business run by professional management at all levels.

In parallel, Li & Fung expanded on the sourcing side by growing a greater presence in the Indian subcontinent as well as the Caribbean and Mediterranean basins which were important given their geographic closeness to the key North American and European markets, respectively. In 1999, Li & Fung also diversified into the distribution business through the formation of a privately held business, Li & Fung (Distribution) Limited (Li & Fung Distribution). Li & Fung Distribution then acquired the marketing services businesses of Inchcape in the Asia-Pacific region and continued to provide services in three core businesses across Asia: manufacturing, logistics, and marketing. Subsequently, Li & Fung Distribution was reorganized to form the Integrated Distribution Services (IDS) Group and listed on the Hong Kong Stock Exchange in December 2004. In its first 100 years, Li & Fung made great strides in export trading.

In 2006, Li & Fung supplied over 1,000 customers in both hard and soft goods from a coordinated network of 8,000–10,000 suppliers through a sourcing network of over 70 offices in over 40 countries and territories. The trading business was divided into soft goods and hard goods. Soft goods were defined as garments and apparel, while the hard-goods category included fashion accessories, toys, travel goods, gift items, fireworks, stationery, furniture, shoes, and so on. The soft-goods business accounted for two-thirds of the total trading business, and the U.S. was responsible for over 69% of customer orders in 2005.

In 2006, Li & Fung was divided into over 170 entrepreneurial profit centers that maintained a customer-centric focus. To further reinforce this customer culture, Li & Fung offered its staff competitive compensation, incentive bonus plans, and stock-option grants based on individual and group performance.

6.8.1   *Li & Fung business model*

Li & Fung makes no products of its own. Rather, it *orchestrates* the production of goods by others, drawing on a vast global network of highly focused providers to arrange for private-label manufacturing, primarily on behalf of US and European clothiers. For a specific product or client, Li & Fung assembles a customized set of specialized providers to handle everything from product development to the sourcing of raw materials, production planning and management, and, eventually, shipping. If glitches pop up at any stage of the intricate process along the network, the company can quickly shift an activity from one provider to another.

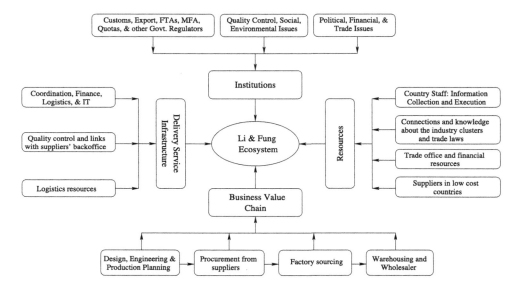

Fig. 6.3   Li & Fung ecosystem

A typical order flow at Li & Fung

When a customer placed an order with Li & Fung, a dedicated team would take the order and work with the customer to clarify all needs and specifications. The Li & Fung manager would next take the order instructions and feed them into its intranet to find the right supplier of raw materials and the right factory to assemble the clothes. The goal was to get top-notch quality at the best price in the timeliest manner. What this meant was that orders could be woven in China, sent to Korea for fastenings, and then sent to Guatemala for sewing. Before each production step, the customer was able to change its orders, for example, before the fabric was dyed the customer could change the color, or before the garment was cut the client could change its design. Li & Fung virtually offered *just-in-time* coordination that allowed the customer more lead time to garner more accurate information on trends. The outcome of this level of efficiency was fewer product markdowns and increased sales. This process reinforced a core Li & Fung philosophy that the company was organized around the customer in a *flat world* [Fung *et al.* (2007)]. The transfer of information in a timely manner was fundamental to the success. Thus:

- Upon receipt of the order within a division, Li & Fung dissects the manufacturing process for the order and attempts to optimally allocate the work at each step to its global supply partners.
- The manufacturing process is divided into two sub-processes: the front-end (sales and design) coupled with the back-end (logistics and banking), and the labor-intensive middle portion.
- The front-end and back-end are typically performed in Hong Kong.
- The middle portion is further decomposed into various segments, and Li & Fung finds the best factory to serve each segment.
- The entire process is tied together in the end with IT and logistics.

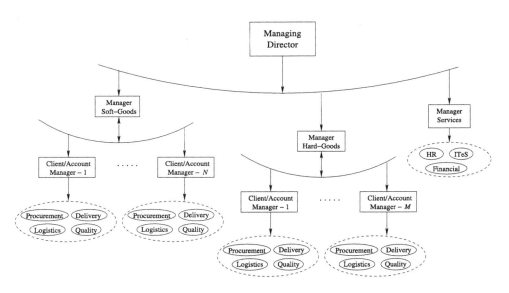

Fig. 6.4   Li & Fung governance structure

The customers of Li & Fung's are U.S. and European retailers and manufacturers seeking low-cost production sites in East Asia and trying to balance precisely their price, quality, and delivery needs. These customers face a bewildering array of supply markets (countries) and suppliers within those markets, all of which offer different combinations of particular manufacturing capabilities, quality, delivery time, reliability, and price. Finding the best suppliers is made even more difficult by the fact that the scene shifts constantly as countries develop and individual suppliers improve their operations. The products Li & Fung offers to the clients are Network, Relationships and Knowledge. The company's sources of competitive advantage lie in the scope and timeliness of its knowledge and in the number and depth of its relationships.

The *network* is not a formally constituted entity. It consists of two important, but intangible assets:

- Relationships with factory owners and managers: Suppliers often gave priority to orders from Li & Fung customers, because they knew they would pay on-time and not reject finished goods for spurious reasons.
- Connections (*government contacts in Hong Kong and Beijing, ability to reduce impact of quota restrictions*).

The extensive manufacturing network and ties with more than 3,000 factories of Li & Fung enables low cost, larger-scale manufacturing (if more than one factory is used for an order), with the added benefit of flexibility (relying on only a few manufacturers risks losing projects because of a drop in quality, insufficient manufacturing capabilities, financial or management problems, etc). To get the same advantage, Li & Fung would need to manage 3,000 factories, each with around 500 workers, which would make them responsible for managing over one million workers! Through its network, Li & Fung gets the benefit without having to manage 1 million workers.

Li & Fung has in-depth knowledge of the manufacturing capabilities, special skills, and business practices of each country and each supplier and can help customers choose among the manufacturing options its network provides. Li & Fung managers keep themselves informed of the changing labor costs in different countries and allocate production to least expensive countries. They also have knowledge regarding the different trade restrictions each country imposes, such as tariffs or quotas, or imports from each of its trading partners and free trade agreements. For example, Li & Fung managers knew which countries made leather jackets most skillfully and which at lowest cost, how easily each factory could obtain raw materials, and what official signatures in each country were required to import raw materials. Both customers and suppliers benefit from the credibility they have with each other as a result of working through Li & Fung. Further, the supply chain communications connecting and sharing information across its headquarters, customers, sourcing offices and factories, warehouses etc., Control of quality (attention to detail) through well-trained inspectors who make frequent trips for ensuring product quality, and managing the consolidation of shipments (logistics) through its own logistics services ensure on-time delivery of quality products as each product travels across supplier countries moving in the most optimized value chain for it to assume the finished form. Five weeks after the order, 10,000 garments arrive on the shelves in Europe or USA, all looking like they came from one factory, with colors and sizes perfectly matched. The label may say *Made in Thailand,* but it is not a Thai product. The logistics and coordination is a new type of value-add, producing a truly global product that has never been seen before. It is about pulling apart the value chain and optimizing each step, and doing it globally.

How does Li & Fung's product differ from products manufactured through traditional traders? By speeding up time-to-market and leveraging supply contracts across factories and product lines, Li & Fung helps customers keep inventory low. It does this by reserving capacity with standard apparel items that it can easily switch to expand capacity for fashion-sensitive orders. One of Li & Fung's major strengths is managing the supply chain and ensuring quality — a particularly difficult task when manufacturing orders are spread among several factories. Li & Fung's different product divisions have quality control managers responsible for different types of products within defined regions. By managing the supply chain and ensuring quality before shipping an order, Li & Fung reduces returns from unsatisfied customers.

6.9 Conclusions

Governance of global supply chain networks is an important subject. Disintegration of supply chains as a follow-up of modularization of products and outsourcing to low cost countries has happened in several verticals. Governance of these fragmented supply chain networks by reintegrating them through collaboration and coordination is happening today. We have studied in this chapter the vertical as well as distributed supply chain from their organization structure viewpoint. Through several examples we have discussed the integrator and orchestrator organization models. Implementation of these models using software-oriented architectures (SOA) is a very active subject in the software industry.

Chapter 7

Global Supply Chain Redesign

7.1 Introduction

As we have discussed in Chap. 1, integrated supply chain networks operating in domestic environments were the order of the day during the 1990s. Estimating or monitoring the demands at the retail shelves, planning the production schedules for the flow of goods through the entire network from suppliers to distribution and retail, and visibility of the goods flow through wireless and Internet were in primary focus. Companies plan the entire goods flow using sophisticated algorithms, manufacturing and assembly using SAP or Oracle package solutions and assume things will work as per plan. But in practice, they don't work for several reasons:

(a) The current supply chain networks are globally dispersed with suppliers, OEMs and service providers spread all over the globe including emerging markets, catering to the rapidly changing global demands.

(b) Several disruptions and delays can originate from the institutions financing the supply chain, governments of countries where suppliers are located, bankruptcy of the suppliers, disruptions due to natural disasters in locations where partners are based resulting in shutdown of factories, piracy, cyber-attacks, port strikes and a number of other unknown and unforeseen factors. One cannot anticipate all the disturbances or risks that affect the supply chain and plan for their mitigation. On the other hand, you cannot ignore their occurrences since they affect both the bottom line and top line.

(c) Innovations of various kinds in new products, new manufacturing and delivery processes, new business models such as outsourcing to low cost countries, home delivery, free trade agreements, special economic zones, government regulations and deregulations and many more affect the supply chain.

(d) Fluctuations in resources' costs such as wages, oil prices, foreign exchange fluctuations, war, terrorist strikes all have an effect on the supply chain performance as well as on cost savings.

The current-day companies have to tread carefully with right products, services, planning strategies such as location and partnership decisions and business models to succeed and grow in the face of the uncertainties in government regulations, the investment climate, and resource availability of the vertical space.

In emerging market supply chains, which are currently under liberalization, globalization, industrialization and infrastructure-building pressures, the supply chain formation becomes a very important step for companies. For example, several infrastructure projects in India had time and cost overruns and some projects are forever under development. In the recent past, there have been many issues over land acquisition for major projects of social importance: SEZs, dams, infrastructure projects, greenfield projects, and steel industries in India. The Tata Nano car project had to relocate the manufacturing plant out of Singur, West Bengal because of land acquisition issues.

In this chapter, we develop a supply chain design which takes into account all the above factors such as role of the government policies and regulations and the pressures from the social groups, the delivery infrastructure for product and service delivery, the human, natural and financial resources in the design of the supply chain. Further, this framework is very suited for modelling, analysis and design of supply chains or service chains in emerging markets which are in early stages of industrial development.

7.2   The Four Phases in Supply Chain Design

Generally the design and operation of supply chains involves four phases: supply chain formation, project planning and management, supply chain planning, and supply chain execution. In established supply chains operating in domestic markets, industries concentrate only on demand-supply matching or supply chain planning. Such supply chains are formed and maintained for long periods of time by means of extensive human interactions. But current supply chain networks are globally dispersed with suppliers, manufacturers and service providers spread all over the globe including emerging markets and catering to the rapidly changing demands for customized demands. They need to deal with all the four phases. In some cases such as apparel industry, each customer order defines a new and different supply chain partnership.

1. Supply chain formation   involves design of dynamic networks — choice of countries to operate in, partners in those countries and establishing a relationship. Formulation of the strategy involving innovations, business models and talent generation is also a part of this step. A comprehensive risk analysis about resources — land ownership in the case of greenfields; labor issues such as productivity, unions, training and industry clusters; available infrastructure and its effects on product or service delivery; effect of changes in Government regulations and pressures from social groups — is needed at the supply chain formation stage to avoid disasters later. A list of feasible alternatives along with their risk factors and mitigation strategies is the outcome of this step.

2. Project planning involves the project definition, construction, and management of the facilities, attracting partners or suppliers, coordinating service providers for goods and information delivery, etc.

3. Supply chain planning and operations involves collaboration between the suppliers, manufacturers, logistics providers, the dealers and retailers for supply-demand matching.

4. Supply chain execution is the stage where the service delivery is monitored in real time and any deviations, departures from promised quality and time deadlines are corrected through monitoring and control.

The two steps of supply chain formation and project planning are generally embedded in an institutional setting involving governments and social groups. In most cases, both project planning and supply chain planning are standard and technology intensive.

To keep connected with all these factors in the supply chain, one needs to look at this entire process in a holistic manner. To address this, we propose an ecosystem approach that comprehensively links all the above mentioned factors on a single platform — *the supply chain ecosystem.*

7.3   Global Supply Chain Formation

Global supply chain formation involves five steps:

(1) Map the Supply Chain Ecosystem.
(2) Formulate the Supply Chain Strategy.
(3) Select possible locations for the suppliers, factories, distribution centers, based on investment climate.
(4) Identify the Supply Chain Risks.
(5) List the feasible supply chain configurations.

We describe in detail each of the supply chain formation steps below. It may be noted that some of the issues that arise in supply chain formation are wicked problems. A wicked problem [Rittel and Webber (1984)] has innumerable causes, is tough to describe, and doesn't have a right answer. Environmental degradation, communalism, and poverty are classic examples of wicked problems. Problems that arise in social context in which every stakeholder seems correct from their viewpoint but collectively all of them fail to arrive at a consensus are wicked problems and they require special methodologies to deal with them. Some of the project planning problems like land acquisition, labour issues, environmental risks versus economic development, culture and social issues that surface during outsourcing and mergers and acquisitions etc are wicked problems. Moreover, because of complex interdependencies, the effort to solve one aspect of a wicked problem may reveal or create other problems.

7.3.1   *Map the supply chain ecosystem*

As we saw before, the supply chain ecosystem can be mapped for any specific company or its industry vertical under consideration. The Ecosystem approach is comprehensive and integrated and depicts all the stakeholders involved with the vertical on a single platform. Supply chain ecosystem has four distinct mechanisms:

- Supply/service chains producing products/services;
- Delivery service mechanisms such as Logistics and IT infrastructure;
- Institutions involving Governments and Social groups that determine the social, trade and economic policies of all countries touching the supply chain network;
- Natural, financial, human and industrial resources such as universities, clusters, banks, power, water, etc.

As we have presented in Chap. 2 (see Fig. 2.1), ecosystem approach calls for a comprehensive analysis that must look at the location, planning, performance, risk, governance and innovation from a systemic viewpoint. The resources arm includes clusters for collaboration and partnership, mines, land, water, universities for training workforce, R&D labs for innovation, FIIs for financing, letters of credit, labour unions and problems, land acquisition and the risks. The delivery service infrastructure is very important for on-time delivery. The logistics and IT infrastructure, the availability of logistics service providers and software developers, soft infrastructure at ports and airports, form the parts of delivery service infrastructure. Customs, trade, tax policies, industry and FDI incentives, labour unions, foreign exchange, legal enforcement form the government side of the institutions. Government policies that directly affect global economic competitiveness also need to be studied. The social groups, farmers and their welfare, NGOs, industry associations all form the societal side of the institutions.

7.3.2   *Formulate the supply chain strategy*

This is an important step. First, one needs to determine the innovations in product, process, business model and other ecosystem parameters needed to make the supply chain a huge success in the industry. Given the information on locations, one needs to determine the value chain architecture with outsourced and ownership details i.e. one needs to identify the strategic areas for partnering and identify the partners. More specifically, one needs to:

- Define the product that is being sold: The knowledge of the ecosystem (Trader) or just the product or solutions (after sales, aircraft engines, Xerox) or value chains (CEMEX: Deliver building materials to site).

- Identify innovations in product, process and other Ecosystem elements to build a blockbuster industry subject to the infrastructure constraints. Some examples include: Prepaid Sim-card, Deregulation of airlines and telecom, Fedex courier services, South West direct routes rather than hub and spoke, Tata Nano, developing industry clusters, digital delivery, home delivery and host of others.
- Identify the strategic areas for partnering or outsourcing in the value chain including the risks of partnering.

At the end of this step, we have the product that is being offered, the innovations in the ecosystem elements to make a big blockbuster industry, and finally we decide what should be done in-house and what should be outsourced and the suitable candidates for the tasks that are being outsourced.

7.3.3 *Select possible locations for facilities*

Investment climate studies from World Bank are available for many countries including India and also for some of the states in India. The three arms — Resources, Institutions and Delivery infrastructure — of the ecosystem map determine the investment climate in the specific location or for the specific vertical. For the industry vertical under consideration, determine the optimal locations for the suppliers, factories, warehouses, and distribution centres etc for the supply chain facilities. There are consultant reports available on location selection. There are several methods available for rank ordering the locations. We deal with this issue in detail in Chap. 8.

7.3.4 *Identify the supply chain risks*

In step 4, we identify all possible social, political and environmental risks that may affect the supply chain and the goods, information and financial flows.

(1) If outsourcing to low cost countries is an option, then outsourcing risks such as the loss of IP, quality issues, transport delays, foreign exchange fluctuations, extra costs due to energy, costs escalation or loss of goods due to theft or piracy, etc need to be identified. Too much dependence on outsourcing and orchestration may be very risky as we saw in cases of Schwinn and Lenovo.
(2) Acquiring global assets is risky for operational and cultural reasons. It also increases the organization's vulnerability to physical attacks as well. Alliances may be the safest form of international expansion. A network of alliances, appropriately managed, is potentially more resilient than a collection of global acquisitions. Alliance partners can retain local management, eliminating the costs and risks of deploying employees around the globe.
(3) In the case of mergers or acquisitions in progress, all the risks associated with the merging supply chain partners must be considered.

(4) One needs to identify the government risks such as change in the government, state-federal government relations, and corruption. Social risks need to be identified if the projects involve environmental degradation or land acquisition or people displacement as in infrastructure projects.

(5) The risk due to resource shortages such as oil, power, water, mining etc, and risks due to infrastructure breakdowns need to be quantified.

During this step, one has to identify the risks that the particular company may face and estimate the risk and determine what it takes for their mitigation.

7.3.5 *List the feasible supply chain configurations*

Here we identify the partners (companies and countries) for the goods, information and financial flows and also the risks of partnering by using the ecosystem information of partners. We map the supply chain for each customer order, identify the possible operational risks and design risk mitigation strategies. We note that the risks that we consider in step 4 are of a different nature than the current ones. Here we consider the operational failures or risks for every possible supply chain configuration. From a list of risk profiles for all possible supply chain configurations, we finally decide on one prospective supply chain. Then, based on the supply chain that is selected, the governance structure is formulated.

What do we have at the end of the Supply chain formation phase after the five steps? The ecosystem map, various network partners (including manufacturing, logistics and IT), their (country and regional) locations, the ecosystem parameters for choice locations, risks that the ecosystem faces, and finally the innovations (product, process, business model) needed to make it big in the industry as well as the value chain architecture with outsourced and ownership details. We also decide on the product that is being marketed: knowledge of the ecosystem, just the product, bundle of solutions or value chains.

7.4 Project Planning and Supply Chain Planning

Any greenfield project has two stages. The first stage consists of the project definition, construction and management of the facilities, attracting partners or suppliers, coordinating service providers, goods and information delivery, etc., which is generally referred to as *project management*. The second stage involves supply chain planning and operations which involves collaboration between the suppliers, manufacturers, logistics providers, the dealers and retailers for supply-demand planning. Both project management and supply chain management are very well-studied subjects and their execution is automated through software available through companies such as SAP, Oracle and many others. Two mathematical project-scheduling models, the Critical Path Method (CPM) and the Program Evaluation and Review

Technique (PERT), are frequently used. Similarly, several planning and execution techniques and software packages such as ERP, CRM are available for planning supply chain networks.

In emerging economies like India where most of the land belongs to small farmers, industrialization and land conversion create tensions between the government, industry and the farmers. Construction of facilities requires several approvals and may require dealing with several government departments. This may result in time and cost overruns. Also, the competencies needed for managing projects and supply chain planning are different. Lack of realization of this fact can impede the development of the project and in some cases it may also lead to abandoning the project itself. Further, the IT and logistics infrastructure could be weak, and service providers to manage the end-to-end delivery processes may not be available.

In the case of both the electronic and apparel manufacturing, which are forerunners in the globalization of supply chains, there are contract manufacturers who are globally distributed. The second step of project planning may be very simple and limited to partner selection depending on the destination of the order. In cases such as auto or contract manufacturing in electronics where there is a land acquisition requirement, then this step of project planning should be treaded carefully.

7.5 Supply Chain Execution

This is the stage where the service delivery is monitored in real time and any deviations, departures from promised quality or time deadlines are corrected through monitoring and control. This can be done through use of call centers or decision support system based cockpits. Use of discrete event system models, hybrid systems, or decision support systems with case-based reasoning are all possible solutions. The practices used in airlines, power systems and procurement could be adopted. In the apparel and electronic industry, the traders or big retailers act as orchestrators without ownership of any facilities including manufacturing. For them the execution step is very important. While the importance of the problem is well-articulated, there is very little analytical work on this topic.

The core competence of logistics companies is execution and 3PLs are specialists in execution. Genpact (India and Mexico) helps Penske in execution. Genpact manages the logistical services of Penske, such as just-in-time delivery of components to US factories and shipping finished goods to retailers and home consumers. BPO workers in India and Mexico:

(i) arrange for titles and registrations for the trucks leased by Genpact in the United States;
(ii) check the customers' credit status and arrange for all the necessary permits. If the truck gets stuck at a weigh station, failing to fulfill some permits, the truck driver would call an 800 number, and the BPO staff transmits the necessary

documentation to the weigh station and the truck would be on the road within a half-hour;

(iii) After the trip, the driver's log would be shipped to a Genpact facility in Juarez, Mexico, where mileage, tax, toll, and fuel data are punched into Penske computers and then processed in India. Genpact manages the logistical services of Penske, such as just-in-time delivery of components to US factories and shipping finished goods to retailers and home consumers.[1]

7.6   Talent

Another important element that contributes to supply chain excellence is the people and formation of high-impact teams. In this context, recognition among the stakeholders regarding the four steps involved in the supply chain or service chains is important. More importantly, it is necessary to organize suitable talent in each step. The talent needed for the group working on supply chain formation is more information- and data-intensive and requires use of analytical techniques for location selection and group formation. Project management requires skills to interact and manage with the Government and local communities. Local connections and knowledge will help to get approvals quickly and resolve any dispute that may arise with land owners, local communities and labour unions. The execution step could be routine during normal times and can be assisted with tools such as scheduling packages and geographical information systems.

In case of emergent situations such as natural disasters, terrorist attacks or long-drawn labour disputes, risk management teams assisted by decision support systems should come on board to resolve the crisis. The organization structure that best governs the supply chain is different for the four stages as we see above. One needs to identify the soft skills, R&D, execution abilities, connections, domain knowledge that are needed at each step and recruit the talent. To the extent possible, it is wise to make the product, process and the organization structures modular.

We illustrate the above procedure for real-world food security supply chain design in the following section.

7.7   Food Security in India: A Case for Supply Chain Coordination

Here, we present an innovative food security supply chain design for urban poor citizens in India to provide them with nutritious food at affordable rates at accessible locations. This design involves building a smart business social network consisting of Distribution centers, Kitchens, Hawkers, Primary Schools (with midday meal programs) and other outlets that serve food to the poor. Certified freshly cooked

---

[1]http://www.outsourcing-center.com/2007-03-when-outsourcing-back-office-its-all-in-the-family-for-penske-truck-leasing-article-37517.html

nutritious food is supplied through retailers such as Hawkers from Kitchens. Our aim is to include the existing food providers such as NGOs in midday meal programs and Hawkers selling food in urban areas as stakeholders in the smart food security network. Using cloud computing, a control room monitors the flow of materials and food through the supply chain and monitors the financial transactions as well.

7.7.1 *Introduction to food security*

Food security is important for every country and it has become a critical policy in largely populated countries such as India where two-thirds of its population live in underdeveloped areas and half of its population is below poverty line. One-third of India's population live in urban areas, of which one-fourth of them i.e. 100 million are below poverty line. Lack of food security has spiraling effect on malnutrition, infectious diseases, lack of education and development for generations. Recognizing this, the government of India has launched several schemes with large budgets and created huge organizations for managing the delivery of the rations (as they are called) to the populations. Unfortunately, none of the schemes were effective and were fraught with corruption, adulteration and diversion. Also, the distribution of rations is not designed and treated as a supply chain although it is a classic example of one such.

Here we create a smart business network with small stakeholders that solves the urban food security issue for approximately 100 million Indian citizens below poverty line. In our food security supply chain, the freshly cooked food in certified kitchens is supplied through the private retailers, hawkers, food outlets, etc to the urban poor. While all citizens can procure food from these sources, the eligible poor get a discount. Using a control room on a cloud computing base, all business and financial transactions can be monitored, and fraud (adulteration, diversion, substitution) can be detected and food quality can be assessed.

7.7.2 *Current efforts by the government*

The Government of India has launched several initiatives towards ensuring food security to its citizens. They include the public distribution scheme, the midday meal program for school children, the scheme for pregnant and lactating mothers, Integrated Child Development Services, and Health, Water and Sanitation programs, the National rural employment scheme (NREGAS), and several others to help people below the poverty line and also for improving the literacy rates. These programs have been in existence for decades now with huge budgets. Separate organizations such as the food corporation of India, warehousing corporation, wholesale shops, and ration shops were created. The performance of these schemes has been far below the mandates. One reason is the involvement of both central and state governments and lack of coordination between them. The cost of implementation of the PDS program is high. Further, the Food Safety Standards Authority of India (FSSAI) has found contamination to be quite common among food items.

7.7.3   The street food hawkers

The lower income groups in the country spend a higher proportion of their income in making purchases from hawkers mainly because their goods are accessible and affordable. There are millions of hawkers in all major cities, serving the food needs of the millions of urban poor and lower middle class. According to one study, Mumbai has the largest number of street vendors numbering around 250,000, while Delhi has around 200,000. Calcutta has more than 150,000 street vendors and Ahmadabad has around 100,000. They are self-employed, serving the needy cause.

The cuisine by the sidewalks is a successful story from Kolkata which can be copied to advantage. Kolkata's streets are a gastronome's delight and a heaven-send for the common man. The sheer variety of food on Kolkata's sidewalks and its affordability make this city's street food unique in the world. From delectable biryanis, chowmeins and pastas to mouth-watering Bengali sweets and pastries, it is all there for a pittance. What's more, it is hygienic and nutritious. Kolkata's 150,000 street food vendors cater to nearly 10 million people, many unable to afford restaurants.

7.7.4   Efforts by NGOs

The midday meal scheme was initiated with the objectives of addressing the classroom hunger, increasing school enrolment and addressing malnutrition among children. Voluntary organizations such as Akshaya Patra are therefore encouraged to set up operations wherever possible. They act as the implementing arm of the government. Akshaya Patra reaches out to 1.3 million children in more than 8000 schools in 18 locations across 8 states of India, providing them with freshly cooked meals packed in stainless steel containers on all school days. Similar efforts exist in other states of India.[2] Naandi Foundation is another social sector organization in India working to make poverty a history. In partnership with state governments and through corporate donations, Naandi runs several automated Midday Meal Kitchens across the country. These kitchens prepare and deliver high-nutrition noon meals to lakhs of underprivileged children every day. Naandi even delivers midday meals in many tribal areas in 4 states which include Andhra Pradesh, Rajasthan, Madhya Pradesh and Orissa. With a highly sophisticated centralized kitchen, Naandi delivers food to nearly 0.8 million children on every working day. The Midday Meal menu is decided in consultation with nutritionists from the National Institute of Nutrition. For locations such as Hyderabad, Naandi uses Global Positioning System (GPS) to determine the optimum way to transport food to the schools. Naandi in partnership with the Government of Rajasthan started the Hunger-Free program

---

[2]http://www.akshayapatra.org

on 1 May 2006 by providing cooked meals to the poorest of the poor at a very nominal price.[3]

If one puts all these desperate efforts together and organizes them as an effective food security supply chain, you have a high-impact food security solution that serves millions of below-poverty-line people and also in the process generates millions of jobs.

7.7.5 *Food security indices*

Despite all these decades of efforts described above, the indices released by the world organizations such as Global Hunger index, Human development index and Malnutrition index have become a matter of grave concern. The GHI is composed of three equally weighted indicators: the proportion of the population that is undernourished, the proportion of children who are underweight and under-five child mortality. India's food security situation continues to rank as *alarming* according to the International Food Policy Research Institute's 2011 Global Hunger Index (GHI).

One of the major interventions that the government made to address the high incidence of infant mortality, maternal mortality, child malnutrition, anaemia, etc was the Integrated Child Development Services (ICDS) program. The ICDS was started experimentally in 1975. Recent studies have found that in India, 47% of children below the age of three years are malnourished (underweight). Also, 47% of Indian children under five are categorized as moderately or severely malnourished. Currently, 50% of the population (24 million people) in Mumbai and New Delhi live in urban slums. The underlying causes are inadequate access to food in a household; insufficient health services and an unhealthy environment; and inadequate care for children and women. The essential amount of vitamins, minerals and the nutrients are extremely necessary for a balanced diet.

Given the above performance and the importance of the subject, it is necessary to think disruptively, to think of alternatives to the existing grain distribution and replace it with a well-designed and well-articulated smart food security supply chain business network which delivers quality nutritious food to the Citizens. We present our approach below.

7.7.6 *Literature survey*

Food supply chain networks and food security are both very well-studied subjects by economists and organizations such as World Bank. References [Rao (2000); Ruben *et al.* (2006); Kadiyala *et al.* (2011)] deal with food security with reference to India. Their presentations bring out the shortfalls of the current implementations in India. In [Umali-Deininger and Sur (2007)], the comparative advantages of India in agribusiness and current failures in supply chain and logistics management were

---

[3]http://www.naandi.org

discussed. In [Gandhi and Jain (2011)], the authors discuss the relationship between food availability, nutrition and health. Indeed, we concentrate on making nutritious food available at affordable prices.

7.7.7 *Our analysis and approach for food security*

From the above discussion, it is clear that the food security issue is not properly defined, the processes not well-designed and the traditional implementations are faulty and their executions are not monitored. The process is more complicated by the involvement of several state and central ministries. The problem is highly complex involving 600 million lives which is almost half the population of India. What has been done so far by all the schemes of the government is provide grains to people for them to cook. It is grain security rather than food security. Also, the PDS scheme has been operational since 1950 and family ownership makes any changes difficult. We would like to mention three main points in this context. First, the importance of cereals in overall food expenditures is declining, and the importance of high-value products such as fruits and vegetables, meat, dairy products, and fish is on the rise. The share of cereals in total food expenditures in urban areas declined from 36 percent in 1972/1973 to 24 percent in 2005/2006. The same trend is seen in rural areas, where the share of cereals declined from 56 percent to 32 percent. Second, there has been a rapid rise of modern private food wholesale and retail and logistics companies in India. The food processing industry is also supported well by the retailers. Third, the distribution of grains is not treated as a supply chain problem and the recent advances in technologies and the food vertical are not taken advantage of. Advances in food processing and packaging, supply chain visibility using the internet, sensor networks for traceability, data mining for fraud detection are all ignored.

Let us start with the well-accepted definition of food security.

Food Security The World Food Summit of 1996 defined food security as existing *when all people at all times have access to sufficient, safe, nutritious food to maintain a healthy and active life.* Thus, food security implies both physical and economic access to food that meets their dietary needs and food preferences. There are two complex issues involved in supply of food as per the World Food Summit definition above i.e. to provide access to sufficient, safe, nutritious food at affordable prices to maintain a healthy and active life:

(1) Creating awareness that food, health and hygiene are interrelated and all three are important;
(2) A well-designed food security supply chain network.

Here we concentrate only on step 2. Regarding step 1, we have the following comments:

(a) Design of nutritious food for children, pregnant women and working young population is a well-researched topic. Manufacturing processed food as per these norms can be easily done following the practices in other countries. The scale of 600 million people as customers provides enough incentive for food manufacturing companies and supply chain stakeholders to develop a highly agile adaptive nutritious food supply chain to provide the products at affordable prices and make them accessible in locations where people live.

(b) Creating awareness regarding health, food and hygiene should be given attention by media, religious organizations, schools, social organizations, etc. Adulteration has no technology solution except from customers and the Government.

Here, we concentrate on the design of the food supply chain for the urban poor that meets the food security specifications taking into account the factors such as accessibility, affordability, while monitoring and eliminating corruption and adulteration. The number of people living in cities is increasing; currently the urban poor in India are about 100 Million. For the rural poor, district-wide distribution centers and kitchens with MacDonald's type outlets or food courts may be a good solution. We will not dwell on the rural poor food security issue in this chapter.

Our approach in detail

Our primary goal is Orchestration of the food security supply chain in urban areas as a resilient network of alliances by streamlining and enhancing the food value chains to Hawkers, Schools, and other food outlets, while ensuring certification of the quality of the food at each stage in the chain and also providing opportunities for vocational training to all the stakeholders. This requires:

- Legalizing current stakeholders such as hawkers and other private food suppliers;
- Obtaining grains through open markets;
- Identification using biometric schemes;
- Crowd sourcing the menu from the customers;
- Certification of quality at each stage in the chain;
- Vocational training for all business participants;
- Micro-finance for small businesses such as hawkers.

Thus, our aim is to design the food security network as a cooperative or orchestrated smart business network of public-private partners in place of government-supported welfare scheme managed by bureaucrats. Monitoring and control by cloud-based control room that has data collection, mining and fraud detection capabilities is also required.

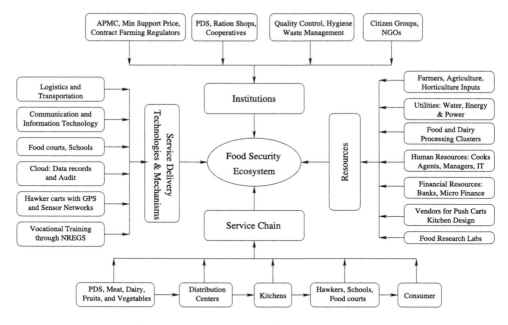

Fig. 7.1 Food security supply chain ecosystem

The food supply chain design

Our primary aim as mentioned before is to supply nutritious food at affordable prices in places accessible to the populations and also make them aware of the food and nutritional benefits by creating a smart business network of existing stakeholders such as Kirana shops, Hawkers, NGOs etc. This does not concern itself with PDS and other programs. It can be an alternate path and if successful can replace the PDS and other schemes for fighting malnutrition. To make this possible we need the intervention of the state government, municipalities, kirana shop unions, and hawkers' union. Also, help is needed from universities, horticultural institutes, micro-finance and other financial institutions, manufacturers of push carts for hawkers, solar heaters etc. The food supply chain ecosystem has four distinct mechanisms (see Fig. 7.1), as summarized below:

- The food service chain consisting of the Food manufacturers, Distribution systems, Kitchens, Hawkers, Restaurants, Kirana shops, Schools, etc.
- Delivery mechanisms include Logistics and IT infrastructure and value-added services for grains transport, Kitchens, Delivery vans, Hawkers, Cloud infrastructure, GPS, Sensor networks, Vocational training, certification of the quality of the food at each stage in the chain, etc.
- Institutions involving Governments and Social groups that determine the public distribution, malnutrition and economic policies of all states touching the supply chain network.

- The resources arm includes Land, Water, Power, Food manufacturers, Universities, R&D laboratories, Hawker manufacturers, Kitchen and solar heater manufacturers, etc.

The strategic partners include Warehouses and distribution centers, Kitchens, Hawkers, Vans to carry food packets to schools, Governments and School managements, Waste disposal, IT monitoring and call centers, Micro-finance companies, Vocational Training Institutes, Hawker vehicle manufacturers, Electrical equipment innovators such as solar or gas-enabled heaters/refrigerators, and Automated Kitchens. A network of alliances, appropriately managed, is potentially more resilient and can provide reliable food supply. Governance models such as orchestration need to be strategically implemented.

Innovations for operational success Several innovations are needed. They include Legalizing the Hawkers and large-scale food sales; Food Processing industry producing protein-rich, vitamin and mineral-enriched food; Product development and Testing laboratories; Independent food chains for various cultures (Halal, Vegetarian, Children, Pregnant Women); Small-size nutritious drinks from soft drink companies such as Coca-Cola, Pepsi and others; Packaging, Green plates for food services; Solar cookers, Gas-fired refrigerators; The delivery business model: Pickup by customers or home delivery; Creating a smart business and social network; Governance model of the entire network for safety and service levels.

Locations for the distribution centers, kitchens, and hawkers Depending on the location of business centers, schools, universities, offices and construction sites, the location of hawkers can be determined. They already exist in busy locations and these locations can be fine-tuned. The locations of distribution centers are up to the businesses and they can be located on paths of goods flow i.e. either on highways or nearer to the railway stations. The kitchens can be in strategic locations accessible to the food courts, food outlets and the hawkers. Based on the demand, center of gravity models can be used for their locations.

The three business processes Earlier we identified all the partners for the goods, information and financial flows and also the risks that the security supply chain needs to face. We have three business processes:

(1) Procure the food material from suppliers (Government or private parties), the processed food manufacturers and meat and milk product suppliers and store in the distribution center.
(2) Transfer the materials from the distribution center to the kitchens on a daily basis or as required or as ordered.
(3) The delivery of the packed food packets from the kitchens (as per the demand) to the hawkers, schools and other outlets is done using delivery vans.

All the above three processes can be standardized and the planning software should be in place. The delivery process for each customer order from hawkers or schools is mapped; the possible operational risks and risk mitigation strategies are documented. Figure 7.2 shows the supply chain architecture.

Our solution

We provide an integrative, co-evolutionary innovation strategy that would lead to high service quality food solutions to millions of people by combining innovations in several of the ecosystem elements and also their convergences. The business processes identified, streamlined, are standardized and automated or semi-automated using IT and sensor networks. Modernization and integration of PDS, midday meal program, and vocational training programs under NREGAS, hawkers, and small food outlets using communication technologies would lead to a blockbuster industry serving the poor and creating millions of jobs for the not-so-well educated. NREGAS can be used for training chefs, cooks, hawker owners, PDS employees, school employees etc. Standardized and automated kitchens and IT-enabled and GPS-equipped push carts can be developed. The push carts can be built following standardized design and equipped with solar or gas-run refrigerators and ovens. The entire process can be monitored, executed and controlled using a call center. The call center can track the Hawkers, the food packets, the consumption patterns, etc. and can act as an orchestrator of the entire activity.

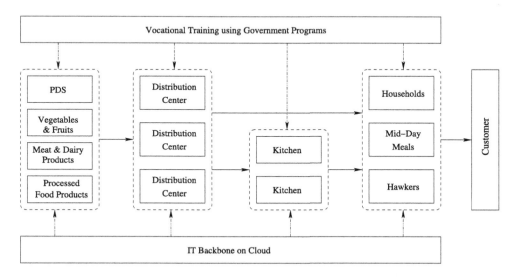

Fig. 7.2 Food security supply chain architecture

The distribution centers can be owned by the big brand retailers and the kitchens can be privately owned by the five-star hotel owners. The food packets can be bar-coded or tagged with RFID as appropriate and can be tracked by the cloud computer servers. Free food can be given instead of ration cards against the thumb print (UID) at the hawker vehicle. The hawkers and small hotel owners can be funded by microfinance organizations. The location and capacity of the Kitchens, the push carts and other retailing outlets can be determined using standard optimization techniques from the demand estimates. The server in the City cloud can keep track of the food packet issued for settlement later. Standardized food outlets with fixed menu can be opened at various places in the city and a take-home facility can be provided nearer to the kitchens.

Is there a need for Proof of concept or a Pilot Project? We do not think so. We put together the above scheme from the best practices of various earlier implementations. We organized them to create a high-impact food security solution that generates millions of jobs. Our concept is already implemented in parts very successfully by NGOs like Naandi, Akshaya Patra for the midday meal program and by more than one million hawkers catering food to millions of people in various cities.

7.7.8 *Supply chain planning*

The project planning is a very important stage in this supply chain. It involves the project definition, construction and management of the facilities, attracting partners or suppliers, coordinating service providers, goods and information delivery, etc. Planning everyday needs depending on the demand and managing the supplies is important. It is important to maintain delivery schedules, conformance of menu items and also quality and hygiene. Perishability of food resulting in quality losses places pressure on time and temperature control for each food actor at each node. Specific food characteristics and large number of product varieties place specific demands on inventory planning and capacity utilization.

The supply chain plans and operations involve collaboration between the suppliers, distributors, Kitchens, logistics providers, the hawkers, schools and others for supply-demand planning. Since one is dealing with highly perishable cooked food items where storage is highly discouraged and its usage is harmful, supply-demand matching is crucial.

7.7.9 *The possible supply chain risks*

Here we need to identify all possible social, political and environmental risks that may affect the food security ecosystem and the goods, information and financial flows. The common risks are: Denial of permission by the Governments, Food/ resources pilferage, Food Adulteration, Compromise on the quality and hygiene, Political/social pressures, Formation of unions among the hawkers, Resistance by other organized restaurant and Kirana shop owners, IT/technology adoption barriers, Waste disposal and Recycling. The risk mitigation is mainly through educating the consumers and businesses regarding the consequences of misuse.

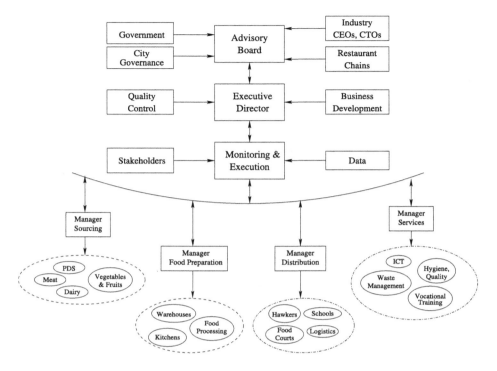

Fig. 7.3   Food security supply chain governance

7.7.10   *Governance and execution*

The management challenge in a FSSCN is the coordination of its activities in sourcing, food production, distribution and variety of services such as vocational training, transport, ICT. The following are the daily activities:

- Selection of Menu for the kitchens and suppliers; what will they supply; how it is used in cooking (e.g., product tastes and quality); the production and delivery schedules (how much to produce and when) of the kitchens; capacity and upgrading of kitchen equipment; new recipes.
- Special foods for children, mothers and pregnant women and delivery in their location.
- Quality assurance across the chain and its maintenance.
- Mitigation of adulteration, pilfering etc.
- Supply of food to the schools and hawkers, etc as per the schedule.

The network consists of half a million stakeholders in big cities. The majority of them are hawkers who are small entrepreneurs. The asset-intensive part of the FSSCN is the Kitchens and the Distribution Centers. The Distribution centers can be a shared service with the big retailers but the Kitchens have asset specificity. The Governance model can be an orchestrator type i.e. the governance is managed by a third party such as an NGO. One of the lead players such as the Kitchen owners can manage the supply chain. It is found that more and more food supply chains are vertically integrated to maintain the quality at every stage in the SCN.

Coordinated food security supply chains are durable arrangements between government, distributors, hawkers, and consumers about what and how much to produce, time of delivery, quality and safety conditions, and price. They often involve exchange of information, and sometimes also help with technology and finance. They are usually initiated by investment of private traders and food companies, who act as chain leaders. Quality management systems (QMSs) provide the standards and monitoring mechanisms for achieving, maintaining, or improving the desired quality level across the supply chain and to end-consumers.

7.7.11 *Talent*

The supply chain consisting of the PDS, Kitchens and the Hawkers and the schools participating in the midday meal program needs trained manpower. The vocational training centers can be funded through the NREGAS to train cooks, chefs, sales people, servers and millions of other jobs required for the supply chain to operate well, given the value and perishable nature of the supply chain. It is necessary to organize suitable talent in each step. People with soft skills to manage and convince local Kirana shops, Hawkers, Farmers, Municipal and local Governments are needed. Local connections and knowledge will help to get approvals quickly and resolve any dispute that may arise with land owners, local communities and labour unions. One needs to identify the soft skills, R&D, execution abilities, connections, domain knowledge that are needed at each step and recruit the talent.

7.7.12 *Institutional interventions*

The implementation and success of schemes require intervention and support of the Governments at various levels: The ministry of agriculture, the food security departments, Commerce ministries, municipalities at the City level, the Unions of various agencies such as Kirana shops, Hawkers, NGOs, health departments, Social activists, Industry associations, small restaurants, etc. There are several small businesses who may misunderstand or feel threatened although the whole process helps them in a variety of ways: in marketing and sales, in financing their business ventures for possible avenues of improvement, and also in food preparation distribution. Convincing the political partners is a heavy agenda item.

7.7.13 *Discussion on the example*

Food security is an important issue for India and cannot be ignored for long. The current systems such as PDS are highly inefficient and corrupt. They deal with grain distribution and do not serve the intended purpose. Our approach presented in this paper links Agriculture, Nutrition, and Health. We provide a real-time supply chain network solution monitored by cloud platform and involving private business networks. The result of our scheme is availability of nutritional high-quality food at affordable prices to the urban poor. We also point out the need to create awareness of the nutritional quality and health through media and other sources. Also there is a need to start giving attention to nutrition at the agriculture level as mentioned in the World Bank 2007 report.

Our solution is implementable and also scalable. Several implementations already exist by NGOs such as Naandi and Akshaya Patra and also through Government midday meal programs. Given the perishable and hygienic nature of the supply chain, the food products made in the day need to be consumed by the night. This requires careful demand forecasting, routing and rerouting of the supplies and monitoring the anti-social activities. The program needs trained logistics and IT manpower. Several product and process innovations are needed and there are opportunities for several small and big private entrepreneurs. This is a unique opportunity for people from all walks of life — Governments, NGOs, Big business houses and small entrepreneurs and micro finance and other FIIs — to come together to make this program successful.

The food security network for any city is a complex system with a large number of independent food suppliers and other stakeholders. Generally such network members are to be given guidelines or rules to follow and in addition their actions need to be coordinated. Here we provide an integrated network design for monitoring and governance based on ICT. Our methodology can be extended to small farmer networks, Milk dairy networks, Kirana shop networks and others.

Coordinated supply chains like the ones described above are rapidly increasing in importance in global service markets. They assure competitive strategies for high quality, safe and better service. However, the share of services in India marketed through coordinated supply chains is very small. The approach presented here can be beneficially used for coordinating small farms, hospitals for public health, vocational training, etc.

7.8 Conclusion

We have emphasized the importance of global supply chain formation strategies and the need for a holistic ecosystem approach. Through this chapter we would also like to bring to the attention of the planners and corporates that they should recognize the wickedness of the Industrialization and Public-Private Partnership initiatives and resolve them amicably in the initial stages of the project using suitable Soft OR/negotiation skills. Moreover, the State or Central Government can appoint a special unbiased committee while sanctioning the projects, to recommend the risks involved in such supply chains, based on the location and environment, during the inception stage of the project. Risks posing from all the components of the ecosystem must be predicted well in advance and corresponding mitigation strategies must be formulated. Otherwise there will be project delays which would eventually affect the economy to a large extent.

PART 2

Applications

Chapter 8

Location Analysis

8.1 Introduction

A global supply chain spans several countries and regions of the globe. Trade liberalization (European Union, NAFTA) and information technology have accelerated the growth of global supply chains, whereby a firm can invest and trade across national borders. It is now a competitive requirement that firms invest all over the globe to access markets, technology, and talent. Firms could trade across national borders either by intra-firm trade (FDI) or arms-length trade (foreign outsourcing). International trade and foreign direct investment (FDI) have been among the fastest growing economic activities around the world. FDI is the movement of capital across national frontiers in a manner that grants the investor control over the acquired asset. FDI includes corporate activities such as building plants or subsidiaries in foreign countries, and buying controlling stakes or shares in foreign companies.

FDI stocks now constitute over 20% of global GDP, which in effect has contributed to the economic growth of developing countries. Firms located in industrialized countries pursue vertical disintegration of their production processes by outsourcing some stages in foreign countries where economic conditions are more advantageous. For example, Intel Corporation assembles most of its microchips in wholly-owned subsidiaries in China, Costa Rica, Malaysia, and the Philippines. With proven results that FDI by multinational corporations (MNCs) increase employment, exports, revenue, and knowledge spillover to host country's private/public sectors, many governments have introduced various forms of investment incentives, to encourage foreign-owned companies to invest in their jurisdiction.

8.2 Location Choice in Emerging Markets: Example — India

Pre-1990, India allowed only up to 40% FDI, selectively in few sectors. The FDI policy reforms that started in 1991 have resulted in tremendous increase of FDI flows into the country. Currently FDI up to 100% is permitted in all sectors except a few. The total inflow of FDI has increased almost 1321% from USD264.1

million in 1991 to USD3.8 billion in 2004 [FICCI (2005)]. The sectors attracting investments are diverse including software, transportation, food processing, chemicals, and metallurgical industries. The top ten countries investing in India include Mauritius, Japan, and South Korea in addition to USA, Germany, France, and Switzerland. One of the strategic decisions faced by an MNC is the location decision of the subsidiary within India. Usually the location choice problem of MNC is only considered at a national level in the literature. This national-level choice is made in tandem with other organizational decisions like mode of FDI (joint venture, acquisition, greenfield), investment budget, level of activities at the new subsidiary, etc. Choosing a nation for FDI is hence related directly with many other firm-level decisions. India is administratively divided into 28 states and 7 union territories. Due to the diversities in geography, climate, culture, language, tradition, resources, and political governance, economic performance of Indian states vary drastically. For example, the gap in per capita income is a lot wider between the states Maharashtra and Uttar Pradesh, or Punjab and Madhya Pradesh, than it is between India and China [World Bank (2005b)]. The investment climate variations within India are very significant. Almost all the FDI were attracted by the following high-performing states: Maharashtra, Delhi, Gujarat, Andhra Pradesh, Karnataka, Punjab, Tamil Nadu, and Haryana. With such diversities in India with respect to economics, politics, resources, and technological advancements, it is mandatory for both business and public policy decision-makers to consider the location choice problem at a more explicitly local level. The development of areas of free trade and free factor mobility, such as EU and NAFTA, have led to researchers taking into account factors pertaining to the level of the region or city rather than at the level of the nation. A decision-making process for plant location in EU [Yurimoto and Masui (1995)] consisted of selection of country, followed by the selection of the sites within the country. Different factors were considered for the above two decisions. Hence, it is important to identify the differences in the location choice problem at the national and the sub-national level.

8.2.1 *Location choice: National versus sub-national*

An MNC faces two kinds of location decisions in FDI. The first location decision of an MNC is to select a nation for FDI from a set of predetermined nations. This decision is a complex one as it subsumes within it the following decisions [Mudambi (2002)]:

- **Mode of entry**: Whether the FDI is implemented through a greenfield investment or an acquisition or joint venture;
- **Industry of entry**: Whether the FDI occurs in the main line of business of the parent MNE or represents a diversification away from this business.

Once the country for FDI is determined, the firm has to choose the location within the country for its intended subsidiary. If the mode of entry is through acquisition, one of the deciding factors is the location of the firm being acquired. However, for greenfield investments and joint ventures (in some cases), the MNC faces the sub-national location choice problem. This problem inherits many of its characteristics from the national-level problem. Based on the nature of the firm, the location choice problem is defined differently. With relevance to current discussion, we identify three different types of firms:

(1) **Single-plant firm**: A MNC which wishes to locate a single plant or business activity. The location choice problem is to find a single location from a given set of potential locations.

(2) **Vertical multi-plant firm**: A firm with a multi-plant production process and plans to locate each plant in a different location. Here the location choice problem is to choose the location for each plant simultaneously, taking into account their interactions.

(3) **Horizontal multi-plant firm**: A firm with decentralized plant locations across the country, catering to the demands locally from the nearby plant. The location choice problem in this case is similar to the classical facility location problem [Drezner and Hamacher (2002)]. Given the demand patterns and a set of production facilities with production costs and transportation costs, the problem is to choose a set of production facilities to open and determine the amount of flow between the opened facilities and the demand points, such that overall cost is minimized.

In this chapter, we focus on the location choice of a single-plant firm. Henceforth, unless specified, the words "firm" and "MNC" refer to a single-plant firm and the location choice refers to the sub-national location choice of the single-plant firm.

8.2.2 *Dynamics of the sub-national location decision*

Consider the example of an MNC interested in setting up a drugs and pharmaceutical plant in India. The industry is clustered in the following four cities: Ahmedabad, Mumbai, Delhi, and Hyderabad. The MNC is interested in locating its subsidiary in one of the above four locations. Given such a scenario, the dynamics of the location decision process can be summarized in the following steps:

(1) Evaluate and rank the four locations with respect to various attributes and the MNC's firm-level characteristics and objectives.

(2) Choose, say for example, two of the top-ranked cities and negotiate with the respective state governments for possible incentives.

(3) Based on the outcome of negotiations, go to step 1 and evaluate the locations using the new information. If further negotiations are not possible, choose the top-ranked location as the location for the plant.

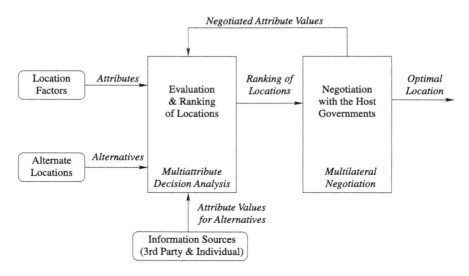

Fig. 8.1 Dynamics of the location decision process

The above dynamics is illustrated in Fig. 8.1. Thus, there are two decision problems: evaluation of locations and negotiation with state governments. The incentives and the hospitality of the host governments play a major role in location decision at the national level. This also holds true for sub-national location choice, as the Tamil Nadu government's hospitality was one of the influencing factors of Ford's choice of Chennai for its integrated manufacturing facility (in addition to other factors like skilled workforce, ports, electricity, water, etc).[1]

The location selection is recognized as a two-player game between the MNC and the host government. The host government attempts to elicit desired behavior from the MNC using direct (through legislative and executive controls) and indirect (through incentives) stimuli [Loree and Guisinger (1995)]. The literature on the interaction between the host government and the MNE is comparatively smaller, since in the international business intellectual tradition, the firm is always assumed to choose amongst several alternative locations, greatly reducing the bargaining power and role of the host government [Mudambi (2002)]. The multi-lateral interaction of the MNC with several host governments simultaneously can also be modeled as an auction game with competitive bidding [Dicken (1990)]. In the following, we focus on ecosystem-based location analysis that can be used for evaluating and ranking locations, which is integral to any location decision.

---

[1]http://www.chennaibest.com/cityresources/Automotive/fordinterview.asp

8.3 Related Literature

The industrial location choice and analysis is addressed by *location theory*. The location theory is concerned with the geographic location of an economic activity and is an integral part of *economic geography*, *regional science*, and *spatial economics*. The MNC location behavior, in particular, has been studied by international business and management science community. We briefly review the above related literature by broadly classifying them based on the conceptual frameworks.

8.3.1 *Location-production models*

Location-production models are the earliest and simplest analytical models, referred to commonly as Weber's and Moses's models. These classical and neoclassical microeconomic models analyze the production behavior of an individual stylized firm in relation to the spatial economic costs. The costs include local labor prices, land costs, transportation costs, and telecommunication costs. The objective is to locate a plant in the plane by minimizing the weighted sum of Euclidean distances from that plant to a finite number of sites corresponding to the markets where the plant purchases its inputs and sells its outputs. In the sum, the weights represent the quantities of inputs and outputs bought and sold by the plant, multiplied by the appropriate freight rates. Thus the models also consider the production as a decision variable, which often depends on the location. The optimum location and the optimum production are determined in tandem. Interested readers are referred to [McCann (2002a)] for an excellent review of the range of microeconomic location-production models. The classical facility location problem [Drezner and Hamacher (2002)], which determines the optimal set of facilities to open given the demand and transportation costs, is a location-production model for a horizontal multi-plant firm. Facility location problems are popular in supply chain management community. The common feature of the location-production models is the consideration of the firm or plant in isolation without the presence of competing and complementing firms.

8.3.2 *Agglomeration economies*

The inclusion of other firms from the same or related industry in the analysis brings out a new set of factors for location analysis. The regional science community uses the term *economies of agglomeration* to describe the benefits that firms obtain when locating near each other. It is related to the idea of economies of scale and network effects, in that the more related firms that are clustered together, the lower the production cost and the greater the market. The production costs are lower due to availability of specialized resources, such as competing suppliers, skilled labor, and infrastructure. On the demand side, the informational externalities from other firms and the reduction in consumer search costs are beneficial for total market demand.

Several studies show that the agglomeration economies are dominant factors in the location choice of MNCs for FDI [Head *et al.* (1995); Cantwell and Piscitello (2003); Boudier-Bensebaa (2005); Barrios *et al.* (2006); Griffith *et al.* (2006)]. The other related model is *core periphery* model that explains why certain regions or cities attract more industries than the others. Such clustering of industries is explained through cumulative causation or *multiplier effect*. *New economic geography* [Fujita *et al.* (1999)] uses general equilibrium models to explain the location of industrial and economic activities. All these models reinforce that the presence of other firms in the same or related industries is an important location decision factor.

8.3.3   *OLI framework*

Dunning's eclectic OLI (ownership, location, and internalization) [Dunning (1977, 1988)] framework is the widely accepted model for the study of MNCs. While the economic geography models study the location behavior from the host perspective, the OLI framework from international business literature studies the location decision from the MNC perspective. The OLI framework suggests that a firm will prefer FDI to trade and become a MNC if the following three conditions are satisfied. First, the firm must possess *ownership* advantages not available to other firms in terms of superior technology, firm size, brand name, etc. Second, the foreign market should offer *location*-specific advantages like market size, cheap resources, and infrastructure. Finally, there should be *internalization* advantages, which eliminate the transaction and coordination costs associated with market interaction and internalizes these activities by bringing them inside the hierarchy of the firm. The framework is also used in the analysis of location decision [Mudambi (1995)] and mode of entry decision [Brouthers *et al.* (1999)]. Accordingly, the location decision is contingent on ownership and internalization factors.

8.3.4   *Clusters*

Global sourcing is possible today with open global markets, less transportation costs, and reliable IT-enabled communications. Though this implies that the location decision is not important, related industries tend to co-locate. The agglomeration phenomenon, from management science literature, is explained using *clusters* [Porter (1998a)]. Clusters are geographic concentrations of interconnected companies and institutions in a particular field. The linked industries and institutions can consist of suppliers to universities to government agencies. Clusters promote both competition and cooperation. For a firm, location in clusters is a source of competitive advantage. For the region, promoting cluster formation is viewed as the basis for economic development and globalization.

8.3.5 *Investment climate and market attractiveness*

A closely related problem to the location choice is the evaluation of the *market attractiveness* or the *investment climate* of the locations. Any solution procedure to the location choice problem implicitly estimates the market attractiveness of the locations. The difference between the location choice and investment climate is that the former is *firm specific*, while the latter is usually *industry specific*. Investment climate studies are conducted at national levels, comparing different nations, and also at regional and city levels, usually for a specific industry [World Bank (2005b)]. The rankings and measures of investment climate are helpful for public policy [World Bank (2005a)]. The above studies basically combine different parameter values in measuring the attractiveness of a location. The problem with aggregate measures is the implicit assumption that location characteristics have same advantages or disadvantages for all firms in an industry. However, there are evidences that the factors affecting location choices are not identical and do not exist in isolation from the characteristics of the investing firms [Nachum and Wymbs (2002)]. For example, good port and customs infrastructure can be a major advantage to firms engaged in exporting and have only more limited and indirect effects on non-exporting firms.

8.3.6 *Prescriptive decision models*

Most of the above literature studies the decision behavior of the MNCs by using regression models on the data. The models vary in their approach in terms of location factors, data, and regression models. There are few works that take on a prescriptive approach in proposing decision models that can be used by a MNC in deciding its location. A decision support system for location choice is developed in [Yurimoto and Masui (1995)]. It considers the location problem of Japanese firms in the expanding European Union. The decision-making process is carried out in two stages: first is the selection of the countries, followed by the selection of the sites within the country. The location factors pertaining to both the stages were identified and sorted in hierarchical form. The selection process used AHP to select the final location. A similar approach was used in [Saaty and Vargas (2001)] to measure the market attractiveness of the developing countries, which can be used to determine the location for doing business. The factors that measure the market attractiveness were hierarchically grouped under *political* factors and *economic-financial* factors.

8.4 Industry Best Practices

Location consultants help with the location/relocation/delocation of sites. The site selection or location selection can be for corporate head office, distribution centers, R&D centers, call centers, data centers, etc.

8.4.1 *Buck Consultants International*

Buck Consultants International (BCI)[2] provides advice worldwide for selecting locations for call centers, R&D centers, distribution centers, production plants, etc. Starting with the definition of the project and the key location requirements, the search narrows down in careful steps from a wide search area to a limited number of regions and locations. BCI supports the whole process, including negotiations on investment subsidies and agreements on land and/or buildings.

In order to be able to compare different sites, BCI has developed the cost-quality matrix. The matrix has a vertical axis showing all costs for the next 5 years (labour costs, transport costs, occupancy costs, etc. minus investment subsidies/grants), and a horizontal axis showing the quality of the investment climate in a weighted form (labour quality and flexibility, labour regulations, technological expertise available, logistics qualities of the location, availability of suppliers, etc.). In this matrix, by way of example, the present site is compared to the various alternative sites. The top right corner is the theoretical optimum, i.e. a combination of low costs and high quality business environment. The cost and quality factors and the sites included differ from one investment project to another.

Furthermore, BCI has developed a model to calculate the pay-back period or break-even time for the investments required for the relocation to alternative locations or investments in new facilities. Additional labour costs (relocation packages, training costs, recruitment costs, etc.) and real estate as well as workforce-related exit costs are included as well in a detailed manner.

8.4.2 *IBM Plant Location International*

Plant Location International (PLI), a specialized service within IBM Global Business Services for Global Location Strategies, has established itself as a market leader in providing advice to companies on their location decisions, covering all sectors and types of business functions. PLI works with government agencies worldwide for economic development and investment promotion in their efforts to improve and market their locations to investors. The services related to location decision of companies include:

- Strategic location planning and selection;
- Definition of key location criteria for specific operations;
- Screening of multiple locations to quickly identify best options;
- Global resourcing and labor market evaluation;
- Site and facility search, once a preferred country or region is selected.

The IBM globally integrated consulting practice is supported by IBM-PLI's *location benchmarking tool* and *Global Investment Locations Database* (GILD). The location benchmarking tool identifies the best locations based on project-specific

---

[2]http://www.bciglobal.com

location requirements. The tool helps analyze the cost and quality trade-off and relative strengths and weaknesses of locations, as well as evaluating the impact of possible changes in business environments over time.

GILD is the leading corporate investment tracking database, registering *mobile* investment projects around the world and allowing representative and up-to-date location trend analysis on a global scale. GILD records announcements of new and expansion projects by companies. For each project announcement, details are registered on the investor, origin, location of investment, sector and cluster, activity and type of investment, as well as estimated jobs, capital invested and locations considered. Investments through business mergers and acquisitions are not included in GILD, since these investments are not driven by attractiveness of individual locations. Being the most comprehensive and accurate global investment database in the market, GILD provides unrivalled insight into global trends in corporate location decision making.

8.5 Multiple Criteria Evaluation of Locations

The industrial location decision making is a highly complex process with multi-faceted characteristics including tangible and intangible elements that are very difficult to measure and evaluate [Hayter (1997)]. The basic steps involved to arrive at the best possible location recommendation are [Meirler (2006)]:

(1) The basic requirements of the location project are first identified, usually by using an all-purpose location questionnaire. From this, critical and desirable factors for the locations are determined. Critical factors are mandatory factors that play a prohibitive role in identifying locations. For example, if seaport is a mandatory factor, then locations without seaports can be eliminated for consideration.

(2) A list of N alternate locations is short-listed that satisfy the mandatory critical factors. Matching algorithms are sometimes used to determine these locations by estimating matching scores between the locations and the desirable location factors.

(3) Based on the intended investment and the nature of the investing firm, M location attributes are identified. These are the location factors over which the N locations are to be evaluated.

(4) Information about the N locations for each of the M attributes are obtained using public databases, private investigations, and personal meetings with the local authorities. This includes quantitative information like economic cost analysis of non-recurring and recurring costs, prediction of future sales, return of investment, production efficiency, government incentives, etc. Qualitative information like living conditions and political climate are also determined.

Table 8.1   Factors influencing location decisions

Industry Inputs	Industrial electricity charge; industrial water charge; availability of land; land cost; labour wage; overstaffing rate; number of white-collar workers; number of blue-collar workers; educational & training institutes; collaboration with local universities
Agglomeration & Network Economies	Localization economies measure; economic diversity: Chinitz-Jacobs diversity measure and Herfindhal measure; location quotient
Communication Technologies	Number of days to get connections for various technologies: telephone, wireless, internet; bandwidth; network readiness index; mail & postal
Transport	Distance to nearby sea port, airport, railway station; transportation costs for various modes; domestic and international connectivity
Laws & Regulations	Difficulty of interface with various government departments: labour, customs and excise, income tax, pollution control, electricity board, water board; corruption level; amount of time spent with government officials; frequency of government official visits
Economic & Financial	Corporate income tax; imports tax; exports tax; financial incentives; availability of funds and loans; GDP; growth rate; buying power
Risks	Political stability; intellectual property protection; friendliness of the government; conflicts with the neighboring governments; communal disputes
Living Conditions	Consumer price index; crime rate; real estate prices; number of hospitals
Third Party Services	Legal; advertisement; logistics

(5) The N locations are ranked with respect to the M attributes. This is a multi-criteria decision analysis problem.

Our focus here is on Step 3, where M location attributes are identified. The first two steps are relatively easier. They are both dependent on the industry-level characteristics and firm-level characteristics. There are some mandatory requirements for any business investment. For example, it is mandatory that the new manufacturing plant have easy access to a port on the eastern coast. This may be because the new plant will have foreign trade with Singapore and Malaysia. With this constraint, one can list the possible locations.

The analysis of potential locations starts with identification of M location factors. Identifying the location factors depends on the industry- and firm-level characteristics. For locating a R&D unit, *number of research institutions* and *IT connectivity* are important location factors. On the other hand, for locating a manufacturing plant, *land cost, labour wage, electricity charge, water availability* are the factors.

Depending on the firm to locate, the number of factors can vary from 10 to 100. A list of location factors considered in several studies [Yurimoto and Masui (1995); FICCI (2005); World Bank (2005b)] is tabulated in Table 8.1 under different categories. The list is not exhaustive and some of the factors are interrelated. However, it provides a higher level view of the factors that can influence the location choice decision. In multi-attribute decision making domain, organizing the criteria into a hierarchy is called *analysis* and measuring how well the alternatives perform on each criterion is called *synthesis* [Olson (1996)].

The analysis starts with the identification of *criteria* and *attributes*. We use the word *criteria* to refer to objectives or directions along which one seeks better performance from the alternatives. The performance is measured in terms of *attributes*. For example, the criterion economic factors can be measured using attributes income tax, property tax, and sales tax. There is a considerable interplay in the identification of criteria and attributes. This complex creative process is achieved through hierarchically structuring homogeneous clusters of criteria and attributes [Keeney and Raiffa (1976); Keeney (1992); Saaty (1980)]. We provide in the following a generic framework for hierarchical structuring of location factors using the ecosystem-based location analysis.

8.6 Ecosystem-Based Location Analysis

The analysis stage consists of identifying fundamental criteria and sub-criteria therein, to homogeneously cluster the location factors or attributes. This would, to a large extent, depend on the industry and the nature of investment. Our aim is to develop a generic ecosystem-based analysis framework, which would help in identifying and grouping the attributes for location selection in global supply chains. The ecosystem framework will be used to identify the activities and factors along four dimensions that affect the business operations and output. Using the framework, the decision maker (DM) can structure the list of seemingly unrelated and incomparable location factors hierarchically with suitable sub-categories.

There is little work in any area of multiple criteria decision making to advise on how hierarchies should be constructed and what makes a good hierarchical representation [Belton (1986)]. However, there are broad guidelines on the hierarchy development process and the properties that a hierarchical structuring should possess [Keeney and Raiffa (1976); Keeney (1992)]. In general, this phase is entirely under the control of the DM. There are many different ways one can cluster and form a hierarchy of criteria and it is not possible to claim or prove the betterness of one over other. Table 8.2 presents different hierarchical clustering proposed in literature and being used in practice. The list is not exhaustive and it includes location selection problems studied from varying perspectives: locating in foreign countries [Yurimoto and Masui (1995); Atthirawong (2002)], locating manufacturing industries [Yang and Lee (1997); Alberto (2000); Atthirawong (2002)], locating

Table 8.2   Fundamental criteria and sub-criteria of various hierarchical structuring

Fundamental Criteria	Sub-criteria
Location of Japanese firms in European Commission [Yurimoto and Masui (1995)]	
1. Labour	labour force, costs, union;
2. Markets	product market, raw materials;
3. Transport	airways, railways, seaport, roadways;
4. Financial inducement	tax, country risk, loan availability;
5. Living conditions	firms from host country, educational facilities, crimes, consumer price index;
6. Environment for operations	electricity rate, water charge, sewage facilities, rules and regulations;
International location decision for manufacturing plants [Atthirawong (2002)]	
1. Cost	direct costs, indirect costs;
2. Quality of products	labour, infrastructure;
3. Time to market	markets, suppliers, macro-environment;
Industrial location decision [Alberto (2000)]	
1. Environmental aspects	regulations, disposal, taxation;
2. Cost	operating, start-up;
3. Quality of living	climate, crime rate, traffic congestion, living expenses;
4. Local incentives	tax, union, laws, skilled labour;
5. Time reliability provided to customers	proximity to centers, suppliers, customers, waterway, rail, highway;
6. Response flexibility to customer demand	proximity to suppliers and customers, other company's complementary facilities;
7. Integration with customers	post-sale service, co-makership, co-design;
Facility location selection [Yang and Lee (1997)]	
1. Market	growth potential, proximity to market, raw materials;
2. Transportation	land, water, air;
3. Labour	cost, availability of skilled and semi-skilled labour;
4. Community	housing, educational, business climate;
Locating global R&D operations [Jones and Davis (2000)]	
1. Demand factors	proximity to the final market, growth potential, response to local variations;
2. Supply factors	local scientific talent, local technology, know-how;
3. General competitive factors	competitive environment;
Benchmarking of European locations by IBM PLI [IBM (2004)]	
1. Cost	property costs, labour costs;
2. Quality	staff availability, language skills, labour laws, international accessibility, attractiveness for international staff;
Market attractiveness of developing countries [Saaty and Vargas (2001)]	
1. Political factors	turmoil, strategic relevance;
2. Economic-financial factors	risk of direct investment, GDP, inflation rate, growth rate of GDP;
Investment climate of India for manufacturing industry [World Bank (2005b)]	
1. Business environment	regulation, corruption, infrastructure, factor markets;
2. Agglomeration economies	own industry concentration, economic diversity, spatial distribution;

R&D facilities [Jones and Davis (2000)], industry location consultants [IBM (2004)], and measuring market attractiveness of countries [Saaty and Vargas (2001)] and locations within a country [World Bank (2005b)]. There are two things that are evident from Table 8.2. Firstly, the hierarchical structure depends on the particular industry and firm, and for the same type, one can arrive at different structures. The second observation is that there are some common features in these seemingly different location problems. To complement and extend these efforts, we provide here the ecosystem-based location analysis.

The ecosystem framework naturally provides the four fundamental criteria for location analysis:

- Business value chain;
- Institutions;
- Resources and management;
- Delivery infrastructure.

The above are the fundamental criteria in the hierarchical structuring. The sub-criteria under each of them are shown in Table 8.3. There would be uncertainties in any kind of business investment. Those that could be leveraged for growth are *opportunities* and those that would affect the firm negatively are *risks*. Their certain counterparts are *benefits* and *costs*, respectively. To enhance the understanding of the four fundamental criteria, the benefits, opportunities, costs, and risks associated with them are listed in Table 8.4. They are explained in detail in the following.

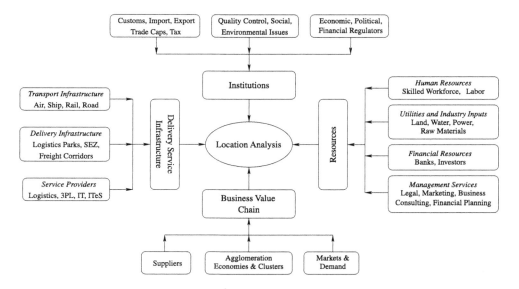

Fig. 8.2   Ecosystem-based location analysis

Table 8.3   Fundamental criteria and sub-criteria using the ecosystem framework

Fundamental Criteria	Sub-criteria
1. **Product/Process value chain**	suppliers, markets and demand, agglomeration economies and clusters, knowledge sharing and collaboration;
2. **Institutions**	economic policies, trade facilitations, laws & regulations, financial inducements and incentives, political factors, living conditions;
3. **Resources and management**	human resources (skilled workforce), financial resources (loans, investors), utilities and industry inputs (land, water, power, educational and training institutes), management services (legal, marketing, business consulting, financial planning);
4. **Delivery infrastructure**	transport (rail, road, air, sea), information and communication technologies (Internet, wireless, landline, data);

Table 8.4 Benefits, opportunities, costs, and risks

Benefits	Opportunities	Costs	Risks
- Local demand - Own-industry concentration	- Market growth - Product/process innovation to meet local requirements (or leveraging local expertise)	- Production cost - Operating cost	- Deviations in demand and supply - Local competition
- Inter-industry concentration - Special economic zones and technology parks	- Spin-offs/ins - Knowledge sharing and collaboration with universities and peers	- Direct and indirect costs	- Ignorance of domain knowledge - Knowledge spill-over and intellectual property rights violation
- Incentives: taxes, utilities, exports, imports - Flexible labour laws - Transparent regulations - Living conditions	- Improving public facilities	- Taxes: income, land, utilities, exports, imports - Delays due to regulations - Corruption - Cost of living	- Exposure of company information while applying for incentives - Anti-dumping - Political instability - Bankruptcy - Breach of promises by government - Crime and terrorism
- Investors and loan availability - Institutions: educational, training, research - Value-added services	- Developing integrated services - Customized training	- Cost of utilities: land, power, water - Cost of raw materials - Services cost	- Sub-optimal quality - Unskilled labour - Exposure of business process - Labour strikes
- Transport infrastructure: airports, seaports, railways, roadways - Network connectivity	- Developing public facilities	- Freight costs - Custom clearance delays - Bandwidth cost	- Disruption of connectivity due to natural calamities - Security in global sourcing - Network reliability and security

8.6.1 *Business value chain*

The investment is intended for some business process like manufacturing a product or providing a service. This criterion is about the value chain dimension of the intended subsidiary. It is not about the entire global supply or value chain, but the part confined to the location. It is concerned about the forward and backward linkages, supply and demand (market conditions), agglomeration economies (competing and complementing businesses) and business process innovation (adapting to local markets, creating new business opportunities). The above aspects of the location are clustered under this criterion.

The important sub-criteria considered are the supply-demand and the agglomeration. The traditional supply-demand factors are enhanced in global supply chains in terms of cheap supplies, local demand, and potential for market growth. However, deviations and disruptions in demand and supply can result in costly discrepancies elsewhere in the global supply chain. Similarly, the stronger agglomeration economies and cluster effects provide many benefits and opportunities and also pose major risks. The presence of related businesses in the location reduces supply costs and provides huge demands. It also enables knowledge sharing and collaboration to make the business process efficient but knowledge spill-over could result in IP violations. Ignorance of domain knowledge will be an added advantage of the locals with added expertise due to knowledge spill-over. The agglomeration, on the other hand, can help in business process innovations by leveraging the global expertise to meet local demands. The DM hence has to take into account the above conflicting factors to arrive at an optimal location decision.

8.6.2 *Institutions*

The economic and political factors play an important role in global supply chains. The interaction between the investing firm and the host government during the location decision has been modeled using game theory in the international business discipline [Loree and Guisinger (1995); Dicken (1990)]. The host government attempts to elicit desired behavior from the investing firm using direct (through legislative and executive controls) and indirect (through incentives) stimuli. The firm is always assumed to choose amongst several alternative locations, greatly reducing the bargaining power and role of the host government [Mudambi (2002)]. However, the economic and political profile of the government plays a significant role in the location decision.

This criterion includes taxes (income, sales, trade, import, export), regulatory framework (labor, environmental, legal), trade agreements, government incentives and subsidies, political stability, and living conditions. The obvious benefits of incentives, subsidies, and trade agreements also come with a great pool of risks like anti-dumping, voluntary export restrictions, and breach of promises. Once the investments are made, the bargaining powers of the firms are lost and are dependent on the functioning of the government. The exposure of the firm's information while applying for incentives is another risk encountered commonly in practice [Meirler (2006)]. The indirect influences of the government like terrorism and crime are other sources of risk.

The regulatory framework is another major sub-criterion that is government-dependent. Many studies [World Bank (2005a); FICCI (2005)] based on surveys have indicated that rules and regulations (labor laws, licensing, environmental) are seen as a hinderance by firms. The bureaucratic framework results in unproductive delays, and non-transparent functioning leads to corruption. Finally, the intangible attributes like living conditions and public attitude also have subtle effects on location selection.

The role of this criterion in location selection is evident at the national level, while choosing countries for investment. They also play an important role at the sub-national level for countries with federal system that is co-administered with several regional or state governments. Incentives, subsidies, and regulatory framework are generally the dominating factors while choosing a location within a country.

8.6.3 *Resources and management*

The third criterion covers the resources and the management of resources. The resources include human (skilled and unskilled), natural (raw materials, land, coast line), utilities (water, electricity), and also financial (loans, banks, venture capitalists). Management of resources is an important sub-criterion that is overlooked. Many global business operations largely depend on resource management skills like global sourcing, global marketing, research and training institutions, legal services, human resource training, and financial planning. The resource management complements with the resources and sometimes even substitutes when the resources are not available.

8.6.4 *Delivery infrastructure*

The final criteria is about how a firm connects to the external world using the transport and network infrastructure. The inbound and outbound flow of materials, manpower, information, and data are considered in this criterion. The obvious attributes include availability of sea ports, airports, railways, road ways, freight forward costs, lead time, network readiness, IT connectivity, mobile networks, postal and courier system, IT-enabled services, etc. The other network components due to globalization are customs clearance and quality tracking systems. International logistics flows are substantially more complex with more documentation like commercial invoices and customs paperwork. Hence, locations that employ automated trade documentation are advantageous.

8.7   Other Applications

In this section, we provide some applications of ecosystem-based location analysis.

8.7.1   *Measuring investment climate*

Private firms invest in new ideas and new facilities that strengthen the foundation of economic growth. They include farmers and micro-entrepreneurs to MNCs, and their investment in a region is mainly determined by the *investment climate*. Investment climate reflects the location-specific factors that shape the opportunities and incentives for firms to invest productively, create jobs, and expand. More specifically it is the *policy, institutional, and behavioral environment, both present and expected, that influences the returns, and risks, associated with investment*. Three main features of the investment climate are:

• Macro-economic factors (including political stability);
• Governance;
• Infrastructure.

   The ecosystem framework, in addition to the above features, includes the *Business value chain* dimension. This is essential for measuring the investment climate of specific industries or verticals like automobiles. The value chain dimension provides the forward and backward linkages like supply, demand, and markets, which are essential in measuring industry-specific investment climates. To be precise, the ecosystem framework can be used for vertical-specific investment climate. If the attributes and weights are derived with industry-specific characteristics, then the methodology can be used to evaluate investment climates at international, national, regional or city level.

8.7.2   *Market attractiveness of tier II cities*

FDI inflows to emerging economies have unilaterally improved the economic conditions of the tier I cities. In India, the tier I cities like Bangalore, Chennai, Delhi, Hyderabad, and Mumbai are over-populated and the infrastructure is overwhelmed. The city limits have expanded considerably and many development agencies are targeting tier II cities for development. The ecosystem-based location analysis can be applied to evaluate and rank the potential tier II cities. The evaluation can also be used to measure the time and cost involved in preparing the cities to be future centers of economic activities. The planning commission and economic development agencies can leverage the proposed methodology to systematically identify, plan, and develop potential tier II locations.

8.7.3 *Location analysis special economic zones*

Special economic zones (SEZs) are geographical regions that have economic laws different from a country's typical economic laws. The goal is usually an increase in FDI in the country. Traditionally, SEZs are created as open markets within an economy that is dominated by distortionary trade, macro and exchange regulation and other regulatory governmental controls. SEZs are believed to create a conducive environment to promote investment and exports. And hence, many developing countries are developing the SEZs with the expectation that they will provide the engines of growth for their economies to achieve industrialization.

One of the primary problems is the location of SEZ, or rather, which location is to be declared as an SEZ. This decision problem, faced by the government, should take into account location- and region-specific factors like availability of labor, utilities, resources, connection to highways and ports, infrastructure, incentives, and governance. Usually the incentive and concession packages are uniform for all the SEZs in the country, but there are certain regulatory framework that depends on the state governments like the labour laws. The ecosystem-based location analysis can be effectively used to evaluate and rank locations that can be potential SEZs. Moreover, this can aid the governments in planning and developing the locations of interest to be conducive to be an SEZ.

Chapter 9

Green Supply Chains

9.1 Introduction

In the 2009 Copenhagen Climate Conference, developing countries India, China, Brazil, and South Africa voluntarily set forth mitigation efforts to reduce greenhouse gas emissions. The Intergovernmental Panel on Climate Change has identified six primary greenhouse gases that impact climate change in the atmosphere: Carbon dioxide, methane, nitrous oxide, hydrofluorocarbons, perfluorocarbons, and sulfur hexafluoride. The common sources of the above gases are fossil fuel combustion, production of cement and aluminum, semiconductor industry, refrigeration gases, and electrical transmissions. The supply chain should be green in order to claim its product as green. There is no unique definition of green supply chain. A popular notion is the extended or closed loop supply chain that includes waste disposal and collection at end-of-life, which are then re-manufactured and re-used [Beamon (1999)]. The most commonly and widely accepted notion of greenness is carbon footprint. A carbon footprint is the total set of greenhouse gas emissions caused directly and indirectly by an individual, organization, event or product, expressed as carbon dioxide equivalent. In a survey among UK consumers [L. E. K. Consulting (2007)], a majority of 56% stated that they would value the information regarding carbon footprint of the products. Also, 44% of consumers would switch to a product or service with a lower carbon footprint, even if it was not their first preference. This is further demonstrated by the fact that 20% were willing to travel to a less convenient retailer in order to obtain a low-carbon product and 15% were willing to pay more for a less-carbon product. The research reveals the growing carbon awareness among consumers and thereby emphasizes businesses' need for including the carbon footprint in their supply chain design. The full footprint of an organization encompasses a wide range of emissions sources, from direct use of fuels to indirect impacts such as employee travel or emissions from other organizations within the supply chain. With increasing pressure from governments, environmentalists, and customers, green initiatives are no more a corporate social responsibility for companies. This chapter deals with the design of green supply chains using ecosystem framework.

9.2   Conventional versus Green Supply Chains

Design, modeling, and analysis of conventional supply chain has primarily focused on optimizing the procurement of raw materials from suppliers, manufacturing of the products, and the distribution of finished products to customers. A supply chain design problem comprises of the decisions regarding the number and location of production facilities, the amount of capacity at each facility, the assignment of each market region to one or more locations, supplier selection for sub-assemblies, components and materials, number of echelons, and distribution network [Chopra and Meindl (2007)]. The primary performance criteria are cost and customer satisfaction (measured in terms of quality, lead time, service, etc). Hence the supply chain practices such as JIT, TQM, low inventory, etc reduce the cost and improve the lead time. However, social and environmental costs such as wastage, pollution, and energy usage are ignored. The common method of inventory reduction in JIT is to produce and deliver in small batches, requiring frequent deliveries, higher fuel consumption, and increased traffic congestion.

These ill-effects have further compounded with globalization where suppliers, production facilities, distribution centers, and markets are dispersed globally. The delivery mechanisms consisting of trains, trucks, ships, aircrafts, and warehouses are major sources of greenhouse gas emissions. In addition, sourcing from low-cost countries with poor technology and non-stringent regulations contributes to the increasing greenhouse gas emissions. Long-term contracts with low cost countries enabled considerable reduction in production cost, but companies are forced to deal with environmental costs. Nearly 17% of the iron ore that China uses to make products for the Americas are shipped across the Pacific from Brazil. China's labor cost advantage is the primary driver for shipping an extra 10,000 miles instead of producing in Brazil or Mexico. However, if the incremental transportation cost, carbon footprint, and inventory at transshipment are calculated, one could question the realized savings from low-cost country sourcing.

Design of green supply chain involves fundamental rethinking of supply chain management practices. The primary focus on reduction in utilities usage and waste, leads to process innovations. Xerox realized that many of the components from its commercial copiers did not change between product generations and hence could be reused. The used machines are now bought back from customers for recycling and using in newer models. The Dutch flower industry was land-constrained and was generating high levels of fertilizer and pesticide waste. A new innovative way of cultivating flowers in rock wool was developed. This process requires less fertilizer, and the flowers are grown and transported in same trays, thus also reducing the traditional performance metrics like shipping time and cost. With the growing concern over the environmental degradations due to carbon emissions, a fundamental paradigm shift is required in designing and analyzing supply chains, spanning across the strategic, tactical, and operational decisions. Such a paradigm shift need not be considered as a threat, but as an opportunity to increase the competitive advantage by businesses and governments.

In the remainder of this chapter, we show that the ecosystem framework with the end-to-end holistic view of carbon emissions at various stages of the supply chain and its interdependency on the stakeholders, can help companies leverage the green mechanisms by making informed decisions in design, manufacturing, sourcing, and distribution.

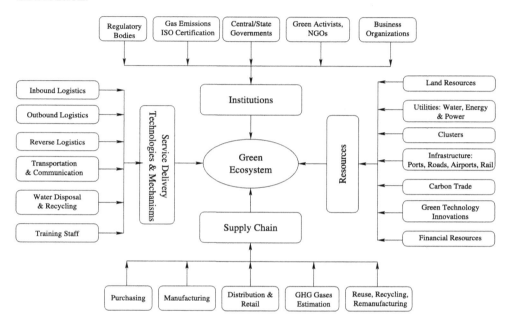

Fig. 9.1   Green supply chain ecosystem

9.3   The Green Supply Chain Ecosystem

Figure 9.1 shows the ecosystem of a green supply chain comprising of: (a) forward-backward supply chains, (b) resources, (c) institutions, and (d) delivery technologies and mechanisms.

9.3.1   *Forward-backward supply chain*

A green supply chain ensures greenness in all the three business processes: procurement, manufacturing, and distribution. Procurement is acquisition of materials or sub-components from suppliers. The procurement business process includes functionalities such as vendor selection, outsourcing, negotiation, delivery scheduling, quantity allocation, inventory management, and in some cases, involvement

in design. Green procurement is essentially taking into account factors like carbon footprint along with conventional drivers like cost, quality, and lead time.
Green manufacturing focuses on decreasing carbon footprint using both product
and process innovations. Green distribution is achieved through fewer shipments,
less handling, shorter movements, more direct routes, and better utilization. These
policies often conflict and trade-off with traditional logistics drivers like delivery
time, responsiveness, quality, and cost. In general, the carbon footprint should be
measured over the lifecycle of manufacturing, transportation, usage, and recycling
or disposal. In addition, green supply chains may include new processes related
to repair, re-use, reverse logistics, re-manufacturing, and recycling. The forward-
reverse supply chain has dual objectives:

(1) Forward supply chain optimizes cost and performance of all the processes in-
    volved from product design through final delivery to the customer;
(2) Environmental management looks at the same processes with a view to optimize
    the environmental performance and create the backward supply chain.

The reverse features add additional complexity to the supply chain design. Recycling involves collecting used products through reverse logistics, disassembling
them into categories of homogenous materials or components, and processing into
recycled materials. Re-use is the process of collecting used materials or components
and selling them at reduced prices. Re-manufacturing is the process of collecting
used materials or components from the field, repair or refurbish, and test for quality
standards, before re-use. The forward supply chain should be so designed to include
the reverse products, which re-enter the supply chain through reverse channels.

9.3.2 *Delivery mechanisms*

Delivery mechanisms for green supply chains include inbound, outbound, reverse logistics, waste disposal, and communications. The above processes directly influence
the performance of the forward-reverse supply chain.

Inbound logistics

Inbound logistics handle the movement of raw materials from source of supply to the
production line. The popular and efficient just-in-time (JIT) practice reduces the
inventory by delivering in small batches. This practice needs less storage space and
thus reduces the necessary overhead and resource consumption needed to manage
the inventory. JIT seems like an environmentally sound practice but smaller batches
mean more deliveries, thus raising fuel consumption and traffic congestion. Green
practices include freight consolidation and mode selection. Freight consolidation
ensures less deliveries and fuel consumption by waiting for freight to have full load
transportation with maximum space utilization of the trucks or containers. However, this adversely affects various metrics like lead time, increased inventory, and

delayed production costs. The transport mode selection decision determines which transport option to use and often affects traffic congestion and air pollution both directly and indirectly. Some transport modes like rail and barge use less energy or use energy more efficiently than other modes like road haulage and air cargo. In this case, flexibility, timing and speed are trade-offs to cost and environmental factors.

Outbound logistics

Outbound logistics is movement of finished products from end of the production line to the consumer and is a part of distribution. It includes transportation mode selection, packaging, warehouse location, and inventory management. Many trade-off decisions in outbound logistics need to be made with regard to the firm's market, customer, product and logistical resources. Typical outbound logistics decisions include direct shipping or hub-and-spoke, central warehouse or distributed network, inter-modal or single mode, and third party services or private fleet.

Reverse logistics

Reverse logistics is the process of retrieving the product from the end consumer and includes collection, sorting, re-processing, redistribution, and disposal. Reverse logistics is a core competency that does not exist with most original equipment manufacturers and organizations. Outsourcing to third-party logistics specialty companies is common. Most logistics systems are ill-equipped to handle product movement in a reverse channel. Reverse distribution costs may be much higher than moving the same product from producer to consumer. Returned goods often cannot be transported, stored and/or handled in the same manner as in the forward channel. Tools and models for disassembly scheduling, planning and control are still in their infancy since return logistics flows are more difficult to forecast and are directly related to the reliability models for the products.

9.3.3 *Institutions*

Institutions are playing a major role in enforcing and enabling the compliance of environmental regulations. New environmental legislations such as the Clean Air Act, the Clean Water Act, the Toxic Substances Act, Comprehensive Environmental Response, Compensation, and Liability Act are adopted in several countries. Environmental management standards (ISO 14000 series) have also been designed to develop operational guidelines and standards to assist organizations in moving towards ecologically sustainable business practices. Kyoto Protocol is an international agreement that established commitments by all industrialized nations to reduce GHG emissions. Targeted at country level, the governments adhering to the protocol have accepted to limit the GHG emissions. The governments, in turn, enforce the businesses to be green. There are three mechanisms to achieve the reduction in emissions: carbon pricing, clean development mechanism (CDM), and joint implementation (JI). Carbon pricing has become widely acknowledged as a significant catalyst in international efforts to reduce greenhouse gas emissions. It is essentially based on the theory of internalizing the externalities. The greenhouse gas emissions are negative externalities caused in production and transportation of products through the supply chain. In order to internalize the negative externalities, the environmental costs are factored into the supply chain costs in the form of carbon pricing. The rationale for using carbon pricing is as follows [Neuhoff (2008)]: It creates incentives for the use and innovation of more carbon-efficient technologies, and induces substitution towards lower carbon fuels, products and services by industry and final consumers. The price signal feeds into individual decisions that would be difficult to target with regulation. It also makes it profitable to comply with carbon-efficiency regulations, thus facilitating their implementation. There are two mechanisms for delivering carbon prices: carbon tax and carbon trading. While both are institutional enforcements, carbon trading is a market-based approach that makes carbon a tradable utility and hence a vital resource in the ecosystem.

Carbon tax

Carbon tax levies a fee on the production, distribution or use of fossil fuels based on how much carbon their combustion emits. The government sets a price per ton on carbon, which is translated into a tax on electricity, natural gas or oil. Taxing basically discourages the usage of high carbon-emitting fuels, thereby encouraging businesses and individuals to reduce consumption and increase energy efficiency. It is an indirect tax that is based on transactions, rather than direct taxes that are based on incomes. Carbon tax schemes were introduced in Sweden in 1991 and subsequently in Denmark, Finland, Netherlands, and Norway. Carbon tax can be levied at different points of the supply chain. Some taxes target the transaction between producers (coal mines and oil wells) and suppliers (coal shippers and oil refiners). Some taxes affect only distributors like the oil companies and utilities. There are also taxes that charge consumers directly through electricity and utility bills. Thus, it is a price-based mechanism — the carbon price is fixed, but the quantity of emissions is not.

9.3.4   *Resources*

In addition to GHG emissions, industries significantly influence the environment in the use of raw materials, energy, water, and land. Use of land in competition with other economic activities such as agriculture is a source of economic and social divide. Also, usage of virgin land such as forests, wetlands and coastal areas, has adverse effect on biodiversity and climate change, leading to natural disasters.

Consumption of water and pollution of water resources with effluents and chemical wastes are a major negligence towards resources and are often implemented with poor resource management skills. Sustainable manufacturing should include Cradle-to-Grave or Cradle-to-Cradle protocols. For a business enterprise, sustainable development means adopting business strategies and activities that meet the needs of the enterprise and its stakeholders while protecting, sustaining and enhancing the human and natural resources that will be needed in the future. The growing awareness among businesses towards natural resource depletion can be observed in process innovations like Levi's WaterLess jeans. Water will be priced in future like carbon. The carbon trading markets have made carbon a resource though it is emission rather than consumption that is priced.

Carbon markets

Carbon markets use cap-and-trade scheme, which is dual to carbon tax where the quantity of emissions is fixed, but the carbon price is determined by the market. Cap-and-trade schemes have four basic components [Neuhoff (2008)]:

(1) Governments set a cap on the total volume emissions of a pollutant and create the corresponding volume of allowances.
(2) These allowances are distributed for free or sold to firms and individuals.
(3) The allowances can then be traded in the carbon market. This creates in principle economic efficiency. Firms that would face high costs to reduce their emissions will buy allowances from firms with lower costs, thus reducing the total costs of emissions reductions.
(4) Emissions are monitored and reported, and at the end of the accounting year, firms either have to surrender allowances proportional to the volume of their emissions to government or can bank them to the following year.

In contrast to carbon tax, cap-and-trade scheme fixes the quantity of emissions and allows the market to determine the price. The largest carbon market is the European Union Emissions Trading Scheme valued at US$50 billion with a volume of 2061 MtCO2e, followed by New South Wales (US$224 million with a volume of 25 MtCO2e) and Chicago Climate Exchange (US$72 million with a volume of 23 MtCO2e) in 2007 [Capoor and Ambrosi (2008)]. Developing countries have not capped their emissions, and therefore do not have cap-and-trade schemes. They participate in emissions trading via the clean development mechanism (CDM). Under CDM, certified projects in developing countries can sell credits from emissions reductions to developed countries that accept these credits within their cap-and-trade schemes. Thus, linkages created by emissions trading can put a price on carbon even in countries that have not capped their emissions. The producers in developing countries do not pay for carbon-intensive production but they are paid for investments to reduce emissions. Thus their production costs and competitive product prices do not increase to reflect the carbon price [Neuhoff (2008)]. To the contrary, where the allowance price exceeds the costs of implementing measures to reduce carbon emissions, this provides a subsidy to carbon-intensive activities.

For supply chain design, the carbon pricing offers three alternatives for locating a manufacturing facility or an emissions-intensive process:

- Locate in a region that offers cap-and-trade scheme with an allowance on the quantity of emissions; Additional emission requirements can be bought from the market or the excess allowance can be traded or saved for future use.
- Locate in a carbon taxable region, paying tax as per the usage with no upper limits on emissions.
- Locate in a developing country with neither tax nor cap on the emissions.

For a global supply chain with many facilities, one can judiciously choose the facilities in different regions such that the emissions can be traded among subsidiaries by balancing carbon reductions with economic justifications.

9.4   GRIP Methodology

As seen in the previous section, the ecosystem of the green supply chains comprises of new entities and elements that conflict with design and analysis metrics of conventional supply chains. The green requirement is perceived as a threat that could potentially change the structure of the global supply chains. With suppliers across the globe increasing the carbon footprint of inbound logistics, hemispheric supply markets are favorable than global sourcing. However, focusing on certain obvious parameters without analyzing the entire ecosystem would often mislead the decisions. For example, consider buying a rose in UK with two alternatives: one grown in Netherlands and the other from Kenya. At the outset, the flower from Netherlands will be more eco-friendly as it would have traveled less miles than the one from Kenya. However, research by Williams (2007) reveals that 12,000 cut stems of roses from Kenya emitted $2,200\,Kg\,CO2$, whereas that of a Dutch operation emits $35,000\,Kg\,CO2$. Roses from the Netherlands required artificial light, heat and cooling over the eight to 12-week growing cycle, whereas the natural weather of Kenya favored the roses without any temperature regulators. Thus a holistic analysis of end-to-end supply chain and its ecosystem can lead to better reduction in emissions. In this section we use the GRIP methodology that leverages the drivers and levers of the ecosystem for the design and analysis of green supply chains. We will only focus on the green factor as the other aspects have been discussed in detail in earlier chapters.

9.4.1   *Performance*

The commonly used metric of greenness is carbon footprint. A carbon footprint is the total set of greenhouse gas emissions caused directly and indirectly by an individual, organization, event or product, expressed as carbon dioxide equivalent.

Equivalent carbon dioxide (CO2e) is the concentration of carbon dioxide that would cause the same level of radiative forcing as a given type and concentration of greenhouse gas. The full footprint of an organization encompasses a wide range of emissions sources, from direct use of fuels to indirect impacts such as employee travel or emissions from other organizations within the supply chain. The carbon footprint as the performance metric thus should be measured over the entire supply chain, right from raw materials to final packing and delivery. Consider the carbon footprint of tomato ketchup from Sweden, studied by Andersson *et al.* (1998). The supply chain of the ketchup is globally dispersed. Tomato is cultivated and processed into tomato paste in Italy, packaged and transported to Sweden with other ingredients to make tomato ketchup. The aseptic bags used to package the tomato paste are produced in the Netherlands and transported to Italy; the bagged tomato paste is placed in steel barrels, and moved to Sweden. The five-layered red bottles are made in either the UK or Sweden with materials from Japan, Italy, Belgium, the USA and Denmark. The polypropylene screw cap of the bottle and plug is produced in Denmark and transported to Sweden. Additional low-density polyethylene shrink-film and corrugated cardboard are used to distribute the final product. Other ingredients such as sugar, vinegar, spices and salt are also imported. The bottled product is then shipped through the wholesale retail chain to shops, and bought by households, where it is stored refrigerated from one month to a year. The carbon footprint for 1 kg tomato ketchup, measured as CO2e in kg, is estimated to be 2290. The footprint is contributed by the following activities in the supply chain:

- Agriculture (190);
- Processing (500);
- Packaging (1275);
- Transport (130);
- Shopping (195).

The evaluation of aggregate carbon footprint and the constituent break-ups open the possibilities for innovation. In particular, CO2e is the performance metric or criterion in evaluating or re-designing supply chains. Aankhen, Inc. creates supply chain visibility providing new source of information and data on carbon footprint using RFID and GPS technologies [Aankhen (2008)]. The emissions visibility identifies the opportunities for continuous carbon footprint reduction and cost improvement by exposing existing supply chain inefficiencies. It creates a surprising *I didn't know we did that!* awareness followed by *What is the impact of changing that?* resulting in action with *Let's change that.*

9.4.2 *Innovations*

The obvious way of reducing emissions is to substitute carbon-intensive input factors with low-carbon alternatives. For example in the electricity sector, using natural gas instead of coal for power generation can reduce carbon emissions by about 50%

per unit of electricity produced [Neuhoff (2008)]. Renewable energy sources can provide near-zero emissions during operation of the plants. Similarly for logistics, one can substitute with low-emission vehicles and transportation modes. Walkers crisps from PepsiCo in UK used the following substitutions[1]:

- Using only British potatoes and cutting down food miles;
- Improving production efficiency by moving to more efficient production line;
- Reducing the weight of packaging;
- Running delivery lorries on biodiesel and using fuel-efficient driving.

With additional initiatives like recycling of waste, Walkers has reduced 4,800 tonnes of CO2 in two years (7% reduction). Another approach is to examine the end-to-end supply chain and identify substitution opportunities. For example, Walkers learned that storing potatoes in humid conditions to soften the skin increases their water content. Further, water content is the main weight contributor to potato, thus favoring farmers to humidify the potatoes. However, prior to frying to make crisps, potatoes had to be dried to remove the excess water content, which consumes a lot of energy. A gain in money for one agent in the supply chain adversely affects the emissions in a different segment of the chain. The solution here is to provide farmers with incentives for dry content of the potato (rather than its weight), thereby creating a win-win scenario. Similar observations were also made for clinker, a main component in cement. Clinker is produced by heating lime stone, which undergoes a chemical transformation releasing carbon. Although carbon emissions can be reduced by using renewable energy sources for heating, the majority of the emissions is due to the chemical transformation that cannot be avoided. After milling, clinker is mixed with other substances to make cement. Walker and Richardson (2006) observed that the main scope for reducing emissions is via the substitution of some of the clinker with other materials suitable for cement production. The above innovations are within a firm's supply chain. The ecosystem comprises of more complementary businesses and also competitors. The greenness is also a challenge to the competitors and hence coordinating with competitors is a win-win innovation that could lead to emissions reduction across the ecosystem. For example, consider the automobile supply chain of India. The Indian auto logistics, largely made up of finished vehicle distribution, is estimated at INR 34.71 billion in 200607 and has been growing at a rate of 18.31% during 200102 and 200607 [Cygnus (2007)]. The auto industry in India is clustered in and around the cities of Chennai (South India), Mumbai (West India), Jamshedpur (East India), and Gurgaon (North India). The demand is distributed across the entire nation. The finished vehicle logistics of moving the finished vehicles from the factories to the retailers is usually done by the companies in isolation without any coordination with the competitors. A truck carrying finished vehicles from a factory in the south

---

[1]http://www.walkerscarbonfootprint.co.uk/walkers_carbon_trust.html

to a retailer in the north of India, usually returns empty or less than a truckload carrying some other cargo. The emissions and cost could be optimized if the truck carries in the return journey vehicles from a factory in the north to a retailer in the south. India has a vast and well-established railway network, which can be leveraged for the nationwide vehicle distribution with reduced emissions. However, this demands a central player who can coordinate the competitors and execute the distribution at less cost and low emissions. The lack of such a central specialist is a business opportunity for a third party logistics provider.

9.4.3 *Risks*

There are several risks associated with policies and strategies for mitigating carbon emissions.

Supply chain

New product innovations in green space require rapid product development, testing and scaled up production, leading to reliability and quality issues that often occur when new products are produced. Successful green products may bring sudden large demands resulting in large and sudden material, operational, and warranty costs. Market uncertainty of products (electric cars versus fuel-efficient cars), unexpected generation of pollutant during the production due to machine malfunctioning, design and implementation problems in waste disposal and recycling resulting in hazardous waste liability are other common risks faced with green supply chains. Unstable governance structure results in opportunistic behavior by partners.

Institutions

Governments play a central role in green technology and industry development. The policies on raw material usage, manufacturing process regulations, limits on gas emissions, encouraging green culture with subsidies, etc are all in the domain of the Governments. Change in the leadership could change the policy affecting the industry. For example, green transportation and electric cars are both green-friendly. However, the change of policy from broad clean environment and waste reduction (green transportation) to support specific technologies (electric cars), alters the institutional behavior and relationships. Also, the difference in perceptions of the central and state governments is a major source of uncertainty. The public and businesses would favor uninterrupted and clean energy supply from a nuclear plant. However, with the natural calamities like earthquakes and tsunamis causing further destruction by destabilizing nuclear plants, every region is opposed to host a nuclear plant. Community campaigns alter customer buying patterns and malicious campaigns could result in huge losses even if short-lived.

Delivery infrastructure

Risk factors include Lack of talent and consequent inability to identify and remedy non-compliance or risk problems, Accidents due to a lack of training or awareness, Criminal/Insurance liability for violations and accidents, Reverse logistics and Waste disposal infrastructure, Operational readiness in case of accidents.

Resources

The most valuable resource is the talent for research, product development, rapid implementation and improvements. The current emphasis is on breakthroughs both in government research and corporate R&D labs, where scientists focus more on novel innovations than on incremental advances, relying on existing technologies that may have far greater impacts than novel innovations.

9.4.4 *Governance, coordination, and control*

From the above discussions, one can infer the following requirements for mitigating carbon emissions:

- Emissions can be reduced by choice of right partners like suppliers and logistics providers in isolation. Further, a win-win scenario with both cost and emission reduction can be achieved by optimally selecting the partners across the entire supply chain.
- Carbon awareness is increasing among the consumers. Even if regulators can be bypassed by producing in developing countries with no emissions cap and tax, companies need to be accountable to the consumers.
- Carbon offsets among the different subsidiaries of the supply chain can be done cost-effectively with the use of carbon markets and taxes.
- A green coordinator is required to ensure that the entire supply chain, along with its functional relationship to the ecosystem, is synched with the objective of emissions reductions.

The green coordinator creates value through an alliance of supply chain competencies, by exploiting information flows and goods flows in the supply chain to optimize costs and carbon emissions. The primary strengths of the coordinator are the knowledge of the ecosystem and the relationships with the stakeholders in the ecosystem. The knowledge comprises of:

- the end-to-end supply chain emission requirements;
- requirements of stakeholders;
- capabilities of service providers;
- innovation possibilities;
- emission regulations;
- carbon market information;

- customers' carbon awareness;
- potential risks.

The second asset is the relationships with the key players and potential partners from the ecosystem:

- service providers (suppliers, contract manufacturers, 3PLs);
- regulators;
- carbon markets;
- low-carbon enablers (like Carbon Trust of UK);
- project-based activities like clean development mechanism (CDM) and joint implementation (JI).

Using the above two intangible assets, one can optimize carbon emissions without compromising on cost and risks. With the knowledge of the differential capabilities of the various service providers in terms of cost and emissions, one can optimally choose a set of service providers, such that the emission target of the entire supply chain is met.

9.5   Conclusions

We have seen from the above discussion that the green supply chain design is a complex exercise with risks of non-compliance from partners. Currently, totally green products using green supply chains are being sought after. This may not be a feasible proposition since it requires collaborative developments across all partners and also may face social issues at the tail end where natural resources are involved. A feasible green solution that is a balance between resource use, carbon footprint, customer acceptance and profitability is the one that should be sought after.

Chapter 10

Smart Villages and Cities*

10.1 Introduction

Mahatma Gandhi, father of the Indian nation, quotes in *Harijan* (18-01-1922):

> *The best, quickest and most efficient way is to build up from the bottom.*
> *Every village has to become a self-sufficient republic. This does not*
> *require brave resolutions. It requires brave, corporate, intelligent work.*

If we interpret "brave" as an entrepreneurial and risk-taking attitude, "corporate" to meeting strategic goals and objectives, "intelligent" with IT-enabled governance models, called "smart" nowadays, we implement Mahatma's vision. Indeed, innovations in a product or service may not matter, but a bundle of services strategically grown can lead to impactful growth. This is the smart village vision in this chapter.

For the overall development of any system growth has to begin from its building blocks. Villages are the building blocks of a country and are therefore essential for the development of the nation as a whole. The need of the hour is a paradigm shift in the design of villages from the traditional approach to the smart villages. We define a smart village as *a bundle of services which are delivered to its residents and businesses in an effective and efficient manner*. Dozens of services including construction, farming, electricity, health care, water, retail, manufacturing and logistics are needed in building a smart village. Moreover, every village is unique in itself based on the investment climate in and around the village. In this chapter, we describe the ecosystem for a village and then map out an integrated design procedure for building a smart village. Computing, communication, and information technologies play a major role in design, delivery, and monitoring of the services. All the techniques and technologies needed to build a smart village are available now and some of them are being used in villages in India, but these are disparate, fragmented and piecemeal efforts. We identify four significant parameters in the design and operation of a smart village: innovation, strategy, integrated planning, and above all, monitoring and execution of the activities using appropriate governance models. Our integrated design is a way forward to deal with the demographic

---

*Sowmya Vedula contributed to this chapter.

deficit and also achieve the goals of inclusive growth. It is replicable and can be used to design and build smart villages in other parts of the World.

Of India's 610 districts, the National Rural Employment Guarantee Act has a list of 200 backward districts. Similarly, out of India's 600,000 villages, around 125,000 are truly backward. There are 78 regions in the country, as per the NSS (National Sample Survey) classification. Based on these regions, the World Bank (2004) identifies 18 regions where human development is low. Currently, there is a lot of public spending to improve the infrastructure, water and sanitation in these areas. The socio-economic dualism in the Indian economy is tackled by the Government by taking responsibility for uplifting the rural and the economically poorer sections. The Government does this by giving subsidies, loan waivers, and quota systems in educational institutions, jobs and offering several other schemes based on caste and profession. All these efforts are disparate, fragmented and piecemeal efforts and not much improvement has been achieved in most of the villages.

On the other hand, the villages themselves are a powerhouse of large pools of manpower. As we perceive, there is a huge scope for the villages to be self-sufficient and sustainable on their own. About 700 million people in India live in villages and at least half of them are below 25 years of age. Availability of this rapidly expanding pool of young workers could and should be a major advantage for India's economy if the new generation of workers is healthy and educated and the government succeeds in addressing social infrastructure (housing, health care, schools, colleges and universities) and generating labor markets for all categories of people primarily for those who are educated up to only the middle school. Hence, there is an imminent requirement for vocational training in villages. Vocational education can be broadly defined as a training program which prepares an individual for a specific career or occupation. The National Sample Survey 61st Round results show that among persons of age 15–29 years, only about 2% are reported to have received formal vocational training and another 8% reported to have received non-formal vocational training, indicating that very few young people actually enter the world of work without any kind of formal vocational training. This proportion of trained youth is one of the lowest in the world. The corresponding figures for industrialized countries are much higher, varying between 60% and 96% of the youth in the age group of 20–24 years.

By not providing attention to this aspect, the planners are creating huge opportunity for several devastating risks of either huge epidemics or diseases such as HIV, TB, and hepatitis sweeping across the country and also for rise of unrests among the jobless. There is no integrated approach for a village design so far and various services are provided in an ad-hoc manner. Most of them are left unfinished or are not maintained properly. Schemes such as NREGAS provide employment for some rural folks but these have become breeding grounds for huge leakages and corruption. Though IT services are provided by leading service providers such as TCS, NIC, HP and others, these automate the existing manual accounting processes rather than streamlining, redesigning, modularizing and standardizing the entire value delivery processes. There are a few initiatives like e-panchayats and e-kiosks, designed to provide information and for payment of bills. While these efforts are really laudable and may be meeting the identified goals, they are still not strategically designed to contribute to the growth of the village in a wholesome fashion. Thus, the design of a village with all the essential utility services such as electricity, health care, water and employment guarantee through farming and small-scale industries is an important issue. Therefore, there is an impending need to reconsider design of a village and hence Smart Villages.

In recent times, there is an immense interest in the development of smart cities [Sankhe *et al.* (2010)]. But as we perceive, in the Indian context, villages are the heart of the nation. Hence, for the development to percolate to the grassroots level, focus must be devoted to the progress of villages. In spite of a large-scale migration of people from rural to urban areas, which is increasing the burden and posing a huge threat to the cities, there are still some villages which are thickly populated. The main aim is to smarten the villages using current wireless, IT and other advanced technologies and also to encourage entrepreneurial attitude among its residents to enhance the self-sustainability.

10.2   Literature Review and Motivation for Smart Villages and Cities

"Smart" is the buzzword these days with initiatives to transform and smarten everything from services, systems, cities and countries. There are a lot of studies regarding smart cities aimed at identifying problems due to rapid urbanization and proposing strategic solutions.

The report *Managing Asian Cities* [Asian-Development-Bank (2008)] talks about Asia's urban challenges and why many cities cannot cope with them and proposes strategies on how to respond by acting on the environment, achieving economic growth and ensuring sustainable communities. McKinsey Global Institute also did a study on *India's Urban Awakening: Building inclusive cities, sustaining economic growth* [Sankhe *et al.* (2010)] that explores many problems facing India's fast growing cities and proposes what policymakers can do to mitigate the strains of urban life in India and maximize the opportunities offered by urban cities.

There are initiatives by technology companies like IBM, CISCO to infuse intelligence into existing state of services in cities and make them smart. CISCO has initiatives to develop smartly connected communities in cities like Amsterdam, San Francisco and Seoul.[1] IBM has initiatives in Stockholm, Dublin, Singapore

---

[1]http://www.cisco.com/web/strategy/docs/scc/09CS2326_SCC_BrochureForWest_r3_112409.pdf

and Brisbane to smarten the transportation system and in New York, Syracuse, Santa Barbara and St. Louis to smarten their policing system.[2] They partner with the local governments to work on improvisation and smartening of services like transportation, traffic control, smart power and water management etc catering to individual services.

Real estate developers and consultants are keen on building smart business townships and residential community projects. There are initiatives for the development of new smart industrial/technological cities like Dubai smart city, Smart City Cairo, Gujarat International Financial Tech City (GIFT).

Though there is a focus in all the above studies, from our research we envisage that this needs a holistic vision considering all the aspects that impact a city under one single framework. In emerging economies like India there could be issues with policies, political and social pressures, availability of resources, penetration and awareness of technology etc. Moreover, a city can be considered as an aggregation of several units i.e. villages and hence we begin working with design of smart villages. We intend to incorporate a holistic perspective towards the development of villages/cities because several services can be interdependent and due care must be taken during the design phase itself so that overheads of rework can be prevented. We thus propose an ecosystem framework that strings together all the aspects of the city/village like services chains, resources, integrating technologies and institutions.

In the subsequent sections of this chapter, we describe what we mean by a Smart Village. We then propose an ecosystem framework to understand the concept of smart villages. Then we suggest a methodology for the design of a Smart Village. In the next section, we propose governance models and performance frameworks for Smart Villages. In the end, we take a case of an agriculture-based village and elucidate the various concepts discussed.

10.3   Smart Village Ecosystem

Figure 10.1 shows a typical smart village ecosystem. This Ecosystem approach integrates all the institutions that are responsible, the resources needed, the services to be rendered and the service delivery technologies and mechanisms. We define smart village as a bundle of services delivered to its residents and businesses in an effective and efficient manner. The Smart Village ecosystem brings all the services of the village and its providers and users on a single platform.

Dozens of organizations need to collaborate across industries to build a smart village. These include governments, social organizations, companies (big and small), farmers, labor etc. Many of these organizations fall outside the traditional value chain of suppliers and distributors that directly contribute to the creation and delivery of a product or service. The ecosystem also comprises entities like regulatory

---

[2]http://www.ibm.com/smarterplanet/us/en/smarter_cities/overview/

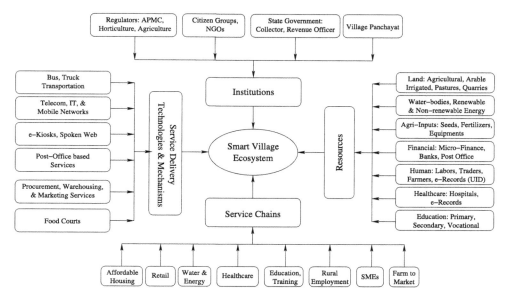

Fig. 10.1   Smart village ecosystem

agencies and media outlets that can have a less immediate, but just as powerful, effect on the business in the village.

The smart village is a formation resulting from co-evolution of four distinct forces and innovations in these four factors. They include:

- Modular services and Modular service chains;
- Service delivery technologies such as logistics and IT and their mechanisms;
- Institutions that influence the governance and regulations;
- Resources and their management.

The basic services offered to the rural residents are supply of purified water, affordable housing, primary education, vocational training, help in farming techniques, procurement of seeds and fertilizers, training and employment opportunities in SMEs like leather, crafts, food processing units, retail/kirana shops. The services delivery technologies and mechanisms like road transportation by bus/truck; IT and mobile networks; procurement, warehousing and marketing for agricultural and SME produce; Food Courts; e-kiosks for bill payment; applications like Spoken web for commodity price broadcast, social networking, etc; and post office based services like ticket booking, e-purchase, etc need to be developed. Existing infrastructures like post offices can be used as village information centers that provide all the information from market prices of various commodities, advice related to agricultural, animal husbandry or health-related issues, educational information for students of class X and XII, employment opportunities, career guidance for young people, to on-line applications for pan card, driving licenses, tax and bill payments etc. They can also have a call center based regular monitoring and grievance system so that their complaints are attended to. This calls for a lot of awareness and training in the initial phases to educate and make people acquainted with the new systems. Vocational training has to be provided on a large scale to make them familiar with IT, maintenance of records, operation of the equipment and managing their finances.

Proven initiatives such as micro finance need to be nurtured more strategically in rural areas. Insurance schemes like crop insurance, livestock/cattle insurance, health insurance, life insurance, insurance in case of natural disasters etc. should be provided. There is a huge gap between the skills needed to work in the agriculture sector for low wages and those needed for working in services such as health care, plumbing, brick making, or other more skilled occupations where the wages are higher. The government has identified about 400 needed skills including in maintenance, operation and repair of various systems so that the villages can be self-sufficient. We must fundamentally innovate, develop new pedagogical tools, and apply technologies in sustainable ways that can help in the betterment of their day-to-day lives.

The government and other agencies have several innovative schemes for providing employment to the rural populations and providing free access to services such as water, power, etc. The effect is not felt because of lack of systematic strategy, planning, developing a group of companies that can work together in a coordinated fashion to reach the end goal of providing the services and also employment. This chapter provides a holistic picture of the smart village and the prioritized execution of various activities.

10.4   GRIP Analysis

The four important criteria that play a significant role for a successful system along with the ecosystem framework are Governance Models, Risk Analysis, Innovations and Performance management (not in the same order).

10.4.1   *Innovation*

Numerous new innovations are needed for building smart villages which include audio-visual interfaces for all applications, equipment that can withstand harsh environments, talented people with capabilities that far exceed those of the current IT workers. We need innovations on the scale of products such as Tata Nano, low-cost medical equipment as done by GE, low-cost housing, re-conceived washing machines or an oven or a school, processed food, food courts with hygienic affordable and nutritious food, etc. Entrepreneurship is absolutely fundamental to design, develop and operate smart villages. Innovations and risk analysis must be carefully looked into for each of the services that is being designed. Developing and nurturing the smart villages is the best way India can reap the *demographic dividend* i.e. the large and expanding workforce. All these innovations can be exported back to both advanced and underdeveloped countries and the models used can be replicated.

10.5   Methodologies for the Design of a Smart Village

The design methodology that we propose for building a smart village consists of:

- Assessment of the Investment Climate of the village;
- Formulate the Growth Strategies for the village.

Assessment of investment climate of the village

Investment climate of a region is defined as policy, institutional, and behavioral environment, both present and expected, that influences the returns, and risks, associated with an investment. We perceive these as location-specific factors like infrastructure, primary occupation of majority of people, nature of industries/business (SMEs) and finance inflow/outflow that impacts the investment and growth of the region. The investment climate of villages differs depending upon the significant occupation of the village and its natural resources. The primary occupation of the villagers can be farming, aqua culture, working for industries such as apparel or leather goods or doll making. The village can be a tourist location, pilgrimage center, or a place of historical importance etc. Mines, Forests, Ocean shores or River banks can be part of the natural environs of the village. So the growth strategy of a village depends primarily on its investment climate. Hence, assessment of investment climate of the village is the first step in design of a Smart Village.

Formulate growth strategies for the village

Providing quality utility services like power, water, sanitation, and essential services such as education, healthcare, transportation, infrastructure (roads, railways, buildings, equipment) etc. for all villages is the primary strategy for the development of every village. Some of the utility services can be managed at a district level and others such as health care, schooling etc need to be managed at village level for proximity and accessibility reasons. Investment climate of the village is also impacted to a very large extent by the availability of the above-mentioned utility and other services in the villages.

The next step is to formulate growth strategies for the village to make it self-sufficient taking into account the investment climate and other factors discussed above. Strategic questions such as what kind of SMEs need to be developed in the village, the kind of vocational training to be given to the residents of the village and how to attract investment as well as entrepreneurs, must be formulated and answered. For example: if a village is a tourist location, then the growth strategies would be aligned towards construction of restaurants and hotels, development of transportation services like cabs or buses, vocational training to act as guides, security, working as chefs in restaurants or kirana shops selling the unique products made in the village, pharmacies and hospital services in a mobile van etc. The residents of the village can be trained to be engaged in providing the above-mentioned services. Once there is a clear picture on the kinds of industries or SMEs that must come up in the village, then the funding agencies Microfinance Institutions or NGOs can be decided. The Business Development comes to the village.

Although we concentrate on self-sufficiency of the villages here, the issue of the village being a part of a SME cluster or a part of the global value chain should not be ignored. There are several villages in India which are a part of the global value chains. Even here, orchestrators who can manage the order to delivery supply chain, with deep domain knowledge and connections with the government and industries, are needed. The Governments need to support these entrepreneurs and enable their success. Once the design methodologies for designing the smart village are formulated, the next aspect is execution of the strategies using appropriate governance models. Then there must be a scorecard to measure and monitor the performance of the services and their overall impact.

10.5.1 *Risks*

All the risks associated with each of the services must be mapped well in advance. Risks in the Service delivery can be: Environmental risks, failure in the supply chain, infrastructure breakdown, non-availability of resources, natural calamities etc. Each of these risks must be analyzed carefully and strategies for back-up measures must be formulated well in advance. Villages also pose some significant risks like lack of awareness and education among the villagers, inertia in taking up anything new, political stigma, operational inefficiencies, mismanagement of funds etc. Moreover, exploitation by political parties and corruption are big risks against progress. Mitigation strategies must be devised beforehand so as to avert any disruption in the service delivery. Villagers must be made aware of all the developments, educated, vocationally trained to participate in the development of their village (community participation), induce transparency and accountability in all processes to tackle with the above-mentioned risks.

10.5.2 *Governance models*

Currently the village panchayats are governed by the president and his team. These are elected representatives of the people. But their capabilities are well below those required to build a smart village. The village governance system should have several orchestrators working together along with the people and the businesses. Water, Power and Retail could be orchestrated at the district level for a group of villages, governed by a group of companies. Schools, health care and farming may need local attention. The knowledge-based technologies which provide the smartness and the relationship with other stakeholders need to be built by people with entrepreneurial talents. Thus we see building a smart village requires talents available beyond the village or district. We discuss below an organizational structure and assign the responsibilities that would make a smart village work.

The Governance model we propose is a collaboratory model wherein various organizations like Funding agencies, Industries, and Business Development units collaborate with Government and local village Panchayats to develop a Smart Village. At the highest level is the Advisory Board with members from the Village Panchayat, Funding agencies, Government and Industry, which sets the agenda for growth and maintenance of high-quality services. The Executive Director who works with the Business Development receives inputs and reports to the Advisory Board and is responsible for planning and execution. At the next level, three managers are responsible for the day-to-day activities of various services of the village which are grouped into three clusters. The services in Cluster 1 are Utility services like water, power, affordable housing and transportation. The services in Cluster 2 cater to the services that are local to the entire village and they are healthcare, education, waste disposal, retail. The last cluster is the employment development cluster that deals with services like government rural schemes, vocational training, post office based services and promoting SMEs among the rural population. Thus the village needs a professional organization structure which collaborates with neighboring villages for mutual benefit.

Information and Communication Technologies (ICT) play an instrumental role in the governance of a Smart Village. ICT can help in streamlining the existing processes and interaction and communication across all levels of people involved in Governance of the Smart Village. New technologies like Cloud Computing can be adopted to maintain huge amounts of data at village level or by groups of villages at district level. This can avoid *Operation and Maintenance* overheads of huge servers at the village level where not much talent would be acquainted with the rigorous server operations. This can smoothen the work of the people involved in governance, giving them the opportunity to focus on the core governance of the village. The execution of various services can be monitored and controlled using remote call centers with trained employees.

10.5.3 *Performance measurement*

Performance measurement is a key step in assessing the effectiveness of the services being rendered. This performance measurement must be oriented towards measuring the performance of individual services as well as measuring the performance of the smart village on the whole. For each of the services, certain parameters/metrics can be identified, which can be used to measure the service performance like timeliness, reliability, responsiveness to complaints, user satisfaction, innovation in the system, usage, accessibility etc.; whereas for the entire smart village, performance

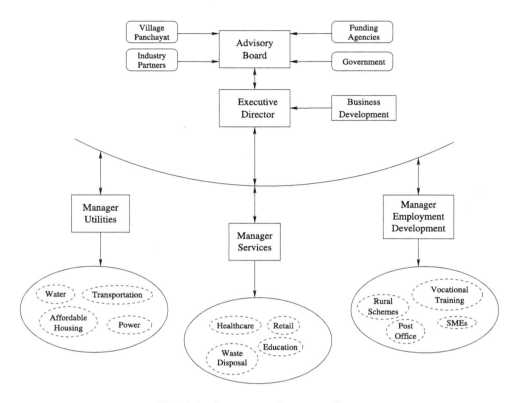

Fig. 10.2   Governance of a smart village

depends on the effectiveness of individual services rendered, the kind of vocational training and its impact on betterment of skill development and employment, the innovations in the systems, increase in connectivity to outside markets, growth in trade and per-capita income, sustainability of the village. To measure the performance of these aspects of the Smart Village, a balanced scorecard approach as developed by Kaplan and Bower (1999) can be used. These scorecards can be used to communicate the information and strategy to all the stakeholders. The components of the balanced scorecard are learning and growth performance, internal processes performance, financial accountability and customer satisfaction. Figure 10.3 shows the scorecard for a smart village.

All the components of the balanced scorecard must ultimately meet the objectives of the Smart Village which are to improve the utility services, improve the investment climate, enhance skill development and promote economic development. Service quality is achieved when all these characteristics hold good simultaneously. These performance measures can be used to improve the system to continuously make it better. The feedback from this balanced scorecard from all stakeholders can be used to revise and upgrade the objectives of the system and to improve it on a regular basis.

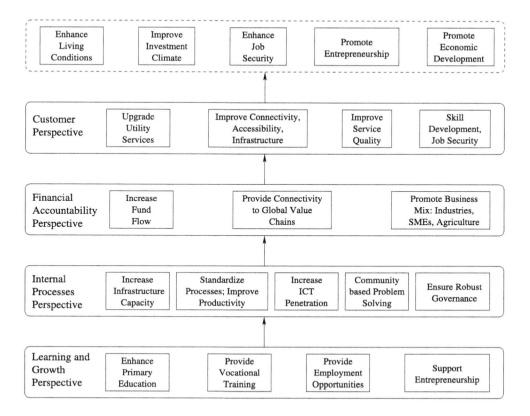

Fig. 10.3   Balanced scorecard for the performance of a smart village

10.6   Pochampally Village Case Study

Bhoodan Pochampally is famous for its Pochampally Patola Tie & Dye Sarees and it occupies prominence as the first village for the Bhoodan movement initiated by Acharya Vinobha Bhave. It is situated 46 km away from Hyderabad. About 1,448 families presently depend on weaving. About 102 families have their own Saree shops and they are mainly into Saree-selling business; 402 families are depending on Agriculture; 109 families depend on toddy tapping; 93 families on washing; 79 families on fishing; and 28 families depend on basket making as their primary livelihood. Weavers are the dominant community in the village.

Weaving is the major livelihood in Bhoodan Pochampally village with an annual turnover exceeding $22 Million. In the weaving livelihood, 650 families are weaving wage laborers, 495 families have their own weaving facilities, 201 families are master weavers and 102 families have their own Saree shops. The famous Pochampally Ikat tie-and-dye sari has won Intellectual Property Rights protection. The certification promotes economic prosperity of producers of goods in the territory, provides legal protection to Indian geographical indications for boosting exports, and prevents unauthorized use of a registered GI certification. The products reach the market through various channels of which Middlemen form a major part and play different kinds of roles. They have 20%–50% margin (on the sale price) on most of the products with exportable products being the high-margin niche items. Most of the weavers sell their sarees to the local shopkeepers/traders who provide them the yarn. Generally, either weavers' cooperative or middlemen in the village supply yarn to the weavers. A few weavers send their sarees to the shops in Hyderabad market and other places. Local traders send stocks to various parts and states of the country like Maharashtra, Orissa, Kerala, Gujarat, and West Bengal etc. These sarees also have international demand. Very few weaving families are also involved in direct selling of their own weaved sarees, which comprises of 5%–8% of the total retail sale. These families participate in exhibitions in various parts of India and abroad and sell these sarees.

Because of its worldwide famous weaves and proximity to Hyderabad, Pochampally has been considered for development by Tourism Development Corporation of India and UNDP. Some significant developments include vocational training institute SRTRI, Self-Help Groups, NGOs, online sale of sarees and dress materials etc. However, there are some issues with regard to weaving — fluctuating cost of raw material (silk yarn), lack of working capital, shortage of pure water for dyeing purpose, competition from the Power looms, tied-up sales to the middlemen etc. The possible opportunities to enhance the weaving livelihood include collective procurement of raw materials; collective processing of the silk yarn to minimize the input cost; collective marketing of sarees through direct selling, through exhibition cum sale shops, Internet, to the wholesalers etc; establishment of reeling machine to ensure regular supply of silk yarn etc. On the other hand there are many other backdrops plaguing the village. There is a price to be paid for the vibrant saris and materials produced in the village. The weavers complain that when they consume water from the bore wells, because of excess fluoride content in the water, their bones ache and so they buy water for their drinking needs. Other areas where focus is needed are the infrastructure facilities, power, telephone connectivity, schools, healthcare etc. The need of the hour is integrated growth strategies, planning, and above all, monitoring and execution of all the services using an integrated ecosystem approach. Governance models can also be proposed for coordinating all these services. Hence, Pochampally can be considered as a prospective case study for Smart Villages. The ecosystem and governance model for Pochampally are given below. The major areas where focus is needed in Pochampally are underlined in the ecosystem:

(i) The weavers and their communities must be vocationally trained to access the latest technology in designing and weaving.

(ii) They must also be trained to take up entrepreneurial initiatives by setting up SMEs. They must have convenient and regular access to the resources that are required like cotton, silk and fabric resources, microfinance and loans.

(iii) More importantly, there is hardly any significant domain research about weaving. Research must be focused on what kind of raw material must be sourced, quality monitoring from sourcing to delivery, design techniques using the latest advances in technology, power looms that can enhance production capabilities, safe and environment-friendly ways of using and disposing synthetic dyes and colors so that they do not affect groundwater, product innovations to cater to diverse national and international customers, pricing mechanisms, marketing strategies etc.

(iv) Weavers and their communities must be trained to be acquainted with Government Regulations of textile industry, sourcing, trade and export regulations. Once they are aware of the regulations that govern their domain, they can keep a check on middlemen.

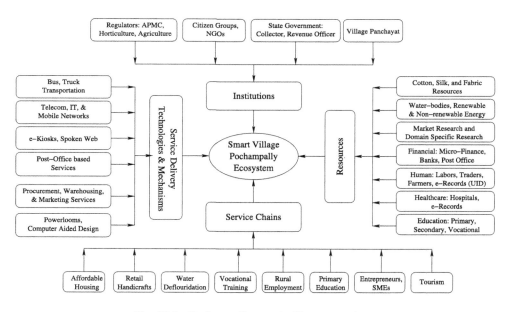

Fig. 10.4   Pochampally smart village ecosystem

More efforts must be directed towards linking their products to the global value chain using product and service innovations, resource availability, regulations, and advanced service delivery technologies. All of them should co-evolve.

10.7   A Case of Agriculture-Based Villages

India is primarily an agriculture-based country with 300 million small farmers and an equal number employed on farms.   12 million Kirana shops supply food to the population employing 30 million people. In this section we consider a case of agriculture-based village and apply the Ecosystem framework discussed above to elucidate the concepts discussed. The farms produce products such as wheat, rice, fruits, vegetables etc., and dairies generate milk from live cattle. These are distributed to the population for consumption. They are either consumed fresh or processed as food. The food supply chain is the vehicle that supplies the farm produce to the consumers via kirana shops or big retailers. We all know that services like logistics, retail, marketing, Internet are integral parts of the food supply chain. Their role is enabling and strategic in moving materials, marketing and inventory management. Currently there is a lot of discussion about the inefficiencies in food supply chain and wastages in warehousing, logistics and in kirana shops. There is also discussion about whether or not foreign direct investment should be allowed in multi-brand retail.

Agriculture is important for providing food security for the country and is a protected part of the economy through various regulations. The scenario that we presented above is very generic. The supply chain is highly inefficient and lots of food is wasted away. The food inflation is another worry. On the other hand, India is well-endowed with highly fertile land and live rivers and good climate. 51% of our land is cultivable whereas the global average is 11% and we have good seasons to produce all the fruits and vegetables that can be produced anywhere in the world. The question then is: can we improve the situation and provide quality food services for local consumption at affordable rates in both urban and rural areas and serve the expectations of younger populations? Can we do this by redesigning and rebuilding the current service networks such as logistics, retail using smart technologies such as IT, sensor networks etc and using precision agriculture? Can we follow an Integrated Service, Manufacturing and Farming to create Food Solutions for the populations?

Breakthrough Innovations are possible with out-of-the-box thinking in terms of product offerings made to various customer segments with booming employment opportunities. The world took notice of the market opportunity and several companies such as Reliance and India's other big corporations Bharti Group, Aditya Birla Group, Mahindra & Mahindra and the Tata Group, and global retailing majors Wal-Mart to Carrefour have entered the market. This affects the food supply chain since 50% of retail in India is food.

The government from its side provides rural employment schemes. There are several acts such as the *Agricultural Produce Marketing Committee* (APMC) Act, the minimum support price announced by the Govt. for 24 crops that acts as insurance for farmers against sharp price fluctuations and provides inputs to the PDS, and the Essential Commodities Act that empowers the Govt. to control production, distribution and pricing, etc to secure equitable distribution and fair pricing. Yet the food retail industry has not made its impact on the country and a lot more needs to be done before it attains breakout status. The two important issues are how do you achieve astounding *breakout growth* and employment generation.

To address the above-mentioned challenges, we propose innovations in food supply chain ecosystem for agri-based villages. All the utility services like water, power, education, healthcare, affordable housing etc are required for the agri-based village as evident in the Smart Village Ecosystem. However, the main focus of the agri-based village will be the food supply chain wherein the farming and SMEs will be the major concern. Hence, we map the food supply chain and enumerate the various innovations in value chain, institutions, resources and delivery infrastructure. The food supply chain eosystem is shown in Fig. 10.5.

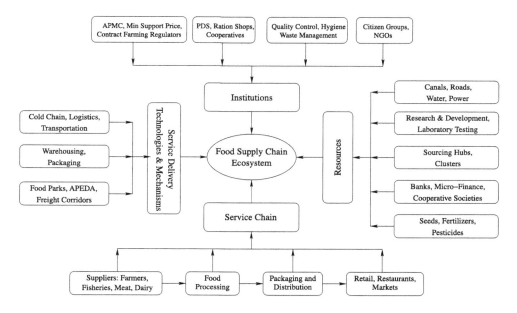

Fig. 10.5   Food supply chain ecosystem

10.7.1   *Innovations in food supply chain in the four components*

Innovations must come from all aspects of the food supply chain ecosystem as elaborated below.

Product and value chain innovation

- Seed-Feed agriculture, Food Processing, wellness and convenience embedded Protein-rich food, Convenient packaging, Standardization.
- Low-cost high-quality food, certified food like Halal, Organic etc., Store formats, Home delivery, e-retail, International markets through JVs.
- Market Channel Innovation.

- Operational Innovation; Outsourcing, Vertical Integration into land ownership & Farming or real estate.
- Developing SMEs in areas of food processing like rice/flour mills, packaging, etc.

Institutions

- The availability, price and quality of the products and services that people use are affected by the Government and Institutional policies. Many successful services companies owe their existence and success to the opening up of markets. Companies such as Airtel, Jet Airways in India and SouthWest, E-bay and others in USA owe their existence to policy shifts in the government. In the agri supply chains there are several Regulatory Innovations that are possible.
- They include Green, VAT, Trade, Hygiene, Regulations on packaging, Pricing, Procurement like APMC Act, Essential Commodities Act, Minimum support price for PDS, FDI in agriculture, multi-brand FDI in retail.

Delivery services infrastructure

- Cold chain, Packaging, Sensor networks for visibility, Delivery with poor infrastructure, Distribution backbone, Product recalls, Local sourcing due to logistics costs.
- There is no well-designed hub-and-spoke distribution network in India and the taxation barriers between states act partly as barriers to efficient regional distribution.

Resources and resource management

- Water, Power, Post-harvest research, Food clusters, Food courts, Product development and Testing laboratories, Talent.

10.8   Smart Cities

The unprecedented urbanization over the last fifty years is overwhelming many of the Indian cities. Inaccessibility to bare essential quality services like water, energy, healthcare, transportation etc. has become an issue of prime concern in these cities. The existing distribution networks were devised several decades ago and scaling up their operations to meet the ever increasing demand has deteriorated the state of these services further. The management challenges they generate are enormous and affect all facets of life: the economy, the environment, and society. Hence there is a need for smart, intelligent and sustainable cities.

A *smart city* as we perceive, is a bundle of coordinated services, both public and private, and is responsible for delivering these services with due quality to the citizens and business organizations in an efficient and effective manner. According to MIT research group, *the smart cities pursue sustainability, livability, and social equity through technological and design innovation.*

Apart from viewing a smart city as a city that provides utility services to its citizens, a comprehensive study of a smart city can also consist of study of the nature of the industries in the Service sector (public, private, MNCs, SMEs), the type of the services rendered (Business-to-Business or Business-to-Customer), the competitiveness of the industry in that sub-sector, service trade, innovation in the industry. Hence, a smart city can further be viewed as a living city and as an industrial city. By living city we mean a city which caters services to all its citizens and their domestic households, while industrial city caters services to all the business units of the city, improves the competitiveness of the city and boosts the investment climate and the economy. This industrial city bears a close resemblance with SEZs. There are many initiatives taken to develop SEZ as a smart city. Gujarat International Finance Tec-City or GIFT is a smart city under construction in the Indian state of Gujarat. Its main purpose is to provide high-quality physical infrastructure (electricity, water, gas, district cooling, roads, telecoms and broadband), so that finance and tech firms can expand their operations from Mumbai, Bangalore, Gurgaon etc., where infrastructure is either very expensive or growth is saturated. It will have a special economic zone (SEZ) status, international education zone, integrated townships, an entertainment zone, hotels, a convention center, an international techno park, Software Technology Parks of India (STPI) units, shopping malls, stock exchanges and service units. The Smart City Kochi project that was taken up by the government of Kerala and Dubai Internet City are also similar initiatives, but the project is stalled over some political and land issues.

We can unbundle a smart city into Smart Living City, Smart industrial or tech city, Smart SEZs, Smart universities, Smart Medi cities etc. Each of the systems in a smart city can be considered as a smart village and can be developed using the above-mentioned ecosystem, STERM frameworks and analyzed through GRIP models.

10.9   Conclusion

There is no denying the fact that we need smart villages that provide welfare to the rural folks. This is the biggest challenge facing all developing countries today. There are technologies available and they are successful elsewhere. But the failure comes from lack of strategy, integrated planning, and above all, monitoring and execution of the activities. The STERM (Science, Technology, Engineering, Regulations and Management) framework can be used to design and build these villages. We need to develop the ecosystem for each village depending on its location and investment climate. Our suggestion is to build smart villages as contracts under PPP for group of companies with mandate to develop smart villages. The gains of success of these smart village efforts are foreseen to be tremendous. They can be replicated to millions of villages around the world in India, China, Brazil, and South Africa to name a few, and this is in line with the inclusive growth that is being advocated by these Governments. Also, these concepts can be extended to small towns and also townships surrounding the big cities.

Chapter 11

Epilogue

We would like to conclude this book with this final chapter which provides insights and research areas which need further investigation. We cite some of our and others' work which can be improved in the context of the ecosystem approach.

Starting with the map of the ecosystem, we have covered the GRIP framework in Chaps. 3–6. We have provided the influence of the Supply chain, Institutions, Resources and Delivery on the performance measures such as Total cost and Lead time. We have also indicated how the four SES elements can be changed to improve the performance e.g. soft infrastructure like trade facilitation improves the time and cost spent in Ports. Real-world examples using data from the field and developing the analytical models such as queuing or discrete event simulation would be very helpful. Currently the policies are made in an ad hoc manner and have political flavor. Quantitative models would be a big help in the actual design and operations.

Collecting data for the entire ecosystem and mining it for variety of applications such as best suppliers, best teams and also best routes, best supply chain links would be an excellent application area adding to the current interest in supply chain analytics. Also this data can be used for multi-tier risk management which lots of companies are trying to address after the financial crisis. The primary issue in applying the SES framework is the availability of data. It would be a valuable contribution to create data format for collection by the industries and organizations such as the WTO, UNIDO, World Bank etc. Companies such as SAP have software to measure the carbon footprint for companies. A useful exercise would be to use this data to design the green supply chain.

The main takeaway from all the chapters and applications is that the network design should include selection of partners, coordination and execution and have an organization structure in place to make things work. This is in contrast to the siloed thinking that studies supply chain separately from international business and organizational design. There is a need as we saw in Chap. 7 to redesign the supply chain network using the ideas in this book. We presented one example in the context of food security system design in developing countries. The chapter on green supply chain deals with a unique way of addressing the green design issues.

We now mention some topics which connect our work with other areas.

11.1   Tax-Integrated Global Supply Chains

The procurement process is undergoing tremendous disruptive changes. In earlier days the supply chain managers and OEMs preferred strong ties with trusted suppliers. Now managers are shifting to customer order configured supply chains particularly in agriculture, apparel and other industries. Here, based on design, the OEM selects or assembles all the players in the chain back to farms growing exactly the right cotton (vegetables) needed for the shirt (nutritious food). To create scale economies, the OEMs are buying through Multi-Tier Purchasing Platform for all the suppliers and their suppliers. OEM or Brand owner or Broker selects their tier 1 suppliers and also influences or selects tier 2, 3, or 4 suppliers for critical materials and components. This creates the need for procurement through supplier factory gate pricing rather than payment on delivery at OEM site.

   With the above changes in mind there is a need to develop optimization algorithms taking into account the taxes, tariffs, logistics infrastructure, labor productivity. The following of our papers can be generalized by adding new cases.

   N. Viswanadham and Roshan Gaonkar, Partner Selection and Synchronized Planning in Dynamic Manufacturing Networks, IEEE Transactions on Robotics and Automation, Vol. 19, No. 1, February 2003, pp. 117–130.

   N. Viswanadham and Kannan Balaji, A Tax-Integrated Approach for Global Supply Chain Network Planning, IEEE Transactions on Automation Sciences and Engineering, Vol. 5, No. 4, October 2008, pp. 587–596.

11.2   Multi-tier Risk Management

The focus of the supply chain managers is shifting from managing immediate suppliers to managing the entire network. Since one is dealing with globally distributed networks, the supply chain is frequently subjected to frequent attacks by nature, terrorists and partner companies. As we have seen in the risk chapter, natural disasters (earthquakes, tsunamis, thunderstorms), Piracy, Financial failures, Govt. regulations can disrupt supplier production or delivery. Also, as can be seen in the case of Mattel, Toyota and other companies, brand owners, OEMs and retailers are being held responsible for what happens in SCN. For these reasons, the managers are moving from reactive expediting to proactive multi-tier risk management.

   In view of the above there is tremendous need to take a relook at the supply chain risk and also design of resilient supply chain networks. Papers like ours can be extended to get some useful results.

   Roshan Gaonkar and N. Viswanadham, An Analytical Framework for the Management of Risk in Supply Chains, IEEE Transactions on Automation Sciences and Engineering, Vol. 4, April 2007, pp. 265–273.

11.3 Orchestrator Model for Governance of SMEs

Small and medium enterprises contribute significantly to the industrial economy of emerging markets. They are adaptable to change and can play a pivotal role in innovations. However, with small workforce, inflexible infrastructure, limited capital, and myopic exposure to the overall supply chain, such enterprises face continuous hurdles for growing amidst globalization. Service orchestration is a business model for inclusive growth of small and medium enterprises to integrate them into the global value chains. Analytical models for orchestration as in the paper below would be a useful addition.

N. Viswanadham and S. Kameshwaran, Orchestrating a Network of Activities in the Value Chain, Proceedings of the 5th IEEE International Conference on Automation Science and Engineering (IEEE CASE '09), Bangalore, August 22–25, 2009, pp. 501–506.

11.4 Social Networks and Supply Chains

The SES framework identifies several actors in addition to the players in the network, from Government, social groups, natural and financial resource groups, education institutions, delivery infrastructure providers with whom any company should develop and also the knowledge about the business, social, political and vertical environments. Tools of social networks can be very helpful in the study of supply chains and social networks. In particular, we feel that the study of supply chain vulnerabilities in the social network framework might provide useful insights.

11.5 Green Supply Chain Design

The countries are moving from uncontrolled GHG emissions to tough environmental regulations. The supply chains should aim at optimal use of natural resources, reusable materials, repairable and recyclable assemblies and above all be sensitive to carbon footprint and the resultant global warming. The current situation in green supply chains is that not everyone is serious about following the rules. There is a tremendous need for active application-oriented research in this area. The use of ecosystem framework to compute the transaction costs and use of scope 1–3 definitions to compute the emissions and also use of reverse logistics to minimize the resource usage and waste will be a good research target. This will extend our work in substantial ways.

N. Viswanadham and S. Kameshwaran, Low-Carbon Logistics Provider, Proceedings of the Indo-US Workshop on Designing Sustainable Products, Services and Manufacturing Systems, Indian Institute of Science, Bangalore, August 18–20, 2009.

11.6   Game Theory and Supply Chain Coordination

Development of simulation games for decision making and resilient designs would be extremely valuable for training managers. The decision-making using the supply chain ecosystem framework can use several of the mechanism design formulations taking into account the uncertainties in the environment, incentives offered to the partners, etc. The above are some of the recent trends within supply chain literature, and this literature can benefit the physics of the ecosystem and make the results more practical and implementable.

We leave this chapter with the confession that the book is incomplete and deals with physics of decision making and needs analytic support. We do hope this will be an extreme help to researchers and consultants.

Bibliography

Aankhen (2008). Carbon footprint reduction by Aankhen Inc. *Supply and Demand Chain Executive*, pp. 24–25.

Abonyi, G. and Slyke, D. M. V. (2010). Governing on the edges: Globalization of production and the challenge to public administration in the twenty-first century, *Public Administration Review* **70**, pp. 33–45.

Adner, R. (2006). Match your innovation strategy to your innovation ecosystem, *Harvard Business Review* **84**, 4, pp. 98–107.

Alberto, P. (2000). The logistics of industrial location decisions: An application of the analytic hierarchy process methodology, *International Journal of Logistics: Research and Applications* **3**, 3, pp. 273–289.

Anderson, J. and Markides, C. (2007). Strategic innovation at the base of the pyramid, *MIT Sloan Management Review* **49**, 1, pp. 83–88.

Andersson, K., Ohlsson, T. and Olsson, P. (1998). Screening life cycle assessment (LCA) of tomato ketchup: A case study, *Journal of Cleaner Production* **6**, 3–4, pp. 277–288.

Andrew, J. P., Sirkin, H. L. and Butman, J. (2007a). The orchestrator: Choosing the optimal business model for innovation, in *Payback: Reaping the Rewards of Innovation* (Harvard Business Review Press), pp. 103–124.

Andrew, J. P., Sirkin, H. L. and Butman, J. (2007b). *Payback: Reaping the Rewards of Innovation* (Harvard Business Review Press).

Arntzen, B. C., Brown, G. G., Harrison, T. P. and Trafton, L. L. (1995). Global supply chain management at Digital Equipment Corporation, *Interfaces* **25**, pp. 69–93.

Arvanitis, S. and Hollenstein, H. (2006). Determinants of Swiss firms' R&D activities at foreign locations: An empirical analysis based on firm-level data, Working papers 06-127, Swiss Institute for Business Cycle Research (KOF), Swiss Federal Institute of Technology Zurich (ETH), available at http://ideas.repec.org/p/kof/wpskof/06-127.html.

Asian-Development-Bank (2008). Managing Asian cities: Sustainable and inclusive urban solutions, Report, Asian Development Bank.

Atthirawong, W. (2002). *A Framework for International Location Decision-Making in Manufacturing using the Analytical Hierarchy Process Approach*, PhD thesis, School of Mechanical, Materials, Manufacturing Engineering and Management, University of Nottingham, UK.

Badri, M. A. (1999). Combining the analytic hierarchic process and goal programming for global facility location-allocation problem, *International Journal of Production Economics* **62**, 3, pp. 237–248.

Bailey, C., Sirkin, H. L., Stern, C., Hemerling, J., Waddell, K., Michael, D., Walter-
    mann, B., Tratz, A., Bhattacharya, A., Bradtke, T., Aguiar, M., de Juan, J. and
    Koh, K. (2009). The 2009 BCG 100 new global challengers: How companies from
    rapidly developing economies are contending for global leadership, Tech. rep., The
    Boston Consulting Group, Boston, MA 02108.
Barrios, S., Gorg, H. and Strobl, E. (2006). Multinationals' location choice, agglomera-
    tion economies, and public incentives, *International Regional Science Review* **29**,
    pp. 81–107.
Beamon, B. M. (1999). Designing the green supply chain, *Logistics Information Manage-
    ment* **12**, 4, pp. 332–342.
Beardsley, S. C., Bugrov, D. and Enriquez, L. (2005). The role of regulation in strategy:
    Companies have everything to gain from linking them, *The McKinsey Quarterly*, 4,
    pp. 92–102.
Beath, A. (2006). The investment climate in Brazil, India, and South Africa: A contribu-
    tion to the IBSA debate, Tech. rep., The World Bank.
Belton, V. (1986). A comparison of the analytic hierarchy process and a simple multi-
    attribute value function, *European Journal of Operational Research* **26**, pp. 7–21.
Bitran, G. R., Gurumurthi, S. and Sam, S. L. (2007). *The Need for Third-Party Coordi-
    nation in Supply Chain Governance*, Vol. 48.
Blanco, E. (2009). Winning in emerging markets: Five key supply chain capabilities,
    Research paper, MIT Center for Transportation and Logistics, Cambridge, MA.
Boudier-Bensebaa, F. (2005). Agglomeration economies and location choice: Foreign direct
    investment in Hungary, *Economics of Transition* **13**, 4, pp. 605–628.
Brouthers, L. E., Brouthers, K. D. and Werner, S. (1999). Is Dunning's eclectic frame-
    work descriptive or normative? *Journal of International Business Studies* **30**, 4,
    pp. 831–844.
Buck Consultant International (1999). Future of foreign investments in North Western
    Europe, Tech. rep., Nijmegen.
Burt, R. S. (1992). *Structural Holes: The Social Structure of Competition* (Harvard Uni-
    versity Press, Cambridge, MA).
Cantwell, J. A. and Piscitello, L. (2003). The recent location of foreign R&D activities by
    large MNCs in the European regions: The role of different sources of spillovers, in
    ERSA Congress (Finland).
Capoor, K. and Ambrosi, P. (2008). States and trends of the carbon market 2008, Tech.
    rep., The World Bank, Washington, DC.
Cattaneo, O., Gereffi, G. and Staritz, C. (2010). *Global Value Chains in a Postcrisis
    World: A Development Perspective*, World Bank Trade and Development Series
    (World Bank).
Chakravorty, S., Koo, J. and Lall, S. V. (2003). Diversity matters — the economic geogra-
    phy of industry location in India, Policy Research Working Paper Series 3072, The
    World Bank, available at http://ideas.repec.org/p/wbk/wbrwps/3072.html.
Chalk, P. (2008). *The Maritime Dimension of International Security: Terrorism, Piracy,
    and Challenges for the United States*, MG (Rand Corporation) (RAND).
Chopra, S. and Meindl, P. (2007). *Supply Chain Management: Strategy, Planning, and
    Operation* (Pearson Prentice Hall).

Cornet, M. and Rensman, M. (2001). The location of R&D in the Netherlands: Trends, determinants and policy, CPB Documents 14, CPB Netherlands Bureau for Economic Policy Analysis, available at http://ideas.repec.org/p/cpb/docmnt/14.html.

Cramton, P., Shoham, Y. and Steinberg, R. (eds.) (2006). *Combinatorial Auctions* (MIT Press).

Cygnus (2007). Indian auto logistics, Tech. rep., Cygnus Business Consulting and Research.

Davidsen, B. (1993). Netpbm, `ftp://ftp.wustl.edu/graphics/graphics/packages/NetPBM`.

de Groot, H. L. F., Linders, G.-J. M., Rietveld, P. and Subramanian, U. (2004). The institutional determinants of bilateral trade patterns, *Kyklos* **57**, 1, pp. 103–123.

Dhanraj, C. and Pharke, A. (2006). Orchestrating innovation networks, *Academy of Management Review* **31**, 3, pp. 659–669.

Dicken, P. (1990). Seducing foreign investors — the competitive bidding strategies of local and regional agencies in the UK, in M. Hebbert and J. C. Hansen (eds.), *Unfamiliar Territory: The Re-shaping of European Geography* (Aldershot, Hants: Gower).

Doh, J. P., Jones, G. K., Teegen, H. J. and Mudambi, R. (2005). Foreign research and development and host country environment: An empirical examination of US international R&D, *Management International Review* **45**, 2, pp. 121–154.

Dollar, D., Hallward-Driemeier, M. and Mengistae, T. (2004). Investment climate and international integration, 3323.

Dornier, P.-P., Ernst, R., Fender, M. and Kouvelis, P. (2002). *Global Operations and Logistics: Text and Cases* (New York: John Wiley & Sons).

Drezner, Z. and Hamacher, H. W. (eds.) (2002). *Facility Location: Applications and Theory* (Springer-Verlag, Berlin).

Dunning, J. H. (1977). Trade, location of economic activity and the MNE: a search for an eclectic approach, in B. Ohlin, P. Hesselborn and P. Wijkman (eds.), *The International Allocation of Economic Activity* (Macmillan, London).

Dunning, J. H. (1988). *Explaining International Production* (Unwin Hyman, London).

Edwards, W. and Newman, J. R. (1982). *Multiattribute Evaluation* (Sage Beverly Hills, CA, London).

Erkut, E. and Morgan, S. R. (1991). Locating obnoxious facilities in the public sector: an application of the analytic hierarchy process to municipal landfill siting decisions, *Socio-Economic Planning Science* **25**, 2, pp. 89–102.

Erocal, D. (2005). Case studies of successful companies in the services sector and lessons for public policy, OECD Science, Technology and Industry Working Papers 2005/7, OECD Publishing.

Escaith, H. (2009). Trade collapse, trade relapse and global production networks: Supply chains in the great recession, in *OECD Roundtable on impacts of the economic crisis on globalization and global value chains* (Paris).

FICCI (2005). FICCI handbook on foreign direct investment, Report, Federation of Indian Chambers of Commerce and Industry, FICCI, New Delhi.

Forman, E. H. and Gass, S. I. (2001). The analytic hierarchy process — an exposition, *Operations Research* **49**, 4, pp. 469–486.

Forman, E. H. and Selly, M. A. (2001). *Decision by Objectives: How to Convince Others That You Are Right* (World Scientific, Singapore).

Fujita, M., Krugman, P. and Venables, A. (1999). *The Spatial Economy: Cities, Regions, and International Trade* (MIT Press, Cambridge, MA).

Fung, V. K., Fung, W. K. and Wind, Y. (2007). *Competing in a Flat World: Building Enterprises for a Borderless World* (Wharton School of Publishing, Upper Saddle River, NJ).

Gai, P. and Kapadia, S. (2010). Contagion in financial networks, Working Paper 383, Bank of England.

Gandhi, V. P. and Jain, D. (2011). Institutional innovations and models in the development of agro-food industries in India: Strengths, weaknesses and lessons, Working Paper Series W. P. No. 2011-04-03, Indian Institute Of Management, Ahmedabad, India.

Gaonkar, R. and Viswanadham, N. (2007). An analytical framework for the management of risk in supply chains, *IEEE Transactions on Automation Sciences and Engineering* **4**, pp. 265–273.

Garg, D., Narahari, Y. and Viswanadham, N. (2006). Achieving sharp deliveries in supply chains through variance pool allocation, *European Journal of Operational Research* **171**, 1, pp. 227–254.

Gereffi, G., Humphrey, J. and Sturgeon, T. (2005). The governance of global value chains, *Review of International Political Economy* **12**, 1, pp. 78–104.

Granovetter, M. (1985). Economic action and social structure: The problem of embeddedness, *The American Journal of Sociology* **91**, 3, pp. 481–510.

Griffith, R., Devereux, M. P. and Simpson, H. (2006). Firm location decisions, regional grants, and agglomeration externalities, AIM Research Working Paper Series 038-May-2006, Advance Institute of Management Research.

Guasch, J. L. and Kogan, J. (2003). Just-in-case inventories: A cross-country analysis, Policy Research Working Paper Series 3012, The World Bank.

Gulati, A. and Reardon, T. (2007). Asian food market transformation: Policy challenges to promote competitiveness with inclusiveness, Tech. rep., International Food Policy Research Institute (IFPRI), Manila, Philippines.

Hagel, J., Durchslag, S. and Brown, J. S. (2002). Orchestrating loosely coupled business processes: The secret to successful collaboration.

Hanink, D. M. (1985). A mean-variance model of MNF location strategy, *Journal of International Business Studies* **16**, 1, pp. 165–170.

Harri Lorentz, P. K.-n. and Srai, J. S. (2009). Configuring manufacturing value chains — responding to an uncertain world, *Internationalizing food supply chains: the impact of emerging market characteristics on supply networks*, September 24–25, Cambridge.

Hasler, C. M. (1998). Functional foods: Their role in disease prevention and health promotion, *Food Technology* **52**, 2, pp. 57–62.

Hausman, W. H., Lee, H. L. and Subramanian, U. (2005). Global logistics indicators, supply chain metrics, and bilateral trade patterns, Policy Research Working Paper Series 3773, The World Bank.

Hawkes, C. and Ruel, M. T. (2007). From agriculture to nutrition: Pathways, synergies and outcomes, Tech. Rep. 40196-GLB, The World Bank, Washington, DC.

Hayter, R. (1997). *The Dynamics of Industrial Location: The Factory, the Firm and the Production System* (John Wiley and Sons, Chichester).

Head, K., Ries, J. and Swenson, D. (1995). Agglomeration benefits and location choice: Evidence from Japanese manufacturing investment in the United States, *Journal of International Economics* **38**, pp. 223–247.

Hedge, G. G. and Tadikamalla, P. R. (1990). Site selection for a sure service terminal, *European Journal of Operational Research* **48**, pp. 77–80.

Hinterhuber, A. (2002). Value chain orchestration in action and the case of the global agrochemical industry, *Long Range Planning* **35**, 6, pp. 615–635.

Hoover, E. M. (1936). *Location Theory and the Shoe and the Leather Industries* (Harvard University Press, Cambridge, MA).

Hoyt, D. and Lee, H. (2003). Cemex: Transforming a basic industry company, CASE GS-33, Stanford Business School.

Hübner, R. (2007). *Strategic Supply Chain Management in Process Industries: An Application to Specialty Chemicals Production Network Design*, Lecture Notes in Economics and Mathematical Systems (Springer).

Huckman, R. S. and Pisano, G. P. (2003). Flextronics International, Ltd. *HBS Premier Case Collection.*

Hummels, D. (2007). Transportation costs and international trade in the second era of globalization, *The Journal of Economic Perspectives* **21**, 3, pp. 131–154.

Iansiti, M. and Levien, R. (2004). Strategy as ecology, *Harvard Business Review.*

IBM (2004). Investment strategies and location benchmarking study, Location benchmarking analysis, Oxford Intelligence.

Immelt, J. R., Govindarajan, V. and Trimble, C. (2009). How GE is disrupting itself, *Harvard Business Review.*

India, K. and FICCI (2010). Indian telecom success story: Broadband for all, DoT (India) annual report, KPMG, FICCI.

Iyer, B. and Venkatraman, N. (2006). The changing architecture of global work: Opportunities and challenges, A White Paper Prepared for the Keane Workshop.

Jones, C., Hesterly, W. S. and Borgatti, S. P. (1997). A general theory of network governance: Exchange conditions and social mechanisms, *Academy of Management Review* **22**, 4, pp. 911–945.

Jones, G. and Davis, H. (2000). National culture and innovation: implications for locating global R&D operations, *Management International Review* **40**, 1, pp. 11–39.

Jungthirapanich, C. and Benjamin, C. O. (1995). A knowledge-based decision support system for locating a manufacturing facility, *IIE Transactions* **27**, pp. 789–799.

Kadiyala, S., Joshi, P. K., Dev, S. M., Kumar, T. N. and Vyas, V. (2011). Strengthening the role of agriculture for a nutrition-secure India, Policy note, India International Food Policy Research Institute (IFPRI), New Delhi.

Kaplan, R. S. and Bower, M. (1999). The balanced scorecard for public-sector organizations, B9911C.

Kaufmann, D., Kraay, A. and Zoido, P. (2002). Governance matter II: Updated indicators for 2000-01, Policy Research Working Paper Series 2772, The World Bank.

Keeney, R. (1992). *Value-Focused Thinking: A Path to Creative Decisionmaking* (Harvard University Press, Cambridge, Massachusetts).

Keeney, R. and Raiffa, H. (1976). *Decisions with Multiple Objectives: Preference and Value Tradeoffs* (Wiley, New York).

Kleindorfer, P. R. and Saad, G. H. (2005). Managing disruption risks in supply chains, *Production and Operations Management* **14**, 1, pp. 53–68.

Kumar, V. and Viswanadham, N. (2007). A CBR-based decision support system framework for construction supply chain risk management, in *Proceedings of the IEEE Conference on Automation Science and Engineering (IEEE CASE 2007)*, pp. 980–985.

Lamarre, E. and Pergler, M. (2009). Risk: Seeing around the corners, *McKinsey Quarterly.*

Lazzarini, S. G., Chaddad, F. R. and Cook, M. L. (2001). Integrating supply chain and network analyses: The study of netchains, *Journal on Chain and Network Science* **1**, pp. 7–22.

Lee, P. D. (2006). Measuring supply chain integration: A social network approach, *Supply Chain Forum: An International Journal* **6**, 2, pp. 58–78.

L. E. K. Consulting (2007). Carbon footprints and the evolution of brand-consumer relationships, Carbon footprint report, L. E. K. Consulting.

Loree, D. W. and Guisinger, S. E. (1995). Policy and non-policy determinants of US equity foreign direct investment, *Journal of International Business Studies* **26**, 2, pp. 281–299.

Losso, J. N., Shahidi, F. and Bagchi, D. (2007). *Anti-Angiogenic Functional and Medicinal Foods*, Nutraceutical Science and Technology (CRC Press).

Magretta, J. (1998). Fast, global, and entrepreneurial: Supply chain management, Hong Kong style, *Harvard Business Review*, pp. 103–114.

Marchand, D. A., Paddack, K. and Chung, R. (2002). CEMEX: Global growth through superior information capabilities, Case Study IMD084-PDF-ENG, IMD.

Mattoo, A., Stern, R. M. and Zaniokni, G. (2007). *A Handbook of International Trade in Services* (Oxford University Press, USA).

McCann, P. (2002a). Classical and neoclassical location-production models, in P. McCann (ed.), *Industrial Location Economics* (Edward Elgar, Cheltenham, UK).

McCann, P. (ed.) (2002b). *Industrial Location Economics* (Edward Elgar, Cheltenham, UK).

McCann, P. and Mudambi, R. (2004). The location behavior of the multinational enterprise: Some analytical issues, *Growth and Change* **35**, 4, pp. 491–524.

Meirler, M. (2006). *Location Location Location: A Plant Location and Site Selection Guide* (Wiley, New York).

Meixell, M. J. and Gargeya, V. B. (2005). Global supply chain design: A literature review and critique, *Transportation Research Part E: Logistics and Transportation Review* **41**, 6, pp. 531–550.

Min, H. (1994). Location analysis of international consolidation terminals using the analytic hierarchy process, *Journal of Business Logistics* **15**, 2, pp. 25–44.

Mohamed, Z. M. (1999). An integrated production-distribution model for a multi-national company operating under varying exchange rates, *International Journal of Production Economics* **58**, 1, pp. 81–92.

Mudambi, R. (1995). The MNE investment location decision: Some empirical evidence, *Managerial and Decision Economics* **16**, pp. 249–257.

Mudambi, R. (2002). The location decision of the multinational firm: A survey, in P. McCann (ed.), *Industrial Location Economics* (Edward Elgar, Cheltenham, UK).

Nachum, L. and Wymbs, C. (2002). Firm-specific attributes and MNE location choices: Financial and professional service FDI to New York and London, ESRC Centre for Business Research — Working Papers wp223, ESRC Centre for Business Research, available at http://ideas.repec.org/p/cbr/cbrwps/wp223.html.

Neuhoff, K. (2008). Tackling carbon: How to price carbon for climate policy, Research report, University of Cambridge.

North, D. C. (2003). The role of institutions in economic development, Discussion Paper Series 2003.2, United Nations Economic Commission for Europe, Geneva, Switzerland.

O'Connell, J. (2006). Li & Fung (Trading) Ltd, Teaching Case 9-396-075, Harvard Business School.

OECD (2003). Emerging systemic risks in the 21st century: An agenda for action, Tech. rep., Organization for Economic Co-operation and Development (OECD), France.

OECD (2007). Staying competitive in the global economy: Moving up the value chain, Tech. rep., France.

Olson, D. L. (1996). *Decision Aids for Selection Problems* (Springer, New York).

Ordanni, A., Kraemer, K. L. and Dedrick, J. (2006). Medion: The retail orchestrator in the computer industry, Tech. rep., Personal Computing Industry Center.

Porter, M. E. (1998a). Clusters and the new economics of competition, *Harvard Business Review*, pp. 77–90.

Porter, M. E. (1998b). *Competitive Strategy: Techniques for Analyzing Industries and Competitors*, The Michael E. Porter Trilogy (Free Press).

Porter, T. B. (2006). Coevolution as a research framework for organizations and the natural environment, *Organization Environment* **19**, 4.

Provan, K. G., Fish, A. and Sydow, J. (2007). Interorganizational networks at the network level: A review of the empirical literature on whole networks, *Journal of Management* **33**, 3, pp. 479–516.

Provan, K. G. and Kenis, P. (2007). Modes of network governance, structure, management, and effectiveness, *Journal of Public Administration Research* **18**, pp. 229–252.

Pyke, D. F. (2007). Shanghai or Charlotte? The decision to outsource to China and other low-cost countries, in C.-Y. L. Hau Leung Lee (ed.), *Building Supply Chain Excellence in Emerging Economies*, International Series in Operations Research and Management (Springer), pp. 67–92.

Ranawat, M. and Tiwari, R. (2009). Influence of government policies on industry development: The case of India's automotive industry, Working Paper 57, Technology and Innovation Management, University of Hamburg, Germany.

Rao, C. H. H. (2000). Declining demand for foodgrains in rural India: Causes and implications, *Economic and Political Weekly*, pp. 201–206.

Reardon, T., Gulati, A. and Minten, B. (2008). The rapid rise of supermarkets in India: Implications for farmers, processors and traders, Discussion Paper 00752, IFPRI.

Rittel, H. J. and Webber, M. M. (1984). Planning problems are wicked problems, in N. Cross (ed.), *Developments in Design Methodology* (John Wiley, New York), pp. 135–144.

Ritter, T., Wilkinson, I. F. and Johnston, W. J. (2004). Managing in complex business networks, *Industrial Marketing Management* **33**, pp. 175–183.

Rodrik, D., Subramanian, A. and Trebbi, F. (2004). Institutions rule: The primacy of institutions over geography and integration in economic development, *Journal of Economic Growth* **9**, 2, pp. 131–165.

Ruben, R., Slingerland, K. and Nijhoff, H. (2006). *The Agro-Food Chains and Networks for Development* (Springer).

Saaty, T. L. (1980). *The Analytic Hierarchy Process* (McGraw-Hill, New York).

Saaty, T. L. (1986). Axiomatic foundation of the analytic hierarchy process, *Management Science* **32**, pp. 841–855.

Saaty, T. L. (1991). How to make a decision: The analytic hierarchy process, *European Journal of Operational Research* **48**, pp. 9–26.

Saaty, T. L. (1994). How to make a decision: The analytic hierarchy process, *Interfaces* **24**, pp. 19–43.

Saaty, T. L. (1996). *The Analytic Network Process: Decision Making with Dependence and Feedback* (RWS Publications, Pittsburgh, PA).

Saaty, T. L. and Vargas, L. G. (2001). *Models, Methods, Concepts and Applications of the Analytic Hierarchy Process* (Kluwer International, Massachusetts, USA).

Sankhe, S., Vittal, I., Dobbs, R., Mohan, A., Gulati, A., Ablett, J., Gupta, S., Kim, A., Paul, S., Sanghvi, A. and Sethy, G. (2010). India's urban awakening: Building inclusive cities, sustaining economic growth, Tech. rep., McKinsey Global Institute.

Sehgal, V., Dehoff, K. and Panneer, G. (2010). The importance of frugal engineering, *strategy+business magazine*.

Services, I. G. B. (2008). Supply chain risk management: A delicate balancing act, White paper, IBM.

Sheffi, Y. and Rice, J. (2005). A supply chain view of resilient enterprise, *MIT Sloan Management Review* **47**, 1, pp. 41–48.

Society, T. R. (2009). Hidden wealth: The contribution of science to service sector innovation, RS Policy Document 09/09, The Royal Society, London.

Srivastava, N. K., Viswanadham, N. and Kameshwaran, S. (2008). Procurement of global logistics services using combinatorial auctions, in *Proceedings of 2008 IEEE International Conference on Automation Science and Engineering (CASE 2008)*, pp. 297–302.

Study, D. A. (2008). Innovation in emerging markets: Managing product sourcing risks in emerging markets, Annual study, Deloitte.

Sturgeon, T. J. (2002). Modular production networks: A new American model of industrial organization, *Industrial and Corporate Change* **11**, 3, pp. 451–496.

Tan, A. and Noori, H. (2011). Inter-organizational collaboration in dynamic, short-term supply chains, in *Supply Chain Management — Pathways for Research and Practice*, chap. 11.

Tempest, R. (1996). Barbie and the world economy, `http://articles.latimes.com/1996-09-22/news/mn-46610_1_hong-kong`.

Thompson, J. D. (1967). *Organizations in Action: Social Science Bases of Administrative Theory*, Classics in Organization and Management Series (Transaction Publishers).

Umali-Deininger, D. and Sur, M. (2007). Food safety in a globalizing world: Opportunities and challenges for India, *Agricultural Economics* **37**, s1, pp. 135–147.

UNCTAD (2005). Transnational corporations and internalization of R&D, World investment report, UNCTAD.

Vidal, C. J. and Goetschalckx, M. (2001). A global supply chain model with transfer pricing and transportation cost allocation, *European Journal of Operational Research* **129**, 1, pp. 134–158.

Viswanadham, N. (1999). *Analysis of Manufacturing Enterprises: An Approach to Leverage the Value Delivery Processes to Competitive Advantage* (Kluwer Academic Publishers).

Viswanadham, N. (2005). Can India be the food basket for the world? Working paper, Indian School of Businesss.

Viswanadham, N. and Balaji, K. (2008). A tax-integrated approach for global supply chain network planning, in *Proceedings of the Annual IEEE Conference on Automation Science and Engineering (IEEE CASE 2008)*, Vol. 5, pp. 587–596.

Viswanadham, N. and Gaonkar, R. (2003). Partner selection and synchronized planning in dynamic manufacturing networks, *IEEE Transactions on Robotics and Automation* **19**, 1, pp. 117–130.

Viswanadham, N. and Gaonkar, R. (2009). A conceptual and analytical framework for management of integrated knowledge-based logistics providers, *International Journal of Logistics Systems and Management* **5**, 1/2, pp. 191–209.

Viswanadham, N. and Kameshwaran, S. (2007). A decision framework for location selection in global supply chains, in *Proceedings of the Annual IEEE Conference on Automation Science and Engineering (IEEE CASE 2007)*, pp. 704–709.

Viswanadham, N. and Kameshwaran, S. (2009a). Low-carbon logistics provider, in *Proceedings of the Indo-US Workshop on Designing Sustainable Products, Services and Manufacturing Systems*.

Viswanadham, N. and Kameshwaran, S. (2009b). Orchestrating a network of activities in the value chain, in *Proceedings of the Annual IEEE Conference on Automation Science and Engineering*, pp. 501–506.

Viswanadham, N. and Narahari, Y. (1992). *Performance Modelling of Automated Manufacturing Systems* (Prentice Hall, USA).

Viswanadham, N. and Prakasam, A. (2006). Decision support system for exception management in RFID-enabled airline baggage handling process, in *Proceedings of the Annual IEEE Conference on Automation Science and Engineering (IEEE CASE 2006)*, pp. 351–356.

Viswanadham, N. and Vedula, S. (2010). Wicked problems and soft solutions, *ISB Insight*, Spring, pp. 22–25.

Walker, N. and Richardson, M. (2006). Developing national standards for durability, performance and environmental sustainability of concrete: an Irish case study illustrating the potential for win-win, Tech. rep., University College Dublin.

Wedan, Q. (2006). Transforming global logistics for strategic advantage in emerging markets, White paper, IBM Global Business Services.

Williams, A. G. (2007). Comparative study of cut roses for the British market produced in Kenya and the Netherlands, *World Flowers*.

Williamson, O. E. (2008). Outsourcing: Transaction cost economics and supply chain management, *Journal of Supply Chain Management* **44**, 2.

World Bank (2005a). A better investment for everyone, World development report, World Bank.

World Bank (2005b). India: Investment climate and manufacturing industry, Investment climate assessment report, World Bank and International Finance Corporation.

World Bank (2009). Systems of cities: Integrating national and local policies connecting institutions and infrastructure, The world bank urban and local government strategy, The World Bank.

World-Bank-2010 (2010). Trade logistics in the global economy: The logistics performance index and its indicators, Tech. rep., The World Bank, Washington, DC.

World-Trade-Report-2008 (2008). Trade in a globalizing world, Tech. rep., World Trade Organization, Geneva.

World-Trade-Report-2010 (2010). Trade in natural resources, Tech. rep., World Trade Organization, Geneva.

Wu, J. A. and Wu, N. L. (1984). Analysing multi-dimensional attribute for the single plant location problem via adaptation of the analytic hierarchy process, *International Journal of Operations and Production Management* **4**, 3, pp. 13–21.

Yang, C. H. (2004). *Identifying and testing the decision making factors related to key industries' choice of location*, PhD thesis, Faculty of Commerce and Management, Griffith University, Brisbane.

Yang, J. and Lee, H. (1997). An AHP decision model for facility location selection, *Facilities* **15**, 9/10, pp. 241–254.

Yurimoto, S. and Masui, T. (1995). Design of a decision support system for overseas plant location in the EC, *International Journal of Production Economics* **41**, pp. 411–418.

Zacharia, Z., Sanders, N. and Nix, N. (2011). The emerging role of the third-party logistics provider (3PL) as an orchestrator, *Journal of Business Logistics* **32**, 1, pp. 40–54.

Zeleny, M. (1982). *Multiple Criteria Decision Making* (McGraw-Hill, New York).

Index